A Thousand Weddings

A Thousand Weddings

THE MEMOIR OF HOPE HART OF WEST TENNESSEE

Edited by Marvin Downing

The University of Tennessee Press / Knoxville

Copyright © 2025 by The University of Tennessee Press / Knoxville.
All Rights Reserved. Manufactured in the United States of America.
First Edition.

Library of Congress Cataloging-in-Publication Data

Names: Hart, Hope, 1897–1985, author. | Downing, Marvin, 1937- editor.
Title: A thousand weddings : the memoir of Hope Hart of West Tennessee / edited by Marvin Downing.
Description: First edition. | Knoxville : The University of Tennessee Press, 2025. | Includes bibliographical references and index. |
Summary: "Hope Hart was the daughter of a traveling Methodist minister, Sterling Hart, who was active in the late nineteenth and early twentieth century. Her father traveled throughout Tennessee, Kentucky, Mississippi, and Arkansas performing wedding ceremonies and preaching. As such, Hart's memoir of her time with her family provides an eye-witness account to a rapidly evolving West Tennessee and surrounding regions. Likewise, Hart's father represents the last vestige of the Methodist circuit riders of the nineteenth century. As populations were on the move after the Civil War, once rural areas of the upper Mississippi Valley were quickly becoming more populated, and Hart's memoir provides a lens into an important history of the state and larger region"—Provided by publisher.
Identifiers: LCCN 2024049502 (print) | LCCN 2024049503 (ebook) | ISBN 9781621909439 (paperback) | ISBN 9781621909453 (adobe pdf) | ISBN 9781621909446 (kindle edition)
Subjects: LCSH: Hart, Hope, 1897–1985—Diaries. | Hart, Sterling Reece, 1862–1956. | Methodist Church—Tennessee, West—History. | Circuit riders—Tennessee, West—Biography. | Tennessee, West x Social life and customs. | Tennessee, West—Biography. | LCGFT: Diaries
Classification: LCC F442.3 .H37 2025 (print) | LCC F442.3 (ebook) | DDC 976.8/105092—dc23/eng/20250225
LC record available at https://lccn.loc.gov/2024049502
LC ebook record available at https://lccn.loc.gov/2024049503

CONTENTS

Acknowledgments   ix
Editorial Notes   xi
Introduction   1
Chapter 1. We Are Gathered Together   23
Chapter 2. A Babe at Little Zion   35
Chapter 3. Disenchantment   45
Chapter 4. "Go On with the Marryin'"   53
Chapter 5. Angel Music   67
Chapter 6. "Oh Dem Golden Slippers"   79
Chapter 7. When Mama Laughed Again   89
Chapter 8. Grandma: Ninety-Five Pounds of Grit   109
Chapter 9. The Mail-Order Bride   125
Chapter 10. A Gambol on the Mississippi   133
Chapter 11. Our Thanks to God   153
Chapter 12. You Learned or Else   159
Chapter 13. The One That Got Away   171
Epilogue   187
Notes   189
Bibliography   237
Index   251

ILLUSTRATIONS

Following page 102
Hope Hart Dressed for the High School Dance
Hope Hart Going to a Congressional Dinner
Hope Hart Announcing Her Retirement
Hope Hart Visiting the *Dresden Enterprise*
Hope Hart Riding a Donkey in Greece
Sterling and Mattie Hart
Sterling Hart
Gravestone of Eleanor Hart Harbert

Map

The Residences of Sterling Reece Hart   22

ACKNOWLEDGMENTS

It seems like working with Hope Hart's manuscript "A Thousand Weddings" began light years ago, although it has been really quite a few. A special thanks goes to the Weakley County Historical and Genealogical Society for preserving Hart's literary piece. Several members in the conservation were Pansy Baker (now deceased), Mary Ann Baxter (now deceased), Janice Crider (now deceased), Elaine Knight, Greg Roach, and Dr. Bill Austin. The later eventually persuaded me to read the story, but neither of us realized the magnitude of the undertaking. (And at our ages perhaps some word other than undertaking would be more polite.) Nonetheless, we persevered. Greg Roach was most helpful with his knowledge of pertinent print and electronic sources.

Of course, professionals also contributed. Dr. Erik Nordberg, the University of Tennessee at Martin Dean of Libraries, contributed invaluable insight along with many encouraging words. Sam Richardson and Karen Elmore of the UTM Special Collections pointed to relevant sources and the UTM Circulation Department also provided services. (It is a point of special pride that I was a part of the early evolution of the UTM Special Collections.) Thankfully Dr. Jeff Rogers, UTM geography professor, generated the map showing the general travels of the Hart family in West Tennessee and Western Kentucky. Naturally the completed work would not be possible without the guidance and prodding of University of Tennessee Press staffers particularly associate director Thomas Wells and editorial coordinator Jon Boggs.

I can only imagine the kind of informational and emotional help my wife Sandra Kay "Sandy" Mitchell Downing (now deceased) could have given me. However, the former UTM Paul Meek Reference Librarian of twenty-eight years died in 2019—before I even became aware of Hope Hart.

Please indulge me as I reach even farther back. Dr. Charles Ogilvie (now deceased), my history colleague at Wayland Baptist College in the mid-1960s and then at UTM beginning in 1969, introduced me to local history and how to do it. Little did I know such local studies would provide background and insights for the Hart endeavor. Of course, along the way Dr. Robert "Bob" Smith, then the UTM dean of Arts and Sciences, later the UTM chancellor, suggested I write a book. Then I did not have a book in me, but, Bob, maybe this is the volume you envisioned, albeit an edited one.

EDITORIAL NOTES

Hope Hart's manuscript contained some editorial challenges. She used ellipses excessively without indicating why. She might have thought about later editing such statements or portions. Sometimes it appears she might have used ellipsis for a reader to pause or to allow space for her reader's own created mood or thoughts. Whatever her intentions, editorially it became necessary to standardize ellipses. She also used underlining in lieu of curse words or for emphasis.

Hart was also much given to aliases. Perhaps she wanted to avoid or soften potential personal embarrassment to family members and friends or avoid legal problems. When names were especially relevant, the editor sought to further identify individuals from external documents if possible. Otherwise, most names had so little accompanying facts that it was not feasible to search further. Thankfully Ancestry.com, FindAGrave.com, and a few other documentary sources helped fill in gaps, especially about her immediate and close extended family.

Where were the Harts? Hope Hart was not too helpful along that line, being mostly vague about places and years of events. However, with clues about her and her siblings' birthdays and slight hints of location coupled with Methodist records, the editor could approximate where and when incidents happened. This editor, at least, felt much better knowing those things and hopefully readers will too.

Introduction

BETWEEN 1929 AND 1975 HOPE HART (1897–1985), A CHARMING AND vivacious former Dresden, Tennessee, high school principal intermingled work and hobbies—especially writing—in Washington, DC. During that time she was successively an administrative assistant to US Congressmen Jere Prentice Cooper (1929–1957) of Dyersburg, Tennessee, and Robert A. "Fats" Everett (1957–1965) of Union City, Tennessee, followed by a stint with US senator Harrison Williams (1967–1975) of New Jersey as Senate Committee on Aging chair. She exulted, "I have been thrilled to be in the midst of the making of history in Washington" and, indeed, she knew many House and Senate notables. She further witnessed "the exciting New Deal days under President [Franklin D.] Roosevelt; the events leading up to and the grim, dramatic days of World War II, and the action-filled sessions of Congress in the post-war period." Additionally, she emoted, "And nobody who has 'seen it all,' as I have done, has enjoyed it more."

In the 1940s, proud of her family heritage, Hope joined the Daughters of the American Revolution. As a lifelong Methodist, she remained active in a Methodist congregation throughout her life. Hope traveled abroad. Perhaps she combined high personal and literary values by making sure her Christmas cards got to friends on the Friday after Thanksgiving. Reportedly, during retirement she penned articles in the *Washington Post* and other print venues and participated in a two-year university radio series. Furthermore, she often visited West Tennessee friends and relatives and maintained a legal residence in Weakley County where she regularly voted for many years.[1] Understandably, with her death receding into the past, probably only a few scattered unidentified elderly folks might remember her. Nevertheless, her life continues through rich and engaging stories.

By 1962 Hope Hart, the daughter of Reverend Sterling Reece Hart (1863–1956), had produced the manuscript "A Thousand Weddings," a colorful chronicle about her pre-adult development and adventures in West Tennessee and Western Kentucky. Through the years, she assembled an account of an energetic and inquisitive young daughter of a traveling Methodist family and their adjustments in the Jackson Purchase's rural settings. She passed along incredible tales, mostly about matrimonial ceremonies, hopefully blissful. In the process, she pictured the youthful folkways of eventful years, roughly 1897 to 1914. Further, she filled the canvas with amusing instances, emotional moments, and even tragic elements she witnessed or learned from kinfolks.[2]

The composition came together in the nation's capital. She created and typed the original copy for personal fulfillment and enjoyment from recalling delightful (yes, fantastic) highlights of her early life saturated with Methodist ministerial matters and recording memorable community events. While other twentieth-century female authors were penning their thoughts and expressing their lives, often in family-related themes, Hope did likewise. But Hope was not a professional author, and no known evidence exists of an attempt by her to contact a publisher.

Whatever the breadth of Hope Hart's literary awareness, she shared a kinship with other Southern women authors. "A Thousand Weddings" is hard to pin with a genre and, in fact, Southern studies scholar Dr. Peggy Whitman Prenshaw decided finally not to distinguish between autobiography, memoir, and life narrative or story in her case. She pointed out "the near impossibility of linear time framing,"[3] a very definitive feature of Hope Hart's approach. Actually, such regional authors of this period were often vague about "their place, locale, the landscape or wherever they are."[4] Without the Methodist records of Reverend Hart's appointments and occasional accompanying tidbits, a reader could be left clueless about location. Southern writers also typically included recollections about geography, foods, and distinctive languages as Hope did about Little Zion and Shiloh in Tennessee and about southwestern Kentucky. In Southern compositions, church-related activities got ample attention, a naturally abundant feature of Hope's composition given the Reverend's calling and Hope's wedding venue. Additionally, like fellow feminist creators, Hart especially exulted ancestors, contemporary kin, and their doings. Unlike many autobiographers, Hope seemed untroubled by jaundiced White images of Blacks and the inhumanity and insensitivity of the de jure and de facto segregation of late-nineteenth- and early-twentieth-century Southern society. Like other scribes, Hope accepted memory, albeit filtered, as "the primary means of knowing" about family and home amid "a web of personal, relational affiliations."[5] And in that milieu she emerges as a sort of relational self in contrast to an individual self.[6] In contrast to other Southern molds, however, Hope's craft does not signal ambivalence toward a dominant male order. In the final analysis it's likely Hope wrote for the joy of it, herself, and the thrill of sharing about her family. She was generally lighthearted, upbeat, and seldom down, perhaps akin to famed author Laura Ingalls Wilder on the prairie.[7]

Upon Hope's death in 1985, the boxed manuscript went to William (Bill) Thomas Killebrew, a cousin in Weakley County, as she did not have children. He died two years later in 1987, leaving that material to his daughter Judith (Judy) Killebrew-Lambert of Medon, Tennessee, near Jackson. In time, wanting "it readily available to the public," she gifted the items to the then Weakley County Genealogical Society in 2009. On January 4, 2010, she made it the property of the renamed Weakley County Historical and Genealogical Society (WCHGS) for whatever use it wished, with any society profits going to promote historical efforts. It is now in the Martin Public Library.[8]

Then the initiative shifted to WCHGS. A dismaying surprise was that Judith's version was incomplete, specifically chapter 2 "A Babe at Little Zion." However, her Colorado relative Basil Brooks discovered a copy in his footlocker stored in the attic. With a full text, WCHGS members—notably Martin residents Pansy Baker (now deceased), Mary Ann Baxter (now deceased), Janice Crider (now deceased), Elaine Knight (now in Florida), Dr. Bill Austin, and Greg Roach of South Fulton, Tennessee—determined their next moves with a digitized typescript completed by Knight. After the society agreed Hope's creation was quite worthy of publication, committee chairman Roach contacted the University of Tennessee Press; there Thomas Wells advised seeking a local historian to edit the volume. After a couple of urgings from Dr. Austin, Dr. Marvin Downing, a retired UT Martin American history professor, assented, not realizing the complexities of genealogy and the undertaking. After lots of time and effort, this is the latest rendition of Hope Hart's "A Thousand Weddings."

Future family biographer Hope Howard Hart, one of seven children, entered the world on Wednesday, September 11, 1897, at Cottage Grove, Henry County in upper northwest Tennessee. Her parents, Sterling Reece Hart and

Martha "Mattie" Kennedy Hart, were longtime residents of Henry and Weakley County where Sterling taught school for many years. After 1899 Hope's father, Reverend Hart, worked as an itinerant Methodist minister in numerous Jackson Purchase locations. She finished high school at Murray, Kentucky, before attending West Tennessee Teachers College in Memphis. Afterward, she became a West Tennessee teacher, and then a Dresden high school principal after World War I.

Hope especially treasured Weakley County. It hosted grandparents and multiple aunts, uncles, and cousins whom she often visited. She might have idealized it in part because it was the only constant in a life, before 1929, frequently on the move. Her educational tenure at Dresden may have heightened that sentimental attachment. Maybe she caught the emotional bug from Reverend Hart who, upon retirement in 1927, "returned to Dresden, in his beloved Weakley County."[9] Presumably other relatives embraced that feeling, too. Throughout fifty-six distant years, she was aware of northwest Tennessee events. She might worship in Washington, but her membership was at the First United Methodist Church of Dresden.

Hope did not learn about family history accidentally. From her parents she became proud of the family heritage. While Sterling spun a good narrative, to the Hart siblings, Martha "was our Homer" who "made distant dramas and comedies come to life for us." She retained their full attention while regaling them about predecessors and their environment. For instance, one distant uncle participated in the Battle of New Orleans in early 1815. After someone stole his horse, out of necessity, the veteran labored mightily to return home. A high fever greatly complicated his long walk. Hope "gagged a bit when Mama told how he ate raw polk [*sic* poke] sallet as a remedy."[10] Seemingly, their Weakley County kin were relatively homogeneous about Christian beliefs and practices, education, society, and kinship. Among them, it was only natural to socialize at church, County Court days, First Monday trade days, and to celebrate "Christmas with eggnog and happy visits among their kin." From nuclear family sessions in the summer on the porch and around the kitchen table in winter, the youngsters gained respect for "the witty Killebrews and thrifty Kennedys, the fun loving McWherters, the bookish Harts," and the Moores. Hope proclaimed, "When a handful of people, with few skills and little money can come into a wilderness and build a society and help establish a nation—they are worth studying, and remembering, and honoring."[11] With such laudatory information, it's little wonder the Hart children believed Weakley County produced the best trees, apples, buggy horses, and well water. Conceivably such accounts contributed to Hope Hart becoming a storyteller and a writer.

According to Hope Hart, her ancestors were among the many Americans who longed to tap the resources of the island circumscribed by the Ohio, Tennessee, and Mississippi Rivers and delimited by the northern boundary of Mississippi.[12] However, only Southeast Chickasaw Indians, mainly in Mississippi, could legally be there, according to George Washington's 1785 treaty. The natives primarily hunted in the area.[13] Hopes of entry brightened after Tennessean Andrew Jackson and Kentuckian Isaac Shelby concluded the Purchase Treaty of 1818 transferring ownership to the US. Following federal and state approval, Americans rushed westward to fill the void.[14]

What spurred large numbers of easterly Americans to migrate? Large coastal planters sought the rich soil to replace their nutrient depleted lands. Others were attempting to escape and overcome the crushing impact of the financial Panic of 1819 and its lingering economic effects. Land speculators hoped to cash in on such eagerness. Among the largest land speculators were famed military leader and treaty negotiator Andrew Jackson and his lesser-known in-law John Christmas McLemore, who held lands in most Tennessee counties. Some northwest Tennesseans knew the latter's name through the land office at Christmasville, Carroll County, just an adjacent southerly county away from northern Henry and Weakley Counties.[15] Such speculators quickly grabbed large portions of the choice acreages not already claimed.[16] Weather played a part in some migration. Not yet nationally famous, Tennessean David Crockett relocated after a flood disrupted his Middle Tennessee income and fed his desire to move into Weakley County.[17] About 1828, a Carolina drought motivated many to relocate westward. Around 1820, Hope Hart's maternal ancestors, the Sampson Edward Kennedys (1787–1845)[18] of northwest South Carolina, claimed a plot near Cottage Grove, Henry County, and Palmersville-Little Zion, Weakley County. Hart traced them through Kentucky into Tennessee "with their livestock, household plunder, slaves, and worldly possessions."[19] They and other eastern itinerants banded with families, friends, and neighbors for mutual travel benefits and settled in plats near each other.[20]

Those Kennedys, along with the other earliest migrants into the Jackson Purchase, entered what appeared to be virgin wilderness. Utilizing animal and Indian paths, commonly along the easiest terrain,[21] they moved through high grass, tall cane, other dense undergrowth, and abundant hardwood trees of oak, hickory, and walnut to a selected spot.[22] All newcomers had to immediately satisfy their basic needs of shelter and sustenance and refine from there. At first, the Kennedys might have merely thrown up little more than a lean-to with more substantial living quarters as circumstances permitted.[23] In a clearing, they planted a garden of corn, beans, and squash, the three most common food plants among migrants. In time, they added many improvements.

By the time Hope Hart's maternal grandfather, Nelson Edward Kennedy (1817–1900), Sampson's son, reached maturity, Henry and Weakley Counties were much different. Scattered communities commonly under ten miles apart were linked by some roads and hosted courthouses, general stores, churches, and—less frequently—schools. As a second-generation resident, Nelson possibly found adjusting easier due to already being familiar with his surroundings. He also had parental assistance, something the first generation did not have. In 1838, he married a Kentucky-born girl, thereby knitting that grandparental unit. Fifteen years later, they delivered Martha "Mattie" Nelson Kennedy (1863–1945), Hope's mother.[24]

When Hope's paternal kinfolk reached the Palmersville-Little Zion scene, they benefited from some of the community developments. Her great-grandfather, Benjamin Umpstead Hart (1802–1886), relocated from Middle Tennessee about 1835. The next year they had their second son, Thomas Green Hart (1836–1863), Hope's grandfather.[25]

Finally, Hope added the McWherter branch to her direct lineage. Her great grandparents, the James McWherters (1805–1854), settled in Palmersville in time for Ruth Paralee (1841–1916) to be born. Thomas Green romanced Ruth Paralee and they married in 1857, becoming the Thomas Green Harts, Hope's paternal grandparents.[26]

By the mid-nineteenth century, residents had transformed West Tennessee.[27] Could it be from "attracting a high grade of settlers?"[28] Although the majority were at subsistence level, the most industrious generated enough products to sell elsewhere.[29] Water levels and other conditions permitting, William Martin of Weakley County throughout the 1840s profitably sent one to three produce-laden flatboats via the North Fork of the Obion River to steamboats.[30] Once attained, railroads facilitated product movement back and forth. Consequently, by 1860, West Tennessee's agriculture, easily its economic mainstay, was doing well,[31] relying on cash crops of corn, cotton, tobacco, and wheat.[32] Gristmills scattered throughout those counties provided cornmeal and wheat flour for locals. The plentiful trees allowed for sawmills to produce lumber and tobacco barrels for shipping.[33] As of 1860, Hope's kin were potentially enjoying favorable economic circumstances.

Slavery played a significant and important part of agricultural activity and society. As American settlers moved into and across Tennessee, they brought the dehumanizing and demeaning institution of slavery. Their slaves were chattel property with no rights and limited personal protection. In fact, slaves comprised 25 percent of Tennessee's population by 1860.[34] By then, Tennesseans relied on slavery most evidently in West Tennessee with slaves being 34 percent of their population, mostly concentrated in the southwestern cotton-growing Shelby, Haywood, and Fayette Counties. Upper West Tennessee's relatively short growing season limited cotton cultivation and necessitated fewer slaves except in tobacco cultivation. Nonetheless, the slave population amounted to 28 percent in Henry, slightly over 23 percent in Weakley, and almost 19 percent in Obion counties. There and elsewhere, slaves filled such basic needs as field hands and domestics, and possessed vital skills as blacksmiths, wheelwrights, barrel makers, boot, shoe, and saddle makers, bricklayers, and seamstresses.[35]

Even so, slavery was most definitely a race problem, for Southern Whites had no plans to grant Blacks equality. Those Caucasians stoutly adhered to their superiority and Black inferiority. In their minds, slavery was the only way the two races could coexist. Accordingly, Whites enforced subjugation through laws and reinforced it with general intimidation for decades before and untold decades after the Civil War.[36] Actually, slavery was "a malignancy" that scarred both Whites and Blacks with consequences well into Hope Hart's life and beyond.[37]

Tragically, the United States suffered its greatest domestic conflict. Major North-South political, economic, and social differences, including the multifaceted slavery issue, brought on that armed clash. Ultimately, eleven southern states, including Tennessee, fought as the Confederate States of America (CSA).[38] Somewhat generally, Middle and West Tennessee were pro-CSA while East Tennessee adhered to the Union. Yet, interestingly, the number of Tennesseans in Federal forces exceeded the total from other Confederate states.[39] Among West Tennesseans, Confederate sentiment was almost five times greater than Union preference.[40] Some of Paralee's Little Zion kin supported secession and enlisted in Confederate ranks. Numerous volunteers joined the gray at Dresden, Cottage Grove, Paris, and Union City.[41] Henry County provided over twenty-five hundred Confederate volunteers.[42] Weakley County sent about eleven hundred men into Confederate forces compared to nine hundred joining Federal companies.[43]

West Tennessee saw considerable military activity, not all of it legal.[44] Bordering both the Tennessee and Mississippi Rivers, the region had a more than passing significance. However, after the fall of Forts Henry and Donelson, the Federal victories at Shiloh and Corinth, and the Federal capture of Memphis, that importance had considerably diminished by mid-June 1862. Thereafter, in many respects West Tennessee was largely a passageway for troop movements, scattered skirmishes, and disruptive swoops especially exemplified by General Nathan Bedford Forrest's raids in 1862 and 1864.[45]

Like their other kinfolks, the Thomas Green Harts felt impacts of the war. Thomas joined Confederate Tennessee forces with officer status, according to family lore. He was in the Confederate defeat at the Battle of Pea Ridge.[46] Nevertheless, maybe sensing more safety and economic opportunity elsewhere, the Harts relocated to Dardanelle, Yell County, of northwest Arkansas. There on May 11, 1862, Paralee gave birth to their second son, Sterling Reece Hart (1862–1956), Hope's father. The next year while on furlough, Officer Hart succumbed to typhus fever on July 30, 1863. The young mother of two babies, stranded by circumstances, got through the war with compassionate local assistance.[47]

After a travel ordeal back to Dresden, Parlee surely experienced mixed emotions. What elation to be back among Palmersville-Little Zion relatives! Yet, grim family realities tempered that joy. Her oldest brother, C.S.A. captain William McWherter, a Shiloh veteran, died at distant Chickamauga, Tennessee, during 1863. Their cousin, Thomas Killebrew (1839–1907), immediately assumed that command.[48] Her brothers James Monroe and Almus were also in CSA ranks. She shared that CSA 2nd Lt. John Mark Hart, her late husband's older brother, maybe saw action in Arkansas.[49] Paralee's cousin, 2nd Lt. William Marion Killebrew (1837–1862), died in Kentucky fighting on April 6, 1862, and Little Zion cousin Calvin Simpson Moore received an elbow injury.[50]

Paralee's widowhood lasted six years before she married Calvin Simpson Moore (1837–1901). About 1830, his father, Middle Tennessean Silas Reuben

Moore (1809–1897), migrated to Henry County and later married Matilda Kennedy (1813–1861), the sister of Hope's grandfather, Nelson Kennedy. In 1838, the Silas Moores added Calvin, their second son, to the family.[51] In 1861, the son wed Sarah Angeline Kennedy (1837–1868), the granddaughter of Nelson Kennedy (1775–1843).[52] They had children born during the Civil War and afterward. Mrs. Angeline died of an unknown cause in 1868.[53]

Deaths deprived two spouses but opened new opportunities. In 1869, Calvin and Paralee, both near thirty years old, blended their separate families.[54] During the 1870s, they added six more to their brood. Surely, that family lived a rather typical rural northwest Tennessee lifestyle of the latter 1800s. Every able-bodied person worked in the house or the field to make a living when income was depressingly low. Sons learned largely outdoors skills whereas daughters developed more household basics.[55] Whether inside or outside the house, those skills immeasurably benefited them then and later.[56]

The Civil War and its aftermath scarred Southern areas like Tennessee tremendously, and northwest Tennessee's mainly agricultural economy was no exception. While over 275,000 former slaves received freedom, their previous owners lost between $100 and $300 million in human property.[57] Military-related action damaged or destroyed much private and public property, especially expensive travel infrastructure. Fields and farm machinery went unmaintained due to family workers being away. Repairs and rebuilding were both time-consuming and financially costly.[58]

Like Henry and Weakley County cultivators, Tennesseans labored long and hard,[59] only to find prosperity elusive.[60] Their ability to grow plentifully [61]negatively affected prices, a persistently growing disparity.[62] Increased farming costs, market forces generally favoring processors over producers, and overproduction made farm prices and profits low and unpredictable.[63] How ironic and disheartening that persistence worsened their financial status! Those Southern farmers were without a viable option, then.[64] Such was the northwest Tennessee environment in which Hope's more immediate predecessors lived.

Naturally, as Sterling Hart moved into adulthood, he looked beyond the Hart-Moore walls. If he stayed around Little Zion, besides farming, his vocational choices were relatively few unless he became a lawyer, banker, doctor, dentist, teacher, or minister. If he opted for the last two, he needed almost no further formal schooling.[65] Successively he went into teaching and and then into preaching. Eventually, livelihood converged with romance. He eyed the nearby Martha "Mattie" Nelson Kennedy (1863–1945), the youngest child of Nelson Kennedy.[66] Among other affinities, they definitely loved God, music, and learning. While likely keeping some tie to farming, "as a young man he entered the field of teaching. At the outset of his career he married his childhood sweetheart."[67] Thereafter, he spent fifteen or so years in a classroom and sixty-one years in marriage. Weakley County instructors taught seventy-four days a year and received $35 a month.[68]

Naturally, family responsibilities increased significantly as they had children and perhaps moved, if children's birthplaces are indicative. Eleanor (1884–1907), formally Eva Elna,[69] came in Weakley County, as well as Ray Kennedy (1887–1967)[70] three years afterward at Cottage Grove, Henry County. In the 1890s, the Harts tragically lost two Weakley County daughters, Martha Reece (1890–1892)[71] and Ruth Lee (1893–1896).[72] The year after Ruth's death, family chronicler Hope Howard (1897–1985)[73] was born at Cottage Grove.

Maybe Sterling kept in mind a ministerial option. From Hope's manuscript, spiritual facets were readily apparent irrespective of formal ministry. Like their parents, Sterling and Mattie might have worshipped at the Little Zion Primitive Baptist Church. They surely gravitated into a Methodist congregation where they regularly attended weekly worship times, Bible classes, and Wednesday prayer meetings. Their family devotions shaped their spiritual experience, undoubtedly enriching God's kingdom, the community, and themselves.

Certainly by the late 1890s he felt a divine calling to the Methodist ministry.[74] More specifically, according to Hope Hart's youngest brother Nelson Key Hart, who edited at *U.S. News and World Report*, "it was an instinctive desire to serve and uplift humanity, along with a deep religious conviction, that led Sterling Reece Hart to turn from his teaching career to the ministry." In due course, "not suddenly or dramatically, but on mature deliberation and through the travail of prayer, and with the help and understanding of his wife, he gave his life to God and applied for" the Methodist traveling ministry.[75] He was joining a noble group because "the civilizing influence of the itinerant Methodist preacher" was well beyond measure, according to a noted cultural historian.[76]

Such Methodist itinerancy, a.k.a. circuit riding, had existed in Tennessee and Kentucky for almost eighty years. That ministry, beginning in the early

1820s, consisted of choosing zealous men of good morals and demeanor committed to evangelism, frugality, and travel.[77] Eschewing dangers and low pay, these men devotedly praised God to listeners while enduring insecurities of food, shelter, transportation, and weather.[78] Their labors immensely furthered God's kingdom and Methodism. Historian E. Harrell Phillips summarized, "The circuit system and the local societies (often meeting in homes), the techniques of revivalism and camp meetings, the acceptance of a ministry not educated beyond the comprehension of a frontier laity, and the democratic emphasis of Arminian theology all contributed to the success of the movement in the Purchase."[79]

During the 1840s, the newly created Memphis Conference, which encompassed the Jackson Purchase, partitioned that area into districts and subsequently circuits. Those configurations created more humane and manageable, yet still challenging, units.[80]

Methodists faced unprecedented challenges from the 1840s forward. In that decade, Methodists split over slavery, so Southern adherents created the Methodist Episcopal Church South. Itself the product of political and economic differences, the Civil War brought still more suffering physically and spiritually.[81] In the war's aftermath, Methodist evangelists strove to reestablish peaceful circumstances.[82] They realized that for education, "the evangelistic outreach of the Sunday School was immeasurable."[83] Those circuit riders pivotally increased God's kingdom by "preaching, visiting, organizing congregations, and distributing books and pamphlets."[84] Ministerial colleagues were not to use tobacco and their spouses were to dress modestly. They opposed divorce except for biblical reasons. To them, the list of improper Sunday amusements included travel and pleasure riding, baseball, hunting, and reading newspapers, especially comics. Dancing was suspect but gambling and intoxication were always beyond the pale. Methodists utilized the Sunday School and Anti-Saloon League to oppose those twin vices; occasionally, their anti-liquor zeal pushed them into the political realm. In reality, the Memphis Conference "reflected the lifestyle of southern Methodists and most other southern Protestant denominations."[85]

As Sterling was winding down his teaching career and Hope was toddling along, the Purchase was on the verge of an ultimately promising twentieth century. It was still predominantly agricultural and rural in a nation trending industrial and urban. Those shifts, though, noticeably influenced the Harts lifestyle as well as many other Americans. Positively, the nation had emerged from the Panic of 1893.[86] Large-plot and middle-class farmers between the Tennessee and Mississippi Rivers were part of "the golden era of American agriculture" of 1900–1918.[87] For many West Tennesseans, though, work remained seasonal in farming, harvesting, milling, and timber cutting.[88]

Transportation facilitated mobility and accessibility. Railroads linked farms, towns, and distant cities together. Through catalog sales, companies like Sears and Roebuck sent finished products to rural locales.[89] The relatively new horseless carriage evolved quickly thanks in large part to Henry Ford producing affordable models. Its emergence fueled sales, road construction, and travel. In effect, cars and trains markedly altered the American lifestyle, even in the Jackson Purchase.[90]

In 1899, Sterling Reece Hart formally entered the Methodist traveling ministry. Previously, the Harts knew preachers moved a lot; that year they met the reality personally. The Conference sent the family over ninety miles to Hurley, Hardin County, Tennessee, in the Shiloh Circuit close to the famed Civil War battle site. In contrast to upper northwest Tennessee, they were going to the southeastern-most corner bordering Mississippi and Alabama. The parents set out with teenager Eleanor, preteen Ray, and two-year-old Hope. Logistics dictated overland travel in two wagons over rough and sometimes muddy routes; and they appreciated the ready and varying hospitality of residents along the way.

At Hurley, the Harts underwent a sort of ministerial initiation. They were barely into the church parsonage before the locals graciously gave a traditional pounding of staple foods. While becoming acquainted with congregants and other residents as best as possible, Sterling learned regular ministerial responsibilities under the supervising district presiding elder. Somehow, feeling the press of necessity, he shoehorned in prescribed studies toward successfully satisfying an examining committee of elders within twenty-four months. In Hope's opinion, the family adjusted quite well in their new settings. Adaptation had to be speedy, considering it was merely a one-year stay.[91] Thereafter, the Harts underwent travels in both Kentucky and Tennessee; they had only just begun. In 1900, the Conference directed them northward to successive stays in Graves County in south-central Western Kentucky. They were first at Pryorsburg, where Reece Green "Joe" Hart (1901–1975)[92] was born, before they sauntered about eight miles to Sedalia. The latter was their first three-year ministerial home and the birthplace of Nelson Key (1904–1998),[93] their last child. In late 1904, they shuffled a mere seven miles to Wingo for twelve months. In total, during the first six years the family was in four separate locations. For seven years thereafter, they were in Tennessee before returning to Kentucky.[94] During the second and last Commonwealth tenure, about 1915, Hope graduated from high school at Murray, in Calloway County, just north of Henry County, Tennessee. Shortly afterward in 1915, the Harts journeyed southwesterly to Mason in Tipton County along the Mississippi's east bank. That transfer of roughly 137 miles, the Hart's longest move, put Hope within forty-five miles of West Tennessee Normal School in Memphis that she presumably attended.[95] At Dresden in late 1927, Sterling became a retiree, or a superannuate, ending the traveling ministry of twenty-eight years in seventeen different places.[96]

Early in Sterling's ministerial career, family issues alone might have caused a lesser ministerial clan "to locate." (In Methodist jargon, "to locate" was to cease traveling or leave the ministry altogether due to circumstances, often personal.) The first issue happened in the fall of 1900, less than a year into the Shiloh Circuit appointment. Mattie's father, Nelson Kennedy (1817–1900), became quite sick in Weakley County. With toddler Hope in tow, Mattie hastily boarded a train in Selmer, a town about fifteen miles from Hurley, for Weakley County. Regrettably, Mr. Kennedy passed away October 5, 1900, and interred at Dresden.[97] The following October, tragedy again beset the Harts as Sterling's half-brother, Leroy Simpson Moore (1870–1901), a.k.a. Uncle Charlie,[98] the first-born of Paralee and Calvin Simpson Moore, received multiple rib fractures when his skittish horse kicked him. While Charlie was, in his parents' opinion, still delirious, an ambitious Weakley County spinster and her more highly motivated father tricked the propertied fellow. Allegedly, they manipulated Charlie into hasty matrimony; he lingered just eight days before succumbing October 16, 1901.[99] Flustered and irate, the grieving Moores[100] resigned themselves to their unfair fate. Compounding his mother's misery, five weeks later the old Confederate veteran died on November 27, 1901, and rested in the Little Zion Cemetery. For a second time, Paralee had become the widow of a Civil War soldier.

Actually, in Sterling's first eight ministerial years, good and bad news often intermixed. On November 17, 1901, at Dyersburg, Tennessee, about a month after the death of Uncle Leroy, Sterling received "Full Connection," meaning he was no longer "on trial"; he was an ordained deacon or minister.[101] Sterling and Mattie had Nelson Key at Sedalia under a month before the reverend's appointment to Wingo, Kentucky. Three years later, on August 23, 1907, at Obion, Obion County, Tennessee, the Harts joyously celebrated Eleanor's marriage to Perry Morton Harbert (1878–1959),[102] a Savannah, Tennessee, lawyer. After their honeymoon, the Harberts lived near Sterling's first ministerial location. Death tragically scarred both families before Christmas. With an undisclosed illness, Eleanor unexpectedly died and the distressed loved ones, especially Mattie Hart, placed her at Sunset Cemetery in Dresden.[103] Death gave the Harts little slack. On January 17, 1908, Laura Jane Kennedy, Mattie's mother, passed away.[104] Altogether, the Harts celebrated two births and two family weddings, and endured five deaths. Their faith unfailingly sustained their spiritual commitment.

As always, the Hart family adjusted to their surroundings. They made do on the meager and sometimes uncertain amounts locals paid.[105] They spent frugally, making their money go far; otherwise, for instance, how could they ever send their oldest son to law school? A new congregation sometimes showered them with necessities that lasted for days. Now and then, extra money from an impromptu or planned wedding, a baptism, or a funeral helped—even a dollar or two was welcome in the early 1900s. A large donation might stimulate a child's desire for a bicycle, though without much parental encouragement. A perceptive, generous church member might bless the family with unexpected cash, enough for a new ministerial suit that Mattie insisted Sterling needed, and clothes for the entire family. At some residences, the Harts had a cow for milk and butter, one or more horses for transportation, perhaps chickens for eggs and meat. They might be blessed with a garden to tend.

Meanwhile, the Harts allotted for cultural and educational matters, too. Hope did say the family musician, Eleanor, learned instruments from a music teacher.

Hope herself was in and out of piano lessons while wondering how they were affordable. Apparently, a girl's bike was neither cultural nor educational. The Harts definitely stressed informal and formal education. In particular, Sterling and Mattie showed their love of literature. At evening family time, they read different literary genres to their children. Hope's reading materials ranged from inspiring McGuffey's Readers to a dry and demanding grammar on diagramming sentences. She dreaded the latter, but a Sears catalog opened up an entire new world. At conferences, in addition to materials for his studies and congregations, Sterling also purchased children's volumes, a treat the youngsters particularly expected and enjoyed. Wonder of wonders, the Harts proudly owned encyclopedias, a rarity for most families.[106] In the Hart clan, individual and group reading sessions helped enhance preparations for school and vocations. The youngsters (in birth order) went on to teach music, practice law,[107] teach school, and perform secretarial work for US congressmen,[108] research agricultural,[109] and edit news.[110]

Understandably, frequent moves affected family members differently. The venturesome ones looked forward to challenges and opportunities. Out of necessity, Sterling sized up a community as quickly as possible in his calm, easygoing manner. Seemingly, Mattie found adjusting more difficult. She might have felt the early impact of losing loved ones more than Sterling. By 1899, Eleanor and Ray seemed quite outgoing and were soon largely away from home. By contrast, their siblings spent many more years in the ministerial setting, naturally homebound through their high school years. More extroverted, Hope and Key relished accompanying their father around the circuit when possible.[111] Joe, the most obviously studious of the trio, preferred reading at home. In time, all three in varying degrees loved reading. Undoubtedly, the family easily favored some communities, churches, schools, and teachers over others. Presumably, all the Hart youngsters adjusted well to their family's lifestyle.

All the family members especially looked forward to the mid-November conference when the presiding bishop traditionally announced the next year's appointments nearing the meeting's end. Considering Sterling moved often, different Hart family members certainly had frequent opportunities to be ambivalent about the bishop's decision. While their reading fantasies created imaginary, faraway vistas, their parents certainly transported them through the real landscapes of West Tennessee and Western Kentucky.[112]

Sometimes Hart wedding attendance was a family occasion, but other times not. As in 1898, infant Hope knew nothing about the first wedding she attended. In later years, an unanticipated evening ceremony might be after youngsters were already in bed for the night. More than once, young Hope only sat properly silent, something not easy for an active and naturally curious girl. In one town, after excitedly viewing a mill fire, the three youngest Hart siblings, along with their sitter's brood, crashed an outdoor wedding to the dismay of their genteel parents. For a Methodist ministerial family concerned about proper amusements, the most unusual setting was a Mississippi River showboat after a play. Occasionally Sterling and Hope were the only Harts at a wedding. They received special invitations to a Mississippi River island ceremony where the locals were probably the most rural or country that Hope Hart would observe. The bride competed with a new cooking range for attention. In adolescence, though, Hope's interest in weddings waned.[113]

Whether consciously or not, author Hope Hart gave the most wedding ink to the marriage of her Aunt Alice Moore and Uncle Billy Killebrew in 1898, during Hope's infancy. The setting was Little Zion church, a Primitive Baptist community. In its traditions and practices were "all-day preaching, foot washing, dinner-on-the ground and sanctified shouting."[114] The couple, especially the bride, opted for "a formal wedding," something never done before there and certainly a putting on of airs, according to Hard Shell critics.[115] Nevertheless, with the staunch backing of her parents, Aunt Alice prevailed and got the coveted venue.-

Yet one surprise was quite pleasant and most unexpected. The officiating preacher, a long-sermon type, "cut the ceremony to its barest bones to win a promised fee," albeit secretly arranged.[116] The wedding supper with the fatted calf and infare were lavish within rural Jackson Purchase expectations. Afterward, various participants looked upon the rowdy hullabaloo with ambivalence for its doubtfully natured, likely hellish pranks. The customary "shivaree" was raucous and elongated, and it "left the North Fork (of the Obion River) country limp."[117]

In mid-1907, age 10, Hope somewhat participated in arrangements for her sister Eleanor's wedding, the most personal family ceremony. In reality, the Harts "were all but overwhelmed by the preparations."[118] Such displacement of the summer calm was not on Hope's agenda nor were the extensive interior and exterior renovations.[119] Of necessity, circumstances pulled attention from young Hope, a situation she greatly detested. She liked that even less than licking the foul-tasting envelopes and two-cent postage stamps.

Naturally, Murphy's Law applied, and the big day had surprises in store. What was the most likely target when toddler Key Hart got hold of the scissors? Sterling managed to avert that potential "tragedy" by quickly restyling the child's freshly snipped mop. Sterling even glossed over the arrival of "an odd, uncouth character." This "religious crank" was an apparently demonstrative presence, at one point entranced by Eleanor's "angel music," and later leaving behind an unused, possibly malfunctioning folding bed.[120] Nevertheless, by straining their budget and possibly borrowing from congregants, the Harts fashioned a first-class wedding. Maybe the situation also showed "God moves in mysterious ways, His wonders to perform," as the family's matrimonial high in August contrasted steeply with their unmatched sorrow at Eleanor's wake in December.

In small communities, some "hitching" circumstances stirred up more interest than others. If some marriages allegedly formed in heaven, at least one resulted from the social media of a Chicago lovelorn column. Hope recounted news of an Illinois seeker who found bliss with a well-heeled Tennessean, only recently widowed. Her neighbors readily cogitated and outright ogled: Was she a hag, especially a bald one, or just a market commodity? The wedding ceremony itself was fleetingly upstaged by the arrival of state militia to combat lawless "night riders" of nearby Reelfoot Lake. The new bride in time discreetly added a then-strange, unknown linoleum in the kitchen. Bless everyone's hearts, just what was the overall outcome?[121]

Occasionally, arrangements came with an unexpected hiccup. Adult fascination with young people falling in love and marrying puzzled Hope in her formative years. Individuals and even a whole community could get caught up in the kerfuffle and do unexpected things, only to laugh about the outcome later. A bride's previously absent father financed lavish wedding plans. Hope's itchy ears strained to keep up with all the rumors and gossip. The arrival of the financier father and his spouse elevated the general excitement; the buzz was immensely greater with citizens sprucing up their property and the addition of a church marquee. Perhaps even God himself waited only vaguely aware of some abounding surprise. And what of the young principals? On the big day, the bride's father reportedly suffered a severe abdominal mishap and miraculous recovery. Hope especially showered him with attention and, in turn, she received a long coveted gift.[122]

Certainly, other unplanned things surfaced. In one setting, Hope thought the bride was a bit plump but, with little further thought, concluded it was baby fat. Sometimes Hope wondered if a person was marriage material, especially "the world's most terrifying principal—a red-headed, terrible tempered 'tiger.'"[123] This same man Hope saw as a sort of Ichabod Crane. Who could have expected Cupid to shoot his arrows through that administrator-teacher's seemingly calcified heart and into the throbbing breast of the town's sweet first grade teacher? In all this, the most pressing matter was what the bride at the last minute would wear.[124] Yes, Cousin Pigg's ceremony went awry, too. At Grandmother Kennedy's house, some parlor substructure gave way, leaving attendees in disarray. How did a wheelchair-ridden invalid fare? Otherwise, pretty much an ordinary day. At her first church wedding "as a starched and beruffled little guest," Hope memorably got a first taste of gelatin, "a marvelous new dessert" supposedly.[125] At another venue, the young, inquisitive Hope covertly learned creatures had discovered the cake.

Reverend Hart had his share of ministry misadventures. Perhaps the most unusual calamity occurred in Kentucky during his early ministerial years. "In an astonishing turn of his pastoral duties," he "whipped the town bully."[126] On the way to a hitching, while crossing a deep creek, Sterling got soaking wet. The redeeming grace was that he dried before eternity rolled.[127] One Methodist candidate elected immersion in a clear creek, necessitating Sterling, in his long white baptizing clothes, leaving the pool to rescue Hope and the buggy from baptism. She and the horse had different messages in mind. Actually, that setting was more natural than immersing an alcoholic Methodist outdoors in the wee late-winter-morning hours. Blessedly, in another town, Sterling's intervention in a love triangle prevented a murder, saved a marriage, and resulted in the interloper's Methodist conversion. Once, along a wedding route, a bluff even gave way. Always something for a family to be thankful about!

All was not sweetness and light in Hope Hart's world. She lived in and pictured a White-dominated society. The account exemplifies smug Southern white supremacy and alleged Black genetic inferiority—beliefs extant from colonial days far into the twentieth century, accompanied by imposed discrimination, in this instance by local and state Jim Crow laws.[128] Her approach showed absurd acts, childlike behavior, simple-minded thinking, and unsophisticated ways. Likewise, in jaundiced White eyes, most Southern Blacks were naturally domestics and field hands, tasks for which they supposedly were most qualified intellectually; yet some rose to steady railroad employment. Similarly, in the Hart household, good and competent domestic "Aunt" Liza was easily "our friend and main comfort," one perhaps somewhat elevated as the owner of a whitewashed house and an attractive yard.[129] For whatever reasons, Hart did not question or criticize the personal, social, and legal perceptions and status quo. She showed what she learned from other

Whites, maybe confirming "You've Got to Be Carefully Taught" to hate and fear, according to the musical "South Pacific."[130] As such, she was a product of her time and environment, when most Southern Whites considered nothing amiss in racial subordination, even as Blacks felt the full brunt of White intimidation. If Whites saw anything unfair, they themselves kept silent to avoid coercion or threats from fellow Whites. Hope may have positively changed her views about Black-White relations as early as after World War II and certainly no later than the Black civil rights movements of the 1950s, evolving noticeably with the 1970s and her senatorially related work about aging in the United States.

Hope Hart took a varied approach to names in the manuscript. Was she debasing Blacks by only giving first names, or did she only know and recall abbreviated monikers? For unknown reasons, of all the Blacks cited, she only identified Dick Hutcherson (c. 1835-?) of Palmersville by family name. Indeed, he was a freedman who married Ann Kennada (c.1835-?) in Weakley County, Tennessee, on May 26, 1866.[131] Hope did mention a Black woman called Bessie Belle who was a competent hotel cleaner in Fulton, Kentucky. Was that really her name, especially Belle? Not likely. It is also improbable even an outstanding chambermaid would have gained much positive public attention; nor did such individuals' names often appear in print, making it virtually impossible to identify them fully.[132]

Generally, Whites got first and last names. Even so: were these real names or merely substitutes? Most appellations are not searchable because of limited personal facts, location, or year date. Furthermore, for unstated social and legal reasons, Hope Hart specifically assigned a few aliases. The earliest notable example was the Elder Maybank, the long-sermonizing minister, in "A Babe in Little Zion." In reality, he was George T. Mayo, who was also a county officer and Hart-Moore family friend. Another incident inspired name and occupational aliases. While Hope Hart's "Uncle Charlie" was dying from a chest injury he perhaps became a victim of a scheming young woman and her father. "Uncle Charlie" was really Uncle Leroy Simpson Moore, the first-born child of the Hart-Moore marriage. Hope named the allegedly devious pair Caroline and Squire Griggs, the latter supposedly a businessman. Actually, "Caroline" was Ida May Brite (a year later a McWherter) and "Squire Griggs" was Lemuel D. Brite, a Weakley County farmer. Consequently, searching for these family-associated personalities is today more often successful because of

Ancestry and Find A Grave websites, Hope Hart's *Dresden Enterprise* series, and, at times, public records.

Despite untoward events and issues, Reverend Hart's dedicated family and ministry spread the Methodist gospel and matrimony to untold numbers of Jackson Purchase residents in their wide-ranging travels. According to the Hart brood, countless times "he mounted his horse, carrying saddlebags, to meet distant appointments in hazardous weather and over seemingly impassable roads." Nor did "floods, washouts, back water from the Mississippi River or other such difficulties" deter him. His only reply when near ones urged him to avoid risk was, "They [people] are waiting for me."[133] Furthermore, as Elaine Knight imaginatively paraphrased Hope, "weddings were a focal point in the parsonage life, memorably among the pleasures and tragedies that made growing up in our part of the world so fascinating."[134]

Decades removed from the early 1900s, Hope recorded recollections about ancestors in northwest Tennessee and her early life events. Understandably, she focused considerably on her immediate family in the early years of her father's Methodist itinerant ministry. At the same time, she included her perceptions of marital, church, and community events in a largely rural Jackson Purchase, a place increasingly influenced by transportation, communication, and modernization.

After 1907, the Hart siblings did well upon leaving the family household and striking out on their own. Hope's oldest brother, Ray Kennedy Hart (1887–1967), graduated from Cumberland University School of Law and practiced law in Claremore, Oklahoma, before joining Sinclair Oil Company for at least twenty-five years. His wife graduated from the University of Colorado. His father, Reverend Hart, united them in marriage on May 18, 1912, at Fort Scott, Kansas. Perhaps not surprising, the Harts were Methodists. They celebrated their fiftieth anniversary in 1962 at Donaldson, Arkansas, to which they moved in 1945. Their two sons were Bill R. Hart of Grand Rapids, Michigan, and Ray K. Hart II of Little Rock. The Harts were justly proud that their grandson Larry M. Hart was a US Naval Academy honor graduate who planned to study atomic science. Ray Kennedy Hart died May 2, 1967, at Pulaski, Hot Springs County, Arkansas, of a cerebral hemorrhage at age 79 and was buried in Dresden, Tennessee.[135]

Of those four Hart siblings, Joe Reece Hart had the shortest life. He was a research chemist generally and a US Department of Agriculture employee at Beltsville, Maryland, specifically. Unlike his siblings, he became a Lutheran.

He shuffled off this mortal coil in early February 1975 at Leigh Acres in Fort Myers, Florida, at age 73. His widow was Edith S. Hart of Leigh Acres. Nelson Key Hart of Chevy Chase, Maryland, and Hope Howard Hart of Washington, DC, survived him.[136]

Nelson Key Hart won the age prize. Both studious and outgoing, he became a journalist and ultimately retired as a magazine editor at *U.S. News and World Report*. A Chevy Chase, Maryland resident, he died in May 1998 of congestive heart disease at age 93 in Washington, DC, and interred at Sunset Cemetery, Dresden, Tennessee. His son, Sterling Reese Hart, preceded him in death.[137]

Like Key, Hope Hart's resting place was Sunset Cemetery in Dresden, Tennessee. Prior to her death, she lived in Chevy Chase House, a Maryland retirement home there. She passed away on June 11, 1985, at Georgetown University Hospital from heart and lung complications. Fittingly, Weakley County relatives and other outstanding residents were pallbearers.[138]

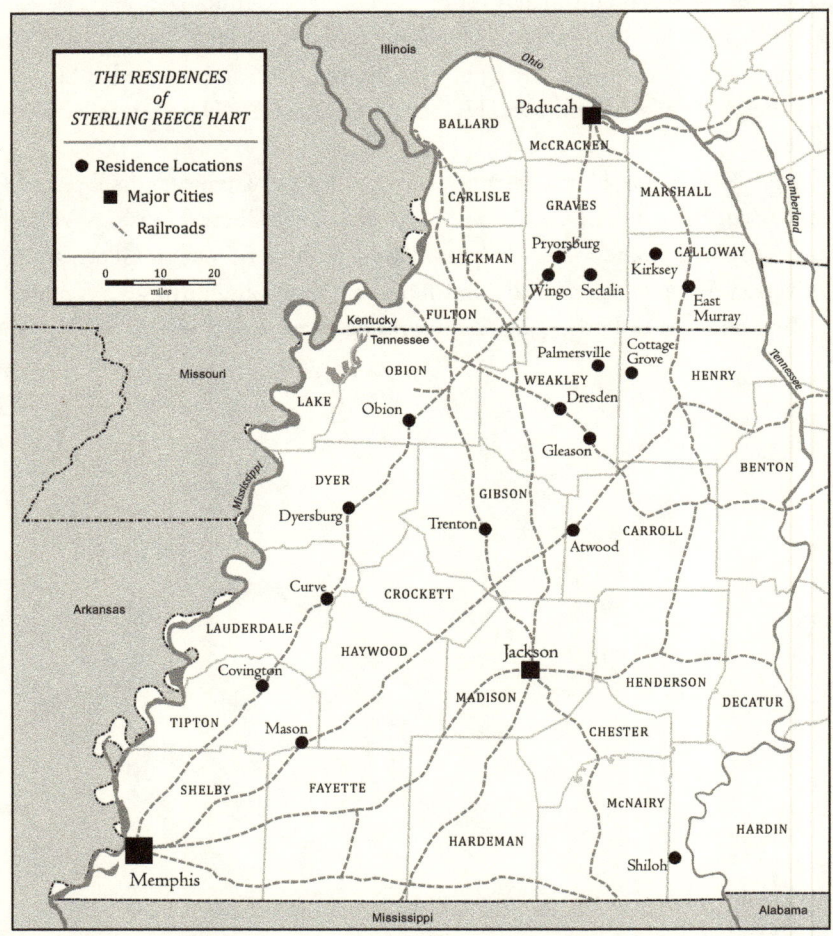

Map courtesy of Dr. Jeff Rogers, Professor of Geography, University of Tennessee, Martin.

CHAPTER I

We Are Gathered Together

IT WAS LATE AUTUMN AND A SOFT HAZE HUNG IN THE AIR AS DUSK settled over our town. The scent of burning leaves lingered from a faintly smoldering fire in the street near the parsonage.[1] The evening was chilly . . .

It all comes back to me as sharp and clear as the tang of that November day: our weatherworn but comfortable old house in a small town in West Tennessee,[2] not so many miles from the Mississippi River: its big front yard, separated from the back by a picket fence: and beyond that an enclosed garden and a barn lot. The barn was for Old Dick, our horse, and Old Bess, our Jersey cow. The garden was the source of most of our fresh vegetables, the cow furnished us with milk and butter, and Old Dick was our means of locomotion.

The house was tucked in close to a brick church. The churchyard and cemetery were on the far side. From our front window I sometimes watched in solemn wonderment when a span of black horses pulled a hearse through the arched gateway for a funeral. The sides of the hearse were of glass, and on the inside were tasseled black draperies. It made me shiver to catch a glimpse of the coffin when the draperies were parted.

Papa was the minister, and this was his church and parsonage.

There were seven of us in all—Papa, Mama, three boys and two girls.[3]

My sister Eleanor,[4] oldest of the children was a grown young lady, teaching music in a nearby town. Ray, my teen-age brother, drove Old Dick to bring her home every Friday afternoon.

The baby, Key, was a superactive toddler of one year, and Joe,[5] with the big brown eyes and quiet manner, was four. I was the rollicking leader of my two little brothers.

We were a happy family . . .

On the day that I recall, I had been home from school a long time. Lessons already were done. In my rocking chair by the big front window I had just finished a favorite story, way over in the back of McGuffey's Reader,[6] about a little girl named Bessie who used her aunt's sewing basket to gather wild flowers and left it out in the rain. The girl was seven years old, my own age.[7]

Now it was time to go help Mama. She had already called.

But, instead, I hesitated, then reached for the Sears and Roebuck catalog[8] on the bottom shelf of the bookcase and turned quickly to page 365. The page was thumb-marked and dog-eared.

I settled back in my chair and gazed long and wistfully at the illustration and description of a "Girl's Acme Wonder Bicycle." I knew the words by heart, but I read them to myself, half aloud, slowly and raptly: "In black or maroon enamel, decorated with gold stripes, strictly high-grade, heavily nickel plated and with ball bearings! For girls 7 to 9, only $12.95."

There it was—exciting and overwhelming in its shiny loveliness—pictured in full color, with a rosy-cheeked little miss holding the handle bars. My heart's desire!

As I sadly and reluctantly closed the catalog, I glanced through the window. A man was hurrying along the sidewalk in front of the parsonage. The brim of his hat was pulled down and his overcoat was turned up, but I knew who he was. He was Mr. Britton,[9] our Sunday School superintendent.

He turned and came up the brick walk to our door.

I called out: "Mama! Mr. Britton is here."

There were two or three light knocks, a pause, then a long, sharp rapping.

Mama came out of the kitchen, moving fast. She was untying and taking off her apron and smoothing her hair.

Mama was a pretty woman—petite, with soft hazel eyes and an abundance of dark hair. Her girlish figure and fair, pink complexion made her look as young as Eleanor. She was lively and full of fun, too, and when only the family was present she could—and did—often entertain us with imitations of characters she had known. She had the gift of mimicry. But of course, she was on guard most of the time to make sure she looked and acted the part of a minister's wife.

"Hurry and pick up your things," she told me.

Please, in a minute, I thought. First, I wanted to know what Mr. Britton's visit was about.

Mama turned into the hallway and opened the front door.

She greeted Mr. Britton and invited him in, but he said he hadn't time, "Thank you, ma'am." They talked for a few minutes. I edged into the hall to watch and listen. I heard Mr. Britton say:

"At six o'clock then—the train leaves at seven-thirty, you know."

With that he turned, started to go, then hesitated and came back a step.

"Why . . . uh . . . Sister Hart, you know Carrie had a right nice cake baked and she was wonderin' if she might send that over . . . and . . ."

Mama said: "Oh I think that would be just fine. Tell her I'll open some of my grape nectar and we'll all have refreshments. There will be plenty of time."

The visitor looked relieved. "Thank you, thank you kindly," he said. "That's mighty nice. Then it's all settled."

Mr. Britton turned again, replaced his hat with both hands, looked closely for the first step at the edge of the porch and quickly walked away, disappearing almost at once in the gathering gloom.

As Mama closed the door behind the visitor I could see she was pleased and a little excited.

"I'm not one bit surprised," she said absently.

I didn't have to ask Mama what it was that had failed to surprise her. The signs were too familiar. Mr. Britton had come to see about a wedding. He was speaking for Papa's services for someone who wanted to get married. That's why Mama was smiling.

A wedding meant the parlor would be opened. There would be visitors, when it was over everybody would be gay and laughing. I would get to watch. There was a promise of refreshments.

And I knew one other thing, too. Mama was thinking of the fee that Papa was almost certain to get. Maybe the windfall would pay for my piano lessons. I had just started "taking" from Miss Randall, and Mama had been wondering where the money was coming from to pay the modest tuition. It seemed that in our family there was never any money.

Papa had said, "Don't worry about it, Mattie. We can manage—someway. Have faith in Providence. Everything will come around in due time."

Then I thought of something else, my heart was racing. Mr. Britton was well-to-do. His store was one of the biggest on the square. Maybe the fee will be enough to pay for my piano lessons and a bicycle, too. The thought was enchanting. Papa said I could have the "Acme Wonder" when his ship came in.[10] Mr. Britton wasn't a ship, but . . .

"They could have picked a more convenient time," Mama continued. "I've already started supper."

With that she glanced in the hall mirror to make sure her hair had not been too much a fright. Then she dabbed for a moment at suspected dust on the stair rail. She hadn't wanted anyone to think for a moment that she might be a slack housekeeper.

These actions were automatic and in stride as she hastily threw a plaid shawl around her slender shoulders and headed for the back porch. There she opened the screen door, leaned out and called:

"Reece! Reece!"

Papa was in the shed out by the barn. He was milking Old Bess. From the shed came a muffled reply.

"Hee-ooh!"

Papa came to the door of the shed and peered toward the house. He was tall, six feet at least, and broad shouldered. He was wearing his "milking clothes."

"Did you want me?" he asked loudly.

"Come in as fast as you can." Mama called back. "Mr. Britton has been here. He wants you to marry his niece."

"When?"

"Six o'clock."

"All right," Papa answered. "I'll be there in a minute. I have to finish milking."

Mama turned and re-entered the house.

Right away things began to happen. Our cat, Whiskers, asleep on the rag rug in front of the sitting room grate, was sent into the night between purrs. With Mama leading the way, we quickly tidied up the room and put everything where it belonged. Then she took me in charge, brushed my curls, scrubbed my hands and face, and helped me change to a fresh crisply ironed dress. She found a matching ribbon for my hair. I was completely transformed in no time at all.

Baby brothers Joe and Key were already asleep. Mama checked their cribs and made sure they were tucked in.

Next Mama did some freshening up herself. She changed to a dark dress, put on her good shoes. Her hair, parted in the middle, was swept up with side combs, and when she returned to the sitting-room, I could see a delicate trace of powder on her face.

Just as Papa came bustling into the kitchen with a full pail of milk, Mama was rushing across the hallway to the parlor.

"I'll open the door and air the room a bit," she called over her shoulder. "Please hurry. I've put your things on the bed. Supper[11] is on the back of the stove, and the milk can wait. I'll strain it later."

In the parlor, Mama struck a match—from an ornamental holder on the mantel—and started a fire laid for such an emergency. Another match lighted our big parlor lamp.[12] It had a fancy rose-colored shade and sat on a claw-foot center table. Mama lighted a smaller lamp and put it on a stand near the piano. I held out my hands to the already crackling fire, enjoying the warmth.

"You may sit on the piano stool," Mama said, "but you must mind your manners and keep your dress pulled down. And don't turn round and round on the stool while the guests are here."

Before anything more could be said the outer door flew open and Eleanor rushed into the hall, making shivery sounds and singing out, "Hello, everybody!" Her cheeks were flushed by the crisp wind. I ran to her.

"Sister! Sister! It's a wedding! A wedding!"

She gave me a big hug and laughed and waltzed me around, I pulled her into the parlor where she could warm by the fire. I adored my grown up sister.

Eleanor, barely eighteen,[13] was a slender brunette, vivacious, cheerful. The open-air drive in our buggy had brought color to her fair skin. She was clad in a light red cloak, with a silk fascinator thrown over her head. Mama quickly told Sister what was about to happen,

"Mama, will I have to play for the wedding?" Sister asked.

"That would be nice if the bride wishes it," Mama replied. "Hurry and take off your cloak and change to your good dress. And please do something about your hair. It's blown all in wisps."

"All right, Mama—but what shall I play?"

"Oh, 'Hearts and Flowers'[14] will do, I guess. Or maybe 'Love is Fair'[15]—the bride liked that, the last time."

Ray bounced into the room with a noisy greeting at that moment. He began to warm his feet in front of the grate. "What's goin' on?" he asked.

"It's a wedding," I told him, "and you have to behave."

"Oh-o-o! So that's it. Say, Mama, if Sister is going to play the piano, how about letting me sing 'Little Brown Jug'?"[16]

We all laughed at that. I jumped up and down and clapped, it was so funny. Mama shooed Ray out of the room and told him to brush his shoes and put on his other jacket before the guests came.

There wasn't time for any more talking and joking. Outside we could hear the wedding party arriving. They were in a surrey from the livery stable. The colored driver yelled "WHOA!" loud enough to be heard by everybody in the parsonage, and the neighbors, too.

In a minute there were footsteps on the porch. Mama opened the door, smiled and invited the group to enter the parlor. Mr. Britton, carrying a package with both hands, guided them in. His niece was a girl about 18 years old. She had on a fur-trimmed cloak and a large velvet hat. The boy with her could have been 20 or 21. He held a cap in his hand, and was wearing a belted overcoat, peg-top trousers, and button shoes.

"You know Essie," Mr. Britton said to Mama. "And this is her fellow, Bob Strong. They've taken a notion to get married."

I had never seen Mr. Britton smile before. It was a weak smile, and it was gone almost before it started.

Mama shook hands with the couple.

"We're so glad to have you," Mama said. "My husband will be here right away. Please have off your wraps and come in to the fire."

Mama wanted to put the boy and girl at ease as they seemed to be quite tense. Her cheerful manner didn't do much good. The boy just managed to say "Good evening." The girl said nothing at all. Mama gave them a little smile as she turned to Mr. Britton:

"Where is Mrs. Britton? Isn't she coming?"

"She wanted to come in the worst way," he said, "but she's been busy all day helpin' Essie get ready, and I guess she's kinda tuckered out. Right at the last minute she took the weak trembles, and just couldn't make out to come. You know her back's been botherin' her a right smart of late."

Mr. Britton suddenly glanced at the package he was holding at half arm's length. "Oh, before I forget," he said, "here's the cake Carrie sent."

"Thank you," Mama said, relieving him of the fresh chocolate cake. "It was so nice of her to send it, and I really appreciate it, but I do wish she could have come, too. A wedding doesn't happen every day."

This seemed to touch Mr. Britton. He said very seriously: "We have raised Essie like she was our own. She was only six when my sister died; been with us ever since." He sighed. "Of course, you know Carrie and were both pretty well took back over this. Bob's been waitin' on Essie off and on about a year now, but we didn't know they were really stuck on one another. But when Bob came out from Memphis yesterday and said he'd landed a new job, the first thing we knew he was down to the store tellin' me that Essie was willin' and askin' if it was all right to go ahead."

Bob was listening to all this. He cleared his throat.

"Asked her as soon as I got here, and she didn't put up any fight," he said. "So here we are."

He started to chuckle, but thought better of it and cut off the sound in midair. Then he glanced around the room to see whether he had said or done the wrong thing.

Essie didn't say anything. She didn't change expression.

Ray came back into the parlor at this moment. His shoes were shined and he was wearing his Sunday jacket. He quietly seated himself at his usual "battle station," as he called it, on the window seat at the back of the room.

Before anything more could be said, Papa opened the door and entered the parlor. He was tall and imposing. His hair, was lightly tinged with silver, was carefully parted on the side and brushed back. His brown eyes had a friendly twinkle and he was smiling broadly.

Papa had changed from his milking clothes to a dark suit, and he was handsomely turned out now. He had on a high stiff collar and gray tie, smooth and nice. This was how he looked when he got up in the pulpit to preach.

This was the Reverend Sterling Reece Hart, pastor of the Methodist Episcopal Church, South.

All eyes turned to Papa, the visitors looking very solemn. He was the one they were there to do business with.

"Brother Britton," Papa said, "I'm delighted to see you, especially on such a very happy occasion." They shook hands.

"I guess what we're here for is all the best," Mr. Britton said, "but it's like I told Carrie when we decided to let Essie go ahead—they're both mighty young."

"Now Brother Hart," he continued, "of course you already know Essie here. And this is Bob Strong. Bob's from Alamo, over in Crockett County."[17]

Papa greeted Essie and Bob warmly. He gave each a big smile and a hearty handshake.

"If you'll just come with me into the other room," Papa said, "we'll talk briefly, and then we can have the ceremony."

I knew about this part. This was where Papa told them what they were getting into. At least, that's the way Ray explained it to me. They always had a prayer, too.

In about ten minutes or so, Papa returned to the parlor with Bob and Essie.

Their entrance broke up a somewhat extended story by Mr. Britton about "Miss Carrie Britton's rheumatism and back trouble." Mama had been listening politely. To me it had been an entertaining recital. The afflicted "Miss Carrie" had been suffering "something awful," he said.

Papa now took over as general manager of the occasion.

"Before the ceremony," he said, "we will have a selection of music."

Sister had just entered the room. She was in a fresh dress and her dark hair was neatly combed back in the pompadour style of the day.

After greeting the company she crossed over to the piano. As I slid from the stool and moved to my familiar place by the lamp, she seated herself, smoothed her skirt, and began to adjust her music.

Papa invited everybody to be comfortable. With all settled and silent he gave her the signal for the music to start.

Sister had decided on "Hearts and Flowers." She played it with tender feeling. The guests were a good audience. Not once did they look away or move a finger. They sat enthralled.

As the music ended, Papa rose and took a position at the right of the cheerfully blazing fire. He motioned the boy and girl to stand opposite of him. Next he opened his Methodist Discipline.[18] This was the book he spoke words from. But before beginning the ceremony Papa had more things to tell everybody.

"Brother Britton, you will be giving the bride away," he said. "Please move over this way."

"Eleanor," he said to Sister, "you may stand with the bride. Ray, next to the bridegroom."

Mama rose and took a position in the background. I returned to my place on the piano stool. I had been through this before.

Now everything was ready.

"Dearly beloved, we are gathered together . . . "

I sat perfectly still and watched. The bridegroom pulled at his tie, then moved his feet a little. I could see that he had on new shoes. Maybe they were hurting. He looked at the book in Papa's hand. He looked up at the flowered border on the wallpaper. Once he glanced at me. I held my breath.

The bride gazed straight ahead. She seemed to be dazed or in some kind of trance. She didn't seem to be alive at all.

Papa was reading the service in his usual way. His voice was serious, yet he sounded warm and friendly. I guess he knew how nervous the boy and girl were and he was doing his best to make them feel comfortable.

The part I like was coming up. The ring. Smiling, Papa lowered his tone and asked:

"There is a ring?"

Bridegrooms, as we all knew so well, sometimes forgot the ring or misplaced it. It had happened right here in our parlor. The question could make an embarrassed young man wish to drop through the floor. Papa was prepared to go on with the ceremony without skipping a beat if the ring had been overlooked.

But Bob Strong had a ring—if he could find it.

It was plain that he had been taken by surprise and was rattled. First he felt in his pants pockets. Then the side pockets of his jacket and the inside pocket. Then he unbuttoned his jacket and tried his vest.

I looked at Essie. She had heard and understood. She came back to life.

"He's got it," she said loudly and firmly, "I saw him buy it down at Anderson's Jewelry Store."

I looked back at Bob. He was still searching.

"It's in a box," the bride added.

"My overcoat," Bob almost shouted, "that's where it is. Where's my overcoat?"

It had been hung in the hall. "Here I'll get it," said Mr. Britton. Mr. Britton seemed upset, too. He stepped into the hall and returned at once with the coat.

The bridegroom first tried the right side. Nothing there. I held my breath again as he reached for the left. His face was set. Then he relaxed and grinned as he produced a small jeweler's box and held it up for all to see.

I wanted to jump and shout but I sat still. Nobody even smiled and nothing was said. Bob opened the box and took out a gold band. After a moment's indecision he handed the box to the bride who placed it gently on the mantel.

Now Papa was reading the words again as if nothing had happened. The room was perfectly still. I decided it was all beautiful and wonderful. The soft lights, the people posing in front of the fire, Papa's musical voice. The world seemed serene and right.

I closed my eyes. I thought: I just love weddings.

". . . whom God hath joined together let no man put asunder. . . . and I now pronounce you man and wife in the name of the Father and of the Son and of the Holy Ghost. Amen. Let us pray."

The prayer was short. At last I could leave my place and stretch and say something. I did all three as the parlor came alive.

In an instant everybody was beaming, laughing, talking merrily. Congratulations were passed. Mr. Britton put his hands on the bride's shoulders and gave her a big buss. He gave Bob a quick handshake.

"Be good to her," Mr. Britton said. He blinked back a tear.

Bob passed his coat sleeve across his moist brow and said, "Whew!" several times. He looked at me and grinned and said, "I sure thought I had lost it."

Essie glanced at me and her face beamed. She was bubbling over. "I thought I was scared, but I wasn't," she said delightedly to nobody in particular. She was chattering in every direction. After a while she calmed enough to say to Sister: "It was the prettiest piece I ever listened to."

With that she crossed to the mantel and took the box that had held her wedding ring. She put the box in Bob's coat pocket.

I could tell it was nearly over. The newlyweds were taking the Accommodation to Memphis. I saw Bob and Mr. Britton step aside and talk in lowered tones. Bob was asking something. When he got his answer, he took some money out of his wallet.

"Brother Hart, Bob wants to see you a second," Mr. Britton said. I saw Bob step over to where Papa was. Mr. Britton moved away. Bob handed something to Papa.

"I sure am obliged for everything," Bob said.

"Thank you," Papa replied. It was a five-dollar bill. "Thank you very much. I wish for both of you a long, happy and prosperous married life, with God's richest blessings."

Papa gave Mama a knowing look and held her eyes for a moment. She knew he was telling her, "Here is the money to pay Miss Crandall, with some left over."

Then Mama disappeared. I ran to the kitchen to find her. In a minute she returned to the parlor carrying a tray with a pitcher and glasses and plate of chocolate cake. I marched behind her with fringed linen napkins.

"Please have some nectar and cake," Mama invited. I passed around the napkins. "I guess I've seen a thousand weddings," I said to everybody there.

I was confident I really had seen a thousand weddings. For, being seven I treasured events such as the marriage of Bob and Essie as part of my own magic world.

The twentieth century was then quite new, and even in a Methodist parsonage, you see, there were many things to keep a little girl entranced. I didn't know exactly why or how it came about, but to me life in our part of Tennessee was wonderful.

Moving to new towns, and going to school, and finding all kinds of playmates . . .

And visiting Grandma, and picking berries in the Obion bottoms,[19] and taking buggy trips to Reelfoot Lake . . .[20]

And sometimes, deep in the night, the courthouse clock struck the hour . . . and from far away I might hear a mellow train whistle to lull me back to sleep.

And there were the joys of pony rides, and Thanksgiving Day programs, and gathering hickory nuts . . .

And once to my delight, Ringling Brothers Circus[21] came to town, with a street parade and countless dazzlements . . . And at the County Fair a man in spangles and tights went up in a balloon and came down in a parachute . . .

And the bicycle drill! Little girls about my age on gaily decorated bicycles riding in fancy formations in front of the grandstand. What a joy it was to watch . . .

There were sad things, too: Toby, my Persian cat disappeared and never came back . . . And I had diphtheria[22] . . . and I was heartbroken when Papa and Eleanor and Ray went to see the World's Fair[23] at St. Louis and left me at home with Mama and my new baby brother . . .

And always there were weddings. My childhood was filled with weddings. That of Essie and Bob was typical.

The procession of shy couples finding their way to our house to hear Papa "say the words" seemed unending.

From my perch on the revolving piano stool, prim and proper under Mama's eye, I watched and reveled in everything that happened. It was as if I were a queen, and each boy and his bride and Papa and Mama and Sister and the guests were players performing just for me.

Pleasant, too, were the weddings I suffered to attend now and then in the homes of the brides—run by fluttery mothers and high-pitched relatives.

At more than one such affair, there were silent menfolks, all but unnoticed by me, hovering in the background, their faces grim.

For sadly some nuptials came about perforce; the ravelings of error could be present.

I only know I rejoiced with the cheerful. I cried with those who wept.

My reward for being good—at least I tried—was the bliss of being there; of sharing in the little misadventures and happy endings. Pridefully, I was part of the show.

Of course, the ceremonies in our own parlor have the front-row seat in my memory. Sister's music, Papa's friendly voice, laughter, a tear or two, hugging and kissing, the going away. Round and round everything went, and, if Mama's eye wandered, I joined in the whirl—on my prize turn stool by our battered upright grand.

CHAPTER 2

A Babe at Little Zion

IF THE FIRST WEDDING CEREMONY IN MY LIFE HAD TAKEN PLACE ON the off side of Sirius the Dog Star, and I had been as far away as Texas, I couldn't have known less about it. I was there—but I was still a babe in arms.[1]

In this circumstance, of course, the story of my debut as a wedding guest was to be handed down to me. It was the wedding of Aunt Alice[2] and Uncle Billy[3], and it took place at hallowed Little Zion.

Little Zion was in the year 1898—and still is—a country meeting house quite a way back in Weakley County, Tennessee. The Little Zion community is where my folks grew up.

It was in this weather-splashed, tree-shaded little church, originally built of hand-hewn logs, that the tight-laced Calvinists who pioneered Weakley County first worshiped. After a long and folksy history, it survives today as the home church of a remaining handful of Primitive, or Hard Shell, Baptists.[4] And this church was chosen by Alice and Billy for a formal wedding, the first of its kind for Little Zioners—that is, the first in which the church was decorated, the bride wore a white gown and veil and a group of attendants took part.

While church weddings were not the rule at Little Zion, a few couples through the years had been bold enough to rise at the end of the Sunday preaching, march up to the "stand" and call on a well-winded parson to unite them on the spot. Such an event almost always came as a surprise to the congregation, and frequently even the families involved knew nothing of what was to happen until they saw the young people step forward.

Formal engagements were unknown. In fact, the prevailing custom was for a Cupid-smitten couple to seek out a magistrate to officiate when they decided to take the final step—without telling anyone in advance. Those considering matrimony often made a game of keeping their plans hidden. If a couple bespoke an ordained minister to tie the knot, they usually pledged him to secrecy until the wedding date.

Aunt Alice, Papa's[5] youngest sister and a belle of the district, was of a different mettle. She had grown up under Little Zion traditions—but she wanted another kind of wedding. So she persuaded Grandpa[6] to stand up in meeting a month in advance and read the announcement of her engagement.

"I beg the indulgence—uh—I arise at this time . . . ," Grandpa began.

He coughed, cleared his throat with a loud "harrumph" then produced a handkerchief from inside his go-to-meeting coat and mopped his brow.

". . . For a special announcement," he finished.

The elder,[7] spent from a long air-flailing sermon on predestination, stood looking at Grandpa curiously.

The congregation, overwhelmed by something unexpected, suddenly was completely still. A pin dropped at that moment would have rattled noisily on the uncarpeted floor. Necks craned. Ear trumpets blossomed in the "amen corner." Those on the front benches turned around for a better look at flustered Grandpa.

Poor Grandpa. He was perspiring profusely.

"Here," he finally blurted, "you read the thing, Elder. I forgot my specs."

With that he stalked down the aisle and handed a folded piece of paper to the preacher.

The original tablets of stone with the Ten Commandments couldn't have fascinated the audience more than that piece of paper. The elder opened it and looked at it fixedly through the lower part of his bifocals. Then he broke into a beaming smile and relaxed. The audience relaxed, too. It was going to be something pleasant.

Grandpas scowled as he marched back to his seat.

The elder proceeded to read a formally phrased announcement of the engagement and impending marriage of Alice Ruth Moore to William Thomas Killebrew.

Alice and her fiancé, a young man from Dresden, had been keeping company for some time and the news that they were to be married surprised no one. But the fact that Alice's family knew all about the approaching event and that it was to be a formal ceremony at Little Zion set the congregation buzzing.

In reading the engagement notice, the good elder of Little Zion was not able to restrain himself from ad libbing a little, extolling the characters of the contracting parties.

". . . No finer young people on God's green footstool . . . nurtured amongst us . . . salt of the earth . . . Beloved by one and all . . ."

These were some of the elder's florid interpolations.

Later Uncle Pete[8] said: "It was so beautiful it sounded like Alice and Billy had just died." Pete was a brother of the bride-to-be. He was the droll one.

To some of the Hard Shells the announcement smacked of "high livin'" and "puttin' on airs." After church let out there was some mumbling about it.

"Don't know what's come over Simpson Moore, lettin' Alice do a thing like that," said one grizzled oldster. "I know'd Simp's daddy. He wouldn't have put up with such."

"Paralee's[9] back of it," grumbled another, "she's the one who's got them high-falutin' notions." Grandma's name was Paralee.

Such crusty comments were minor, however, as Mama recalled. People were far more curious than they were concerned over the proprieties.

The spunky, convention-flouting Alice at once sent for Mama to go with her to select the material for her wedding dress and other finery. They made the trip from Grandpa's in a buggy over muddy roads to Paris—Tennessee, that is—for that purpose.

Back home with the silk and satin, along with the buttons and bows and laces, Alice and various helpers settled down to turn out a trousseau. A neighborhood seamstress was engaged for the fanciest work. For weeks Mama was busy riding Old Molly back and forth, giving a hand. If all the seams that were sewn in those frantic days had been put end to end . . . But there was one mishap. Both sleeves of the wedding dress were made for the same arm hole.

That was the era of muttonlegs at their fullest and flounciest; and for the fine dresses they were so trimmed and beribboned that it was difficult, I'm sure, to tell just which was right and which was left. But the mistake was remedied at the last minutes and no harm was done. None if you discount the years it may have taken off the lives of the toiling needle-and-thread experts.

Uncle Pete again: "It would have looked mighty stylish on a bride with two left arms."

The wedding day was in early spring and the dogwood and wild crabapple were in full bloom. Mama and Sister, helped by various uncles, spent the morning before the evening ceremony decorating the little bare-walled church.

A decorated church!

That was another in a continuing [*sic* continuing] series of jolts for Little Zion—one that left some of the Hard Shells slacked-jawed with wonderment. With the exception, perhaps, of a bunch of stiff prince feathers on the preaching stand hard by the water pitcher, the church up to that time had been innocent of frills or floral arrangements. Now Grandma called it "just heavenly." Before, it was a plain country church, unvarnished, unembellished, austere. Now it was lovely—"a bower of pin [*sic* pink] and white blossoms."

Sister at that time was barely thirteen, but she was the organist in charge of the nuptial music. Her instrument was a parlor organ, moved over from the home of Mama's parents.

This was another innovation—in fact a community-wide sensation.

You see, Little Zion was a little "offish" on the question of musical instruments in the sanctuary. The fact that an organ had been installed for the occasion didn't at all sit well with some of the amen-corner patriarchs. But the Moores were a numerous clan, respected and liked, so the deacons looked the other way and said nothing. But this was not true of Aunt Susie Stone,[10] who had live [*sic* lived] down the holler from the church since long before the War.

She was bound to have her say.

"Might as well bring in a Punch and Judy show,"[11] she fumed. "All that carryin' on and usin' an innocent child to play the devil's music. It's a God's wonder if the church walls don't fall in, with all that squeakin' and squawkin'."

She shook her head, and cluck-clucked and rolled her eyes.

"They can bring on a banjer player and get old Dick Hutcherson's boy[12] to rattle the bones and do the back step for what I care. It's nothin' but pyore scandal. Catch me gawkin' at sech like."

Dick Hutcherson was an elderly ex-slave on Grandfather's place. His boy, a virtuoso of the bones and a noted jig dancer had long since cleared out for Mobile and greener fields.

Aunt Susie vowed she would never set foot in Little Zion church again—but she did. She was down front at the wedding, sitting straight and stiff in a corset that she could scarcely see over, and her married daughters had to restrain her from going into a shouting spell at the end.

The church, of course, was jammed beyond belief for the novel event. Grandpa and Grandma—who had driven over with the bridal party—had trouble reaching their seats. Winding their way down front, they were forced to step over children who overflowed the aisle. There had been a complication an almost a serious hitch in plans before they left home. Grandpa wanted to wear his Confederate uniform. He had ridden with Nathan Bedford Forrest and was proud of that uniform. Hadn't he always worn it to funerals when old comrades were laid away? And to the Weakley County Fair when he judged the stock? And to the county seat on First Monday?[13]

It required Grandma's firmest persuasion to settle the matter and get him into his Sunday clothes. He mumbled all the way to the church and looked pretty grim during the ceremony.

At last all was ready. Uncle Potter escorted Sister in and the music started.

The organ was so wheezy and hard to pump and Sister was so little that Mama was afraid both might "give out." But Sister kept pumping. First she played two "instrumental solos" announced by the parson, Elder Maybank, who was stern and resplendent in a frock-tailed coast, light vest and black string tie.

If the audience was a little bemused by Sister's instrumental selections, it was shaken and stunned by what followed. A member of the bridal party, a young matron from the county seat, rose, stood by the organ and "sang a love song right in the meeting house!"

It was unheard of. There were gasps and whispers. The deacons present stared straight ahead. It was revolutionary, they knew, but they were committed and there was no turning back.

"O Promise Me"[14] poured forth through the last languishing note.

Finally Sister sounded down with a flourish on the wedding march just as her music teacher had instructed her. It was her big moment. Proud of being soloist and accompanist[15]— and of the new silk dress she was wearing—she felt almost as important as the bride.

The two couples who "stood up" with Alice and Billy came down the aisle, followed by the bride on the arm of her brother, Uncle Jim.[16] She was joined by the bridegroom in front of the stand.

The ceremony was brief, a circumstance that was to be told and retold.

Billy had skirmished and lost on the issue of a church wedding. His preference was to drive over to Ellum Tree[17] on the State line and have the "marryin' squire" tie them up without any fuss. The odds were against him. Alice had gone to school at the Palmersville Academy[18] and was independent in her outlook. She had a different notion. She was marrying an important young man, one who was handsome and popular, and who recently had been elected to a county office.[19] She wanted a proper wedding.

Grandma sided with Alice. Born of pioneer parents when this part of Tennessee was newly opened, Grandma had married during the Civil War[20] and had endured the hard times that followed, yet she had been reared to gentle ways. She encouraged Alice's plans.

There was not much the beleaguered Billy could do about it.

So Billy had agreed reluctantly to a church affair, with Elder Maybank to officiate.

The Elder was famous for his long-windedness. Those who had sat on the rigid, back-cracking pews on preaching day were aware that he could roll out a two-hour sermon on one glass of water and preach twice as long without a second pitcher. His prayers, even to the long-suffering Hard Shells, were excessively drawn out, covering everybody and everything in his entire field of thought.

So when Billy took Elder Maybank aside to give him the license they had a talk. Billy told him that if he produced a long ceremony and prayer, there would not be one red cent for the fee. But if he cut the proceedings to a reasonable length, he might get five dollars. If it turned out to be a real short ceremony, there was a good possibility that the fee would run to ten dollars.

The good man of the cloth pondered well his conversation with the bridegroom and he took no chances: After the couple had squared away at the altar and the bride had received her ring and they had joined right hands, he raised his eyes to the ceiling and quickly said, "I pronounce you man and wife. Amen."

Uncle Billy told me years later that he paid the good brother with a ten-dollar gold piece.

"It went off so fast," he said, "there was always some doubt in my mind as to whether it was a really legal."

The best man was a young lawyer from Dresden and it was his wife who contributed Little Zion's first love song. She had been to finishing school in Nashville. She sang beautifully. Mama was proud of the fact that Sister could play the accompaniment. Asleep in a babe's dreamland, I didn't hear it. If I had heard it I could not have been more thrilled than I was twenty-five years later when, as an attendant in the wedding of Aunt Alice's daughter, I stood in the church at Dresden and heard the same voice sing the same song.

The nuptials over, the happy couple and their party drove away in washed and polished buggies to the bridegroom's home for the wedding supper. As only the attendants and close relations were invited, the crowd at the church had to make the most of this whip-cracking exit. They stood chattering and squealing congratulations till the last bit of dust had settled.

They didn't feel left out. They knew the really big occasion was still to come—the "infare" to be given the next day by the parents of the bride. All the kinfolks and practically everybody else within horseback distance would be present, and the bride would wear that creation heralded far and wide as the "second-day dress."

For this event Grandpa killed the fatted calf and barbecued it, along with a pair of shoats and a sheep. And he probably had a jug or two hidden in the corn crib. Uncle Israel—called "Unkissle" by the children—an elderly Negro on the place, and couple of his boys stayed up all night tending the barbecue. Grandpa charged them on pain of sudden demolition that it had to be done to a turn, crisp yet tender and juicy for "that hungry sheebang" he was expecting.[21]

The reassuring Israel had dug a trench in the side lot. It was about three feet deep. He laid a fire in the trench and let it burn until the bed of coals was ready, across the trench he had placed green hickory limbs. After the meat was dressed and had cooled out, he placed it on the hickory cross pieces over the coals. From time to time he added to the bed of coals from a fire he had going a few feet away. In this way he kept the temperature regulated and the slabs of meat slowly sizzled all night. As he turned the dripping section of pork and beef and mutton, he basted each piece with a barbecue sauce of his own devising, for which he had local fame.

The night air around the barbecue pit was filled with a rich, tangy, tantalizing aroma, a sure promise of a wonderful feast to come.

Grandma, with Charlotte and Ann, her kitchen helpers—wife and daughter of Israel—had been cooking for days. To supplement the barbecue, enough food had been prepared to feed a Methodist camp meeting.

It was the kind of feast the "Old Country"—as Mama and Papa always called the community where they grew up—loved and reveled in: hearty and robust, and noisy and gay. The newlyweds held the center of the stage, of course, leading the merry-making. But it was a big day for Grandpa, too. How he strutted in his rebel uniform!

Alice and Billy drove away about mid-afternoon—the barbecue was at noon and caught the train at Dresden for the State capital and their honeymoon. But wait—I must go back a bit and tell you about the shivaree, the boisterous event that came after the wedding supper.

※

The shivaree was as much a part of a wedding affair along the North Fork[22] of the Obion as the license and the preacher. If the young bucks knew of an impending marriage they made elaborate preparations. Perhaps that was the reason for so many elopements.

The sporting bloods had been known to waylay a bridegroom and lock a cow bell on a heavy chain round his neck. The hapless victim would require the services of a blacksmith to get it off. They nearly always rode the bridegroom on a rail. Sometimes they tossed him in a corn crib and nailed the bars on the door while the bride languished alone and bereft. Billy had often been a ringleader in such pranks. He and Alice feared the worst.

Papa and Mama were among the guests at the bountiful wedding supper, and as usual, Papa entered heartily into the fun. If he didn't actually cut the pigeon wing,[23] he sashayed around at a pretty lively clip when Uncle Clabe another hand on the place, brought in his fiddle and scraped away at "Old Dan Tucker."[24]

It was all in jolly good humor. The wedding party, magnificently dined, finally drifted into the parlor and our Aunt Annie[25]—Alice's sister—strummed her guitar and the guests sang the bride's favorite songs.

Finally it was bedtime.

"Get ready everybody," warned Billy's father, grimly. "They'll sure be a-coming. I thought I'd better name it to you. Be prepared!"

He was speaking to the remaining group of close friends and relatives who were staying overnight.

The old gentleman knew. The last light hadn't been blown out five minutes when the mock serenade broke loose. All the young folks from miles around were there, beating on tin pans and wash tubs, ringing bells and yelling like Morgan's raiders.[26] Those who had no "musical instruments" had cut switches from the sumac bushes along the country road and with these they raised a tremendous racket, rapping the sides of the house.

One bold serenader tried to climb a post at the corner of the porch to reach a second-story window. He was just "acting the fool,"[27] which was standard conduct at a shivaree. The reaction from within was more or less standard too—a bridesmaid opened the window suddenly and doused him with a bucket of flour.

The din lasted perhaps twenty minutes; then it ceased as abruptly as it had started and the hoarse merry-makers appeared to straggle off down the road. An uneasy silence settled over the Killebrew manor.

Squire Killebrew,[28] a little elderly for coping with a really rowdy situation, wasn't fooled.

"They'll be back," he told Aunt Sammy,[29] his wife, as they eased themselves into bed a second time. "Those fellers wouldn't give up that easy."

Again he was right. What they had heard was merely the overture. The boys actually had been setting the stage for a roof-raiser.

Their first maneuver, covered by the preliminary clamor, had been to drag a fresh fox skin across the yard, and around the house several times. Then a daring young man pulled it through the open hall, along the side porch and finally up the back stairway that lead to the guest's bedrooms. The skin left a strong scent.

With that accomplished, the conspirators were ready for the grand finale. From a cooperative source over in Henry County[30] they had borrowed a pack of fox hounds. The hounds in closed wagons were being held nearby. At the right moment, just long enough after the lull, the pack was released. That was the moment that turned the bridal retreat, as Uncle Pete put it, into the "biggest uproar since the battle of Shiloh."[31]

Squire Killebrew saw it this way:

"Hell didn't exactly turn loose on us, it exploded all over the place."

The new tumult hit the yard with the force of a cannon blast. The baying hounds were everywhere—in the house, under it, even upstairs.

Scores of excited voices urged on the dogs: "Yip, yip, yipee!"

"Eat 'em up!"

"Get in there, Rusty! Tear 'em up, boy!"

"Sic 'em Rattler!"

"Hoo-hOO-Hoo-EE!"

The yard dogs joined in the scramble, roosters crowed, hens cackled, peafowls screamed, livestock in the barnyard became disturbed and excited and joined in the clamor.

Mama and Papa, among the overnight guests, never forgot the bawling, bleating, braying and neighing, mingled with the hair-raising baying of the fox hounds in full tongue.

The old Squire stormed into the hallway in his long nightshirt, wielding an iron poker, yelling at the dogs and vowing murder.

It was a rouser while it lasted—it had to be—but in another half hour all was quiet and peaceful again. In the far distance could be heard the last faint sounds of retreating hounds. Upstairs there were still a few stray giggles. That was all.

Squire Killebrew next morning allowed himself a wry chuckle over the fun; but he was put out about the corn and tobacco that had been trampled in his fields when the stock broke out of the barnyard gate.

His loss was negligible, though, compared with that of a guest, a weeping young lady. Her magnificent new flower-trimmed hat worn with pomp and glory to the wedding and placed with loving care in a ribbon-bound box, somehow in the excitement of the night had been knocked out of the window and crushed into utter ruin in the melee below.

Sleep was wrecked, crops mangled, nerves shattered—but the tragedy of the mashed bonnet would live longest.

CHAPTER 3

Disenchantment

THE FIRST CHURCH WEDDING THAT I ACTUALLY REMEMBER WAS TO me a disillusioning flop. I was as disappointed as the bride might have been if her betrothed had sent a note to the altar saying that he unexpectedly had been called out of town.

It turned out that way because at my tender age I had allowed fanciful notions to lead me astray.

I already knew, of course, what home ceremonies were like. Those affairs, with Papa reading a solemn rigmarole out of his book to stony-faced couples, were part of my life. The very word *wedding* spelled exhilaration and gaiety. The air seemed to tingle when people were being married.

But when the scene shifted to the church and for the first time I was a starched[1] and beruffled little guest—well, for reasons that were more than sufficient to me, I felt I had been "taken in" and defrauded.

Mama had an uncanny prescience for nuptial events. She could glance out of the window when a buggy stopped at the gate and by the time the visitors alighted and walked to the front door she had Papa in his frock coat, the floor cleared of books and toys, the hearth swept, her apron off, and her hair smoothed, and every child's hands washed and every nose wiped.

And when she opened the door, there would stand an ill-at-ease boy and a blushing girl looking for the preacher.

If they had a license and another couple to stand with them, and if Papa felt that all was correct, the parlor would be opened for the ceremony.

After the ceremony was over and the guests had gaily departed we liked to stay in the parlor till the fire burned out; and I might be allowed to look through the stereoscope² at colored views of *Venice by Moonlight*,³ while Mama and Papa talked.

These weddings were also an economic factor in our family. Even a little impromptu wedding in the parlor was worth a couple of dollars to the house treasury; but if the ceremony took place at the bride's home and was an ice-cream-and-cake affair, or in the church with attendants and a supper later, it could run into big money—ten dollars maybe. There was one red-letter day that Papa liked to remember—when a ceremony netted him twenty dollars and a pair of kid gloves.

Occasionally a couple drove up to the parsonage, called Papa out to the gate and asked to be married while seated in their buggy. Papa did not perform that kind of ceremony. But he usually persuaded them to come into the house for a dignified service, and thus the fee was saved. That helped.

A dollar bought twenty pounds of sugar or a pair of shoes for me in that post-Cleveland era.⁴ Every wedding fee was a windfall that added to the joys of the parsonage lives and provided some of the necessities.

Of course, the bridegroom's gift to the parson wasn't a hundred percent certainty. Cautious customers looking for a parson might ask in advance about the cost. Papa invariably, and in his kindest manner, told them that payment was not required.

"It is a solemn and serious step you are about to take," he would say. "You are entering into a holy estate, a new way of life. As your pastor and friend, I make no charge for my services."

Such matrimonial candidates as a rule left two dollars. A few cut it fine and handed out a single dollar bill. Others took the parson at his word, and brazenly departed with the barest "thanks." One parishioner with great warmth of feeling for the almighty dollar "took" Papa in a two-for-one deal.

One Sunday afternoon the son of this widely known "tightwad" drove up to the parsonage with a girl. It was obvious they had matrimony on their minds. His father and a small party came along to see the ceremony.

Papa greeted them. "Well, Brother Griscom," he said, "everybody is most welcome. Come in."

"Thank you, Brother Hart, Thank you. I hate to trouble you, but you know how it is—Jake and Fanny Sue finally decided to try workin' in double harness⁵ and they wanted you to do the hitchin'."⁶

Mr. Griscom frowned. He was thinking about the cost.

"It's certainly a pleasure to accommodate you." Papa told him.

The guests were arranging themselves in the parlor, but Mr. Griscom wasn't through with Papa.

"Oh, Brother Hart," he said in an aside, "could I see you a second?"

"Yes, of course. Brother Griscom."

"How much is it goin' to cost me?"

Papa smiled broadly. He made his usual reply to such a question

"Not a thing," he said. "There is no fee. You and your family are all members of our church and it is my duty, as well as a pleasure and a privilege, to serve you."

"Well, Preacher, you see I want to do what's a right," the blacksmith said, dropping his voice to a confidential tone, "I've been askin' around and they tell me that the legal free [*sic* fee] at the Squire's[7] is two dollars. Would you be willin' to take care of us for two dollars, say?"

"That is perfectly all right," Papa said.

The blacksmith fished inside his jacket and came out with a long pouch-type pocketbook, folded over several times and closed with a snap fastener. He inserted two stubby work-stained fingers in the pouch and after poking around produced a wad of crumpled bills. He examined these, finally extracting a one-dollar bill. Probing farther, he brought up a number of coins. As he peered through his steel-rimmed spectacles he assorted these in one palm till he had a dollar in change. He checked his count a second time to make sure it was right, then he handed the crumpled bill and change to Papa.

"There you are, Preacher," he said, "two dollars on the barr'l head cash in advance. That ought to fix us up good."

"Thank you," Papa said.

Jake and Fanny Sue were soon one. In the midst of the gay exchanges that followed. Mr. Griscom approached his pastor again. This time he was wearing a sly or perhaps sheepish grin.

"Brother Hart," he said, "I was thinkin' . . . as long as we're here . . . well, I've paid you for the job and I thought maybe I'd get you to tie a knot for me, too."

"You?" Papa's eyebrows went up.

"Yep, you see, I figger it this way, Batchin' is all right for some, I guess, but I've been wantin' a woman in the house ever since I lost my first old lady seven years ago. So me and Miz Crawford here thought we'd . . ."

He jerked his head toward a lumpy, red-faced woman in a faded print dress who was fanning herself briskly with a palm-leaf fan. She was a widow, the landlady of a boarding house. She said nothing but increased the temp of her fan.

Mr. Griscom produced the marriage license and handed it to Papa.

"This is quite a surprise," Papa said, "but a happy one of course."

Before starting the second ceremony, Papa paused and said to the company:

"It has been a pleasure to marry Mr. Griscom's son; now I will do as much for Mr. Griscom. I am reminded of the old proverb: Two can be married as cheaply as one.[8]

※

The affair that disenchanted me took place when I was four[9]—a small girl with a big imagination. The bride was a next door neighbor and Sister's bosom friend, the bridegroom, a young ministerial student, was a protégé of my father's. For these reasons I heard a great deal about the event.

Mama, Sister, the bride and the bride's mother seemed to be in unending conversation and agitation about it. The dress with a train; the veil; the invitation list; the music; the wedding supper. Such momentous things to be decided every day. The biggest question of all, as I interpreted the conversations, was whether everyone would catch his death of cold.

It was midwinter and Mama was set against letting Sister lay aside her union suit[10] and wear a low-neck dress. Sister vowed she would not play the organ if she could not wear her pink chiffon, without winter underwear. Mama finally consented, but on the condition that Sister was to keep her coat on in the Church vestibule till the last possible minute.

Mama had firmer control over me.

"I know it will put you in bed with pneumonia if you wear your white organdy Children's Day[11] dress," she said. Children's Day in our Sunday School came in the spring, and was an occasion for which all the kiddies blossomed out in white frocks and lighter raiment generally. "You'll just have to wear the white ruffled pinafore over your Sunday red woolen dress."

After much inward searching Mama compromised a bit further and permitted me to have white stockings instead of the regular winter kind—long black-ribbed stockings that buttoned to my "drawers-body."

Talk of the refreshments added to my excitement. They were going to have ambrosia[12] with the wedding cake—which seemed normal enough—but they also were to serve a new sort of dessert, something called "gelatin."[13] Sister had been to Mayfield[14] recently to visit our Aunt Nannie,[15] and she reported gelatin to be the newest craze in the bustling city. It not only tasted good but was elegant in appearance, she said. It shook like jelly when finished and was red and sparkled. To me it sounded like a rare adventure in eating. I was beside myself with curiosity.

The bride's mother sent to Mayfield and bought several packages of this marvelous product. I was present when these arrived. There was a picture of a calf's head on each box. Our neighbor had a skeptical look as she read the directions, but she had been assured it was stylish and she was determined that the wedding guests must have it.

As far back as I can remember Papa often returned from a wedding with a piece of candy-decorated cake or a dainty of some kind from the refreshment table for me. This had led me to believe—especially after Sunday School lessons about Belshazzar's feast[16] and the Canaan marriage ceremony[17]—that if I could just get to a Church affair I would be able to wallow in a boundless supply of goodies. Then, too, from all the talk I heard, I decided it probably would be something quite wonderful like a circus, which was by far the most dazzling event I had ever witnessed. During the past summer Uncle Jimmy[18] and Aunt Nannie had taken me to Barnum and Bailey's Circus in Mayfield. It had been so breath-taking I even forgot I had on my "hurtin' shoes"—my Sunday patent leathers.

So through the last week before our neighbor's heralded event, I was a little girl in a frenzy of imaginings and expectations.

One of Sister's school friends from a nearby town was a bridesmaid and she came to our house several days in advance. She had visited us before. She was one of my favorites. In turn, she always gave much of her attention to me. The first piece of mail I had ever received was a colored postcard from her. It had my name on it with the prefix "Miss" and it wasn't "in care of" anyone. I kept it in my doll trunk with my gold bracelet. Her coming added to my excitement. Of course, I was underfoot most of the time.

The day before the great matrimonial triumph, Sister and her chum had to shampoo their hair. That wasn't a chore to be taken lightly. Sister was a brunette, her friend a blond, and each had heavy tresses that hung below the waist.

Mama wouldn't take a chance of giving me a cold, so she had already worked me over with a fine-tooth comb and a stiff brush. I don't suppose she ever actually drew blood in her zeal to cleanse my scalp, but it must have been close. When she finished my dry shampoo, she would take a fresh grip on me—pressing me between her knees as in a vise—and roll my hair on kid curlers. After a day and night she would take down my locks and brush around her fingers the long curls that were her pride and joy. Maybe that's why I became gray so early.

It was too cold for the girls to operate anywhere except in the warm kitchen. They dipped hot water from the reservoir in the wood range and scrubbed and rinsed their mops, one dark and one tawny, in the basins on the kitchen table. Finally they were through except for drying. For that they went in the dining room and pulled up chairs before an open fire.

Enter: an active little darling with not too much to do except to make sure she didn't miss a moment of anything. The little darling, of course, was I.

In my efforts to be entertaining and get attention from our guest I brought out all of my dolls. And then as a special treat I got down my greatest treasure of all—a little "banty" egg that Grandmother had sent me several months before. Grandmother—we called our grandparents[19] on Mama's side "Grandmother" and "Grandfather"—had a flock of bantams. One of the tiny hens was a pet I loved. On our summer visit with my grandparents, Grandmother wanted to give the hen to me, but Mama, for some reason, vetoed the idea. So Grandmother sent me one of the pet's eggs. I kept it in a match box on the mantel, where it was not likely to be broken.

I sat on the arm of my dear friend's chair while she admired my egg and talked with me about it. Lovingly I stroked her beautiful hair, now dry and glistening. When she handed back my egg I reached over and, as further evidence of my fondness for her, gave her a little love pat with it on the crown of her head.

It was such a tiny little tap but what a tremendous "to-do" it caused.

Of course, the egg, rotten and vile smelling, broke with a splash and ran over the young lady's freshly laundered locks.

Now our visitor was a proper girl, well brought up and reserved in manner. Nevertheless, her uninhibited words are etched in my mind.

"Great God Almighty! Hope's broken a rotten egg in my hair!"

The girls screamed, hands were raised to heaven, the Lord's name was invoked. There were alarms and excursions all over the house, and Mama disappeared in search of a switch.

Into the confusion came Papa—strong, steady, safe, reliable Papa. He had been out in the woodshed, busy with the hammer and saw putting together a home-made sleigh.

"Let everybody be right easy," he said.

Papa was the great pacifier in times of stress. When others ran in circles, he stayed calm, smoothed those who were ruffled, sought to fix the difficulty and quiet the commotion.

"The world hasn't come to an end, the damage can be repaired."

I was scared, the tears were flowing. He gathered me up, put me in my bonnet, warm coat, mittens and leggings and took me out to the side gate where he quickly hitched Old Dick to the newly fabricated sleigh. Away we went, leaving behind a greatly relieved Mother and two girls with fiddle-string nerves, on a cold but pleasant jog over the deep snow and crust of sleet.

It was stark, crushing tragedy one minute, joy the next. Such a big [treat] was unusual and it was my first sleigh ride; and it was a grand ride even if the vehicle was made of odd pieces of lumber and furniture crates and an old buggy seat and was little a shaky. Away we went around by the schoolhouse and over to the cluster of general stores and post office that we called town. Papa bought me a sack of gum drops.

Mama and Sister helped our visitor recleanse her scalp. When Papa and I returned, all traces of the morning's disaster had been removed. The odor, too.

At last, the big day arrived and with it more bad weather—freezing rain and crusted snow. By early evening—it was a six o'clock wedding—streets and sidewalks were so icy, it was difficult for anyone to stand up. Ray was an usher; he and other youths formed a human chain to help guests from the street up the church steps. Mama and I got to ride right up to the entrance in the sleigh.

With my heart pounding, I entered the sanctuary holding tight to Mama. By special invitation of the bride's mother we were seated on the very front row. As I gazed around everything seemed to be perfectly normal, exactly as it was every Sunday when I sat there for the closing exercises of Sunday School.

I looked up and the same lamps were swinging from the ceiling, with not a piece of candy in sight. I had expected them to be festooned with bonbons and little coconut flags.

Around the altar were the same faded cushions—no oranges or nuts or wedding cake. Nothing.

In my flights of fancy I had even thought circus ladies in tights might be scampering about or swinging on a trapeze, or maybe clowns with funny noses would be making everybody laugh. But no such entertainment was to be seen. Instead of a glittering band in red coats and gold braid playing a lively tune, there was just my sister at the organ playing "Oh Promise Me"[20] and a man who lived across the street was standing up to sing. It was a cruel letdown.

I began to look around at the crowd as far as Mama would let me squirm and to my surprise all our friends and neighbors appeared eager and expectant. I spotted a little boy I know who may have been bored too; but by the time I had stuck out my tongue and he had wiggled his nose both Mamas took over and ended that meager source of fun.

I wished I were at home with Daisy. She was tending the baby, and if I were there she would fold a strip of paper and cut a long string of dolls holding hands. She could make little birds too, by folding a square of tissue just right and cut all kinds of fancy designs and make Valentines. Oh dear!

By this time Papa had taken charge but there was nothing new in that. He was standing there reading the service and the bride and bridegroom were mumbling some words. And then something did happen—not much, but a little something.

I watched fascinated as a wide gold ring slowly rolled across the varnished floor toward me. I recoiled to grab it, then Mama's hand tightened on my arm. The ring continued to travel in an ellipse, passed within inches of me, curved back toward the altar and came to rest at the feet of the bridal party. That was my small measure of interest in the whole event, the only time in my life I was to see a wedding ring dropped by a nervous bridegroom.

I must have become drowsy; I don't remember anything about getting to the reception. I do recall, however, that the gelatin was triumphantly served and that it was ruby red and shimmered in the light. It seemed to get almost as much attention as the bride.

I wasn't impressed. I didn't like *it* either.

CHAPTER 4

"Go On with the Marryin'..."

FOR THE PEOPLE WHO CRAVED MATRIMONY PAPA[1] OFFICIATED IN FAIR weather and in flood time; at high noon and at sundown; by daylight and once by the light of our town's most disastrous fire.

There was also the time he had to swim to keep a matrimonial appointment—or at least Old Dick, our faithful buggy horse, had to swim.

Ray was along on that occasion. He was good with horses, and he had been drafted to drive. Besides, he always liked to get on the "doings."

It was during a hot, dry spell. Along the way they came to a fairly large branch [of a river or a creek], now low in its banks, spanned by a rickety wooden bridge. Papa told Ray to take the buggy down through the water, instead of using the bridge, to tighten the spokes of the wheels. It was also a good chance to let the horses blow a minute and get a drink.

Ray pulled off the road and drove down to the stream. It looked as it might be about knee-deep.

At the water's edge Ray drew back on the reins and hesitated.

"Go ahead," Papa scoffed. "Drive him on in, it's not deep."

"Gee whiz, Papa, I don't know . . ."

"Giddap [*sic* Giddup], Dick!" Papa reached over, took the reins and gave Old Dick a smart slap across the rump.

The horse took a couple of mincing steps and plunged in.

Almost instantly they were water up to their necks. Old Dick had stepped into a deep hole, pulling the buggy in behind him. All they could do was hold on. The horse took the bit, half swam, half floundered for the opposite bank, The buggy didn't go all the way under—a few inches of the top remained visible most of the voyage across. Somehow, Old Dick managed to scramble out, drawing the buggy and two chagrined passengers back to dry land.

Papa and Ray were soaked and bedraggled. So was Papa's "happy satchel"—the small valise in which he carried his Bible, Discipline[2] and spare collar button, among other equipment. They hitched Old Dick to a convenient rail fence and went under the bridge to wring out their clothes. They were late for the wedding.

How Mama and the rest of us shrieked with laughter when Ray told about it.

"Papa's back was turned to a room full of guests when he lined up the couple for the ceremony," Ray reported.

"His coat tails were still dripping. Left a puddle right there on the parlor floor.

"When he tried to find his place in the Discipline, the book was wet and the pages stuck together. It was a wonderful mix-up."

Papa had to read from memory, which ordinarily would have been easy enough; but he was still a little flustered from the misadventure at the creek. Everything got turned around.

"The bride and bridegroom finally broke down," Ray said, "and everybody quip [sic quit] trying to be polite and just split their sides."

"How perfectly terrible," said Mama. "I feel sorry for that poor bride."

"It was rather embarrassing for all of us," Papa admitted.

"It was so confused [sic confusing]," Ray continued. The couple didn't know whether to say "I do," or join hands, or call for a new deal."

The joke was on Papa, but he, too, enjoyed it. He joined in the merriment as Ray sketched in the lurid details. He brought home four dollars and a watermelon for his fee.

❧

"Old Dick," we called the hero of the ducking episode, wasn't just one horse in our tribe's history—he was a whole line of horses in various identities. He pulled us through the fragrant lanes of childhood and kept us mobile throughout a fascinating area.

With Old Dick in the shafts, we knew the joys of cross-country jaunts to visit aunts, and cousins, and grandparents of fishing and camping expeditions; and of delightful trips to rural churches for dinner on the ground. We knew, too, the soul-trying experiences of coping when Papa took the reins, flicked Nelly lightly with his tassled [sic tasseled] whip.

"Giddap [sic Giddup], Dick!" he said.

I laughed and laughed. Thereafter the family forgot all about Nelly. We cheerfully called her Old Dick.

Papa was a frequent, if not good, horse trader and we had all kinds—trotters, pacers and just nags. Some were gentle and easily managed; others were jumpy. A nervous horse usually was quickly traded or sold. Mama was scared of nervous horses. If she had to ride behind one, she became alarmed every time he switched his tail. This annoyed Papa, who liked to demonstrate his control by cracking the whip in the air and sailing away at a lively clip.

When automobiles first appeared on the roads, and horses trembled and reared at the sight of the monsters, Mama would insist on getting out until the danger was over. But Papa was firm; he usually prevailed on her to sit tight. He got by the devilish machines somehow without ever having a run-away.

A big gray horse in the Old Dick line was once shied at a piece of paper and threw brother Joe violently from the saddle. It was frightening. His foot hung in the stirrup, and he was dragged several hundred feet along a gravel road. Miraculously, he escaped without serious injury, but he was pretty well scraped over.

Papa hitched another Old Dick to a neighbor's wagon to haul a new bookcase from a carpenter's shop to our house. Key, then four, was left on the seat of wagon to hold the lines while Papa stepped inside the shop. Suddenly the horse bolted.

Papa ran out of the shop yelling "Whoa! Whoa, there!" He was too late. Old Dick was headed down the middle of the street at a dead run.

Key clung to the jouncing seat, screaming in fright. Old Dick only ran faster. The fattest man in town waddled across his yard and vaulted a paling fence in an effort to head off the runaway. He wasn't close. The wagon finally hit a bump and tossed Key in a neat arc to the ground, where he lay relatively unhurt. A few feet farther along the street the spooked horse turned a sharp corner and the wagon hit a telephone pole. The wagon bed flew over a fence and landed upside down. The horse stumbled and fell, and the wheels and chassis rolled on top of him, pinning him to the earth. That old [*sic* Old] Dick was soon traded.

There was another Old Dick that nearly broke up a baptizing.

Papa on rare occasions found it necessary to administer baptism by immersion. While this form was used in some denominations, it was not the custom in the Methodist Church. But if an individual requested immersion, instead of the usual sprinkling, Papa honored the request. Such a baptizing was a solemn religious rite; nevertheless it could be fun. For example, when a fat lady shipped water and spouted like a whale, or the minister, wresting with a wiry farmer seized by the Holy Ghost, got ducked too. So I persuaded Papa to take my little brothers and me with him on one such occasion.

This event was to take place in a clear stream near the church. The congregation and the candidate for baptism were already assembled on a bridge overlooking the water when we arrived. Papa retired at once to a nearby thicket to change to his "baptizing clothes." He left me in the buggy to hold Old Dick. For some reason, probably a buzzing horsefly, Old Dick switched his tail and stamped his foot. Whereupon, thinking I should do something. I gave the lines a tug and said "Whoa!"

Feeling the tug, Old dick backed up a step. I tugged harder and then yelled "Whoa!" loud and clear. Old Dick responded to the harder pull on the reins and began to back steadily— straight into the creek.

I yelled bloody murder.

"Papa! Papa! Old Dick's pushing us into the water. Come and get us! Oh-o-O! We'll drown!"

Papa, clad in long white drawers and nothing else, came tearing out of the thicket in time to catch the horse by the bridle and yank him forward before the buggy went all the way under.

The congregation tuned up on the old Methodist hymn, "Throw Out the Life Line."[3]

The last of the Old Dicks was with us when Papa managed to get the family its first car. That one stayed on about a year, as a sort of supernumerary.[4] Key, by that time in high school,[5] had the last full-time association with him. He rode Old Dick to school, making a round trip of about five miles each day. Perhaps he wasn't too considerate; in his exuberance he ran the horse too hard, and the animal turned up lame. After that the final Old Dick was honorably retired to pasture. When he recovered from his lameness, Papa sold him and that for us closed the horse-and-buggy days.

⁂

Much of the fun with Old Dick happened while Papa was "riding circuit" in Kentucky.[6] This was a time of many interests for me. I had started to school[7] and was absorbed most of the time with new playmates, games and lessons— in that order. Although I can recall no great thirst for knowledge, I soon learned to read. This opened a new and wonderful world. I eventually learned to spell, too—somewhat after a fashion—but only at the cost of pain and anguish in the classroom and Mama's eternal vigilance at home.

I had piano lessons prayerfully and hopefully, but after I was billed first in a couple of recitals—the prize pupils always played last—and demonstrated prolonged resistance to notes and scales, the teacher became discouraged and advised my parents to wait until I was "a little older."

These interests seemed to take some of the fascination from such events as weddings. When a couple drifted by and asked for Papa's services, I didn't bother to watch. I preferred to remain with "Alice in Wonderland" or "Sinbad the Sailor."

There were other diversions though—for instance, the time Papa beat the town bully. That's how he got to be known in some parts of Western Kentucky as "The Fighting Parson."

The incident had its origin in a bitter controversy between Old Bill Sullivan (not his real name) and the local school board over Old Bill's somewhat wayward daughter. The girl had been accused of misconduct, with the result that she had been barred from returning to school. Papa in simple humanity and in an effort to help the unfortunate girl, attempted the role of peacemaker.

Bill Sullivan was a character of wild and evil reputation in those parts. I thought the stories I heard he must be an ogre like the ones in my storybooks. Later I was to learn he really was a brutish sort of man, extremely profane and sometimes downright mean to his wife and children. He was a mule skinner and logger by trade, driving a six-mule hitch into the bottoms and hauling out logs in the nearby sawmill. He was a hard drinker on pay day, a hard swearer every day, and an all-around tough customer, frequently in trouble and generally despised and feared. In short, he was the town bully. The town was in a great uproar over the matter of Old Bill's daughter, and the dispute was about to break up the school.

Papa, without taking sides in the controversy over the girl, went to see Old Bill to discuss the situation and, if possible, find a means of softening the bitterness that had developed in the community. For his pains he was met at the door by the bully and roundly cursed.

That might have ended Papa's contact with Old Bill—but Old Bill began to broadcast.

He told the villagers he had "cussed out" the preacher; that the preacher was a "yellow belly" and had "tucked his tail and run" instead of standing up and "fightin' like a Man." He began to curse Papa whenever he passed the parsonage—loud enough for the neighbors to hear.

At first, Papa determined to ignore Old Bill's fulminations. Soon, however, he realized that his standing both as a man and as a shepherd of his flock was suffering; that he would have to reach an understanding with this bully or he no longer would be respected in the community.

A few days later Old Bill was driving by the parsonage just as Papa came out to the front door. That did it.

The logger ripped out a vile oath and roared "Whoa." He slid to the ground from the lead mule he was riding. Still cursing, he strode to the gate and squared himself.

Papa stood quietly on the porch—not moving, saying nothing.

"I can lick any _____ that says my daughter's not good enough to go to school," Old Bill fumed. "I can lick the whole damn school board and the preacher to boot."

Papa still didn't move.

"You _____ yellow-bellied, psalm-singin _____." He pointed the stock of his rawhide whip at Papa. "You ain't got the guts to come here and fight."

Papa stood unmoved by the taunt.

"All right, by ____, I'm comin, after ya!"

Old Bill put his hand on the gate, starting to enter. Mama, standing inside the door behind Papa, screamed. I was the [sic] one of the frightened children and clinging to her skirts. Then Papa acted. In one motion he threw off his coat and thrust back his cuffs. In three steps it seemed he was halfway to the gate. There he and Old Bill Sullivan met.

Both were big powerful men. Papa, a six-footer, weighed two hundred pounds. He had long arms and big hands. Old Bill was of a stockier build. He also weighed two hundred pounds. He had a powerful body and massive shoulders.

Old Bill closed with a rush and a wild swing that never landed. Papa in the first and only physical encounter of his career met the rush with a solid, smashing fist to the jaw, carrying the full weight and forward momentum of his body. Old Bill's head snapped back and this [sic his] body spun completely around. He didn't go down but the fight was over. He flailed blindly a few moments without landing a blow, while Papa crashed home a few more deadening licks that left the bully dazed and helpless.

Old Bill's face was battered and bloody as neighbor [sic neighbors]—who had gathered as if by magic—watched his wife and daughter, hastily summoned, lead him away. He looked as if he had collided with the butt end of one of his oak logs. Papa's hurts were a broken thumb and torn sleeve.

At the trial before the town Magistrate there was considerable tension. Old Bill's brother, who ran a saloon at the county seat, reportedly had sent word that the preacher had better "bring a coffin" if he showed up at the hearing. Some of Papa's parishioners urged him to arm himself. And one pillar of the Church, faithful to his pastor, came with a butcher knife in his bootleg.

It was all a false alarm. The Magistrate assessed nominal fines for disturbing the peace. Old Bill meekly paid up and departed. Loyal churchgoers paid for Papa. Old Bill's brother followed Papa home, leaned over the fence with both hands empty, and apologized for the bully's actions.

The excitement was hard on Mama. She had to have a new bottle of smelling salts.

A good ending would be that Old Bill got religion and joined the church. Such was not the case. However, he did come to see Papa later. He shook hands with Papa and told him that he was "the best man that ever hit Kentucky." Soon after that, he asked Papa to officiate at the wedding of his daughter, who had decided she would rather marry than stay in school. With that, peace was restored to our town.

❦

Then Papa was appointed to a charge[8] back in Tennessee,[9] closer to our old home grounds. Parsonage affairs at once took on a fresh and different tone.

This move had brought us to a thriving little town[10] on the main line. We felt we were edging a bit closer to "civilization." And to give a new flip to our routine, the second of my baby brothers—Key[11]—had just arrived. With his debut, there were three small children and two grown ones in the family.

This was the line-up:

Key, the baby; Joe, whom we often called Little Brother, and me—we were the small fry. Then Ray, our big brother who was now a law student at Cumberland University[12] across the State, and Eleanor—who was Sister to the family—the oldest. Sister was following her true love; she was a music teacher and away much of the time.

The town folks promptly renamed the men of the family starting with

Papa and working down to the baby: Big Preach, Little Preach, Preachie and Baby Preach.

Also, they soon came to know me as little girl with long curls—the scourge of the plank walks on roller skates.

With our change to the new town, a wonderful thing happened to me: now I was in a new kind of seventh heaven. I learned to ride a bicycle.

Oh, it wasn't mine. Our ship still hadn't made port, but a neighbor boy about my age had a bicycle, and although it was not a girl's type, it was small enough for me to manage and at last I knew the thrill of pedaling alone. This pleasure, however, was short-lived. Mama did not approve my riding a boy's bicycle and I was soon back on my skates doing fancy pirouettes along the plank walk.

⁂

Mama was especially overjoyed to be back in Tennessee. She felt more "at home" and she found it easier to get good help—and with a young baby she needed it.

"Aunt" Liza, a good, competent colored woman, lived in a whitewashed house, almost in sight of the parsonage, and in less than a week after we moved in she was our friend and main comfort. She lived with her two small granddaughters Jinsey and Viney, and her aged father, Ike, for whom she was the sold [*sic* sole] support. Every morning she helped Mama with the housework, and occasionally she kept the children in the afternoon.

Sometimes on summer afternoons Mama would send me over with a message for Aunt Liza, and I would play a while in the clean-swept yard with Jinsey and Viney while their grandmother washed and hung out clothes.

One evening Aunt Liza was called over to sit while Mama and Papa went to a wedding. Papa was to perform the ceremony for the only daughter of the town's most affluent family. The daughter had been educated in private schools and finished off in the East. The attendants in what was to be an ultra-smart home affair mainly from out of town. In fact, only a chosen few of the local people were invited. The family appeared to be trying to keep the general run of people out; and, of course, there was a great curiosity about it among the uninvited.

Flowers and ice cream had come by express. The wedding cake had been baked in Memphis. The gown was from St. Louis. The double parlors of the big brick house where the ceremony was to take place were decorated to the ceiling with evergreens from the river bottom and blossoms from city greenhouses. We got this straight from Aunt Liza, who had seen it all when she delivered the fresh curtains she had washed and stretched.

Papa and Mama left with a flourish for the formal affair. They had been gone only a short while when we were struck rigid by a blood-curdling sound, the fire siren.

It made us tremble with fear. Aunt Liza hurried out on the porch but she couldn't see anything. People were rushing and shouting.

In five minutes or so, the siren screamed again—this time with definite authority. While it was still wailing, Jinsey and Viney burst in, squealing with excitement.

"Flour mill on fire" they shrilled. "People say whole town burnin' up!"

"Glory to God!" exclaimed Aunt Liza. The words which might have been a Plea to the Almighty for his works were her way of expressing consternation. The flour mill and the adjourning grain elevator were the town's biggest plant. They were important.

I ran out on the porch with the others. There was a great red glare in the sky. I thought the world was on fire.

The sight was too much for Aunt Liza. If the town went up in flames and smoke, she was going to be there to watch.

"Get ready every'body," she sang out. "We're goin' to the fire!"

"Is the baby going too," I asked.

"Ever'body goin' to the fire," she said. "I'll fix the baby. You help yo' little brother put on his coat. Jinsey, you and Viney stop that jabberin'. Come and he'p these chillum get their wrapps [*sic* wraps] on. We're goin' to that fire. Hurry, Hurry-up, chi'l!"

In no time at all she had Joe and me bundled into warm clothes—it was early spring and the night air was sharp—and the baby out of his crib and wrapped like a cocoon. With that she lit out for town with the baby in her arms and Jinsey, Viney, Little Brother and me in tow.

The mill and elevator were going up in a spectacular blaze. The high leaping flames only a block or so beyond the town square illuminated a wide area. Next door to the mill a bucket brigade was fighting frantically to save the electric-light plant. Already the power was off, but people scarcely notices [*sic* noticed] that the lights were out.

While this was happening, the wedding in the brick mansion, also a short way from the square, was starting. The wedding march had been played and the couple and their attendants had taken their places. Papa's book was open. Then the current failed and all went black—except for the red glare at the windows.

Papa's and the bride's father hastily conferred. In a moment the wedding party and guests, a little shaken, moved on [*sic* onto] the veranda, where the ceremony continued in the illumination from the flour-mill fire.

Hundreds of people were milling about the square and crowding into the street leading to the burning plant. Soon someone spotted the scene on the veranda of the big house across the way and the word quickly passed through the throng.

In a twinkling a drove of spectators, deserting the fire temporarily, rushed up to the exclusive family's yard. The ceremony that had started in privacy now had hundreds of witnesses, all goggle-eyed with the overwhelming excitement of twin spectacles—a super-fire and a super-wedding.

The bantering crowd jostled for position at the fence, everybody straining to hear as well as see what was taking place on the veranda.

"Tell Big Preach to tie the knot good," came a voice from the fringe.

Small boys yodled [*sic* yodeled] and croaked.

"Oh you kid!" and "Some baby!" the big boys shouted at the bride.

"Hey, fancy pants, have your got a ring?" they jibed at the bridegroom. It was fun for all.

As soon as the ceremony was over, the crowd turned back to the fire. Not so, Aunt Liza. She had seen the burning mill and had caught the tail end of the wedding near the front gate. Now she began to work for a vantage point from which to see the goings on at the reception.

With her brood she edged around to the alley side of the house where there was a low hedge and an iron fence. Aunt Liza held up the baby; Little Brother and I were with Jinsey and Viney clung to the top of the fence. We could see everything they were doing and eating on the wide porch.

"Mama! Mama!" I called before Aunt Liza could stop me. "Over here! Looky! We came to the fire and saw the wedding too!"

My startled Mother looked over the shoulder and saw peeping over the hedge six pairs of eyes popping out of six faces—three white and three black. Only Papa thought it was funny.

That wasn't the only time I was caught off base. I wasn't exactly meddlesome at the age. Put it this way: I had an inquiring mind.

We jogged out in the country a few miles to the home of one of Papa's parishioners where the young lady of the family was to be wed. While Papa and Mama were waiting for the main event to start, I became bored and decided to go into the kitchen where, I felt sure, the refreshment goodies were being made ready.

I just opened the door and drifted in. There I found the women of the family huddled and distraught. I sensed some kind of disaster.

The wedding cake had been baked the day before and set aside in a cupboard on the back porch. During the night an enterprising colony of black ants got wind of the nuptial feast and moved in. The bride's mother, poor soul, had just discovered this fact. The cake looked as if it had been sprinkled with mobile particles of black pepper. The ladies were completely crestfallen.

They were right up against starting time, and had to do something fast. The only course, they decided, was to pick off as many ants as they could, scrape off the rest and add a few new decorations. The decorations consisted of "red devils" and candy hearts inscribed "I Love You."

"No one will know the difference," said the bride's mother hopefully.

The ant pickers were already at work when someone looked around and saw me standing there wide-eyed.

This time the ladies became more agitated than ever. *Maybe they are going to lock me in the closet*, I thought. Before they could initiate any such step or even say a word, I took the offensive.

"A little mouse got on top of a cake at home one time," I said, "over on its back. It couldn't get up."

"For mercy's sake," said one of the women. "What did your mother do?"

"She threw up."

I went back quickly and sat down by Papa. Afterward I didn't eat any cake and nobody insisted.

There was one other memorable stop on the matrimonial trail that season.

One day Aunt Liza asked Mama's permission to use our cake pans. She seemed excited; she needed the pans that afternoon to bake two cakes.

It was not necessary for Mama to ask why. Aunt Liza was ready to volunteer everything.

"Like I ain't got all this work to do already," she said. "Washin' and ironin' and cleanin' workin' myse'f to deaf [sic death]. Ain't nobody doin' nothin' fo' me."

"Well, Liza, what is it?" Mama was familiar with her helper's roundabout approach to her troubles. "What's happened?"

"That Bessie Belle . . . that gal . . ."

Aunt Liza broke down and let out a long, low moan, and then she sat in a kitchen chair and began to rock from side to side, her arms clasped.

"What has Bessie Belle done now?" It couldn't be too bad, Mama thought, if Liza was baking two cakes.

Bessie Belle, Aunt Liza's daughter, was a chambermaid in the hotel in Fulton.[13] The colored woman was proud of the fact that her girl had a hotel job in a thriving town where she kept up with everything going on. At the same time Aunt Liza professed fear that Bessie Belle was "carryin' on with not tellin' who, way off there by herself" and, in fact, was in constant danger of slipping into the path of iniquity. She spent most of her spare time praying about it. It was a familiar theme with Aunt Liza __ fretting over the dire things that could be happening to her daughter.

"Now, she done sent word she's home to get married," she wailed.

"Well, that doesn't sound too bad, "Mama soothed." "Maybe it's for the best." "She so young!"

Aunt Liza wasn't easily consoled.

"Who is the man?" Mama asked.

This turned loose a new torrent of moans and wails.

"Railroad man. Pore Bessie Belle! He ain't never gonna be home none. She be her lone se'f. I know his kind. Ain't no good."

"But he has a job—he's working, isn't he?"

"Yass'm Miss Mattie. Bessie Belle say he do work steady. That's sump'n."

With that Aunt Liza regained her composure. She had carried her disavowal of Bessie Bell's choice as far as seemed appropriate. To Aunt Liza it just didn't seem right for a parent to be too happy about gaining a son-in-law. The game, as she understood it, was to show a long face for appearance's sake.

Actually, Bessie Belle's man was a porter on the Accommodation that ran between Fulton and Memphis—a coveted job among the colored people. If he had been Mayor of Philadelphia, Aunt Liza and Ike couldn't have been elated.

Aunt Liza was beaming and chattering gaily when set out for home with the cake pans.

About mid-afternoon, Jinsey and Viney came to "borrow" some flavoring and asked me to go back with them.

Mama consented, but gave instructions that I was to be home in an hour. When we got there, Aunt Liza already had one cake finished, and was waiting to pour the batter for another when she "seasoned it up" with vanilla. That out of the way, she got busy with frosting and decorations.

In the meantime, Jinsey and Viney had to take turns with the fly bush. The house had no screens; the children fanned and swished while the cook poured and mixed.

The fly bush was a long cane with a strip of fringed paper fastened to the end. Aunt Liza saved the pink wrapping paper from store packages that came to our house for making her fly bushes. She would arrange four thicknesses of the paper over the end of the cane, and sew the paper in place with a darning needle. She then fringed the paper with scissors. With this device, a child could stand halfway across the room and shoo flies off the table.

Aunt Liza had cut the tips of small branches from a cedar tree, and had washed and dried them carefully. Now she was dipping them in a bowl of stiffly beaten egg whites and sugar, swishing them around until they were covered with the frosting. She hung each little piece on a wire that had been stretched across the room to dry. I was permitted to wave a peach-tree branch over the wire as Viney was using the fly bush. The whitened cedar sprigs soon were stuck on top of the frosted cakes, and I thought the effect was the last in word of elegance.

Old Ike had whitewashed the fireplace in the front room and placed cedar bough on the hearth. They were going to take down two beds the next day to make space for the wedding. The cakes finished, Aunt Liza let me lick one of the pans. Jinsey and Viney got the others.

When Aunt Liza left our house the next morning, I begged Mama's permission to go to see Bessie Belle's wedding.

"No, indeed," said Mama. "Aunt Liza will be too busy to bother with you."

"Miss Mattie," she said, "if you let her come, I'll take good care of her myself, and send her right on home."

Mama wavered, they consented. I was curious to taste a cake with cedar trees on top, and that wasn't all; Jinsey had told me that the "Reverend" who was to say the words had a gold toothpick on his watch chain. That was something really worth seeing.

Late that afternoon, just before the festivities were to begin, I ran down to the Negro woman's little house. There was a whitewashed paling fence around the yard. The gate was fastened with a latch, and a loop of wire, too complicated for me to open, so Aunt Liza came out and let me in. A brindled hound dog trotted over and barked once; when he recognized me, he retired to his place under the house and lay down again.

The guests were beginning to arrive. One of them, who I recognized as Lattimore, the man who delivered ice to our house, chatted with us as we walked to the porch. Across the porch was a low railing with a row of tin cans and snuff bottles in which geraniums were blooming.

Lattimore was quizzing Aunt Liza about Bessie Belle's catch.

"Hear he got a mighty fine job," he said. "Makin' big money."

Aunt Liza sniffed.

"Ain't so much. Jus' a railroad man."

Her tone indicated great disdain for railroad workers, but Lattimore wasn't fooled; he carried out the end of the banter.

"You crazy?" he scoffed. "Wish I had me a porter job. I'd go down to Memphis and marry me one of them struttin' gals on Beale Street."

"You go away from here, Lattimore," said Aunt Liza, scandalized.

We went inside, and Aunt Liza held me by the hand, and never let me stray off while she talked to her friends. Finally, the "Reverend" came in. There was a great round of "howdies" and hand shaking and joshing with the parson.

CHAPTER 5

Angel Music

TWO MORE YEARS IN SCHOOL . . .[1]

I was finding myself quite self-sufficient, and entirely independent. For couldn't I read anything I wanted to, and hadn't home in the parsonage by some enchantment now become merely a way station, a place of temporary abode as I busily escorted myself on new and fabulous journeys through the world of books?

Yes, it was true. The processes of public-school education in Tennessee were gradually depleting my early store of indifference, and in spite of a gingerly approach, I was being drawn closer to the springs of learning—well, anyway, closer to the hard facts of the 3 R's. And along with a little more interest in my classes, I had acquired an unquenchable thirst for reading— anything from the Almanac to "Pilgrims Progress"[2], from "Twenty Thousand Leagues beneath the Sea"[3] [*sic* Under] to "Thanatopsis."[4] And if I could raise five cents I might go to the corner store and buy a copy of "Tip Top Thriller" magazine[5] to devour in my secret place up by the attic window.

To Mama's delight I had reached the point at which I not only could entertain myself without menacing the family constantly, but also be deployed to reel off nursery classics and adventure stories by the score to my little brothers.

Key, the baby, was now walking and talking. He never grew tired of "The Three Bears"[6] and "The Little Tin Soldier."[7] He shrieked with delight at the antics of "Br'er Fox and Br'er Rabbit."[8] He became a faithful friend of th2e Little Boy Blue,[9] of unhappy fate. He learned with somewhat shrill assistance from me to hum the tune of "The Owl and the Pussycat."[10]

Joe and I were, of course, far past such trifles. On a rainy day we could be outward bound at the creak of the attic door on "Gulliver's Travels,"[11] and without a pause head right on toward "Treasure Island."[12]

Along the way we might take time out to taste the delights of "Hero Tales of All Nations,"[13] or dally on side excursions with James Fenimore Cooper[14] and G. A. Henty.[15] Sometimes we went into semi-retirement to shake hands with Horatio Alger[16] and his synthetic heroes. "Little Women"[17] was not far off, but I was to learn that my brothers wouldn't stay hitched for sentimental stories of that sort—I would have to go that one alone.

Vacation time soon rolled around. My joy seemed unbounded. We were knee deep in the bliss of care-free living, accentuated by the pleasures of our big shady yard where we could sit on the lawn swing, facing each other, gently gliding to and fro as we chattered and enjoyed our books.

About the middle of that dreamlike, delightful summer, the peace of our home life suddenly changed.

One day all was calm and serene; the next the atmosphere tingled with breath-taking news: Sister, the musical member of the family, was engaged and was going to have a church wedding. She had been busy with her teaching duties away from home; now she was back wearing a ring and Papa and Mama had announced her engagement and approaching marriage in the weekly "Clarion."[18] Everybody in the neighborhood seemed to be running in and out and talking about it.

Sister had met her fiance a year or two before, but I couldn't remember him very well. There had always been beaux in the parlor when she was at home. I was conscious of this because early every morning after she had entertained company, I scampered downstairs to see what had been left. Sometimes it would be a nearly full box of bonbons; perhaps a gay basket of fruit and nuts only partially depleted; or there might be a sheet of music for a new popular song. Such things were windfalls that I treasured. If I found only a slim volume of poetry or new views for the stereoscope,[19] I felt let down.

This game of looking for the leftover prizes in the parlor was part of my life. I didn't imagine that someday sister might marry one of the gift-bearing swains and end forever a lush source of treats.

But here she was, getting ready to do just that. A little of my private world was caving in. Another of my daydreams such as owning a circus, or a trip around the world, or possessing even a second-hand bicycle and new, ball-bearing skates was shattered.

I should have known what was coming when the young man of her choice had visited Sister that Christmas before. He gave her one of the new cameras—a Kodak.[20] It sat on a tripod, and it fascinated me because it folded up and the whole works could be put in a case.

He took a lot of pictures—me with my doll, the baby in his high chair holding up his Teddy Bear,[21] and Joe on his velocipede.[22] I knew where some of these snapshots were. I got them out, but they didn't interest me now.

I had never known Mama to be in such a frenzy of house-cleaning. We had gone through the usual window-washing, carpet-beating, floor-scrubbing routine back in the spring. Here she was doing it again and with a great many extras.

When Mama announced the list of things that would have to be done to the house, Papa's eyebrows shot up, way up—a sure sign he was thinking fast. Whatever he thought, in [*sic* it] availed him not in the least.

"We'll have to repaper the hall and parlor," Mama said, "and the front bedroom too."

"Well, now, Mattie that's fine, but—." Papa started to make his demurs.

"No buts about it," Mama scolded, "these things simply have to be done. Why I couldn't ever hold my head up again if we had a wedding here with the house looking so run down."

"All right," Papa said, "just be easy . . ."

But the "just be easy" line didn't work that time. In fact, the first list was just a starter.

"The old woodshed out back is a disgrace," Mama said. "It will have to be torn down and hauled away."

I heard that part of the bad news with a sinking feeling. The woodshed had been a wonderful place to play in bad weather.

"The porch will have to be painted, the brick walk out to the front gate needs mending, and there's an awful lot of work to be done on the yard."

There were really dozens of things to be done in the repairing and refurbishing line. I was pressed into raking the yard and picking up odds and ends and storing away toys, but, in truth, not very willingly. That's why I was overjoyed when Mama engaged Aunt Liza full-time. She told this good helper to come early and stay late "till it's all over."

The question of invitations came up immediately. Mama and Sister discussed it for days.

"They'll just have to be engraved," Sister said. "I know that's more expensive but . . ."

She and Mama were thinking about Papa's pinched resources. "I'm sure Mr. Crandall can print them so they will look just as well(,)" Mama mused, but she didn't sound convinced.

Mr. Crandall, publisher of the "Clarion," was also the job printer. Wasn't he a member of Papa's church? He might do the invitations free.

Of course, the upshot of it was that they sent to Memphis and had them engraved. The panic[23] was on that year, but Papa said he could find a few dollars—somewhere. He remained a firm believer in a practical kind of Providence.

The list of those to be invited required many prolonged consultations. There were relatives and church people and friends in the various towns where Papa had served as pastor. Nobody knew where to stop.

Finally, after much soul-searching, the winnowing of names was finished and all invitations were addressed. I was sent to the Post Office with a five-dollar bill to buy two-cent stamps. That was an outlay in those hard times that had to be in cash. No scrip was acceptable at the stamp window; nor could stamps be charged and paid for in the fall when the cotton began to move and there was a little money for the preacher—and eagerly awaited change from quarterage paid with cord wood and roasting ears.

I was very conscious of the responsibility I bore on my stamp mission. In ordinary times Mama would never have let me go. When I was given permission to put the stamps on the envelopes, the last drop was added to my already brimming cup, and my self-importance could not be contained. I licked every stamp at one sitting.

At that time stamp mucilage was unedible [*sic* inedible] and unflavored—still right out of the horse's hoof. By late afternoon I was glassy-eyed and the world had changed to a hideous hue. Soon I had a fever, and Mama called out of the front door for the doctor; he lived right across the street.

I had a miserable night promoted by our neighbor's drastic potions, but by noon the next day I was fairly chipper again and everybody relaxed. However, I wouldn't go to town with Papa to mail the invitations—I wouldn't even touch them—and I've never licked a stamp since. I lick the letter instead.

The whirling weeks that followed were high clover for me. Laura Lewis —a young woman who did plain sewing, such as underwear and everyday clothes—was there constantly. While Laura ran the sewing machine, Mama and Sister rolled and whipped lace and did the handwork. Between them they turned out a great assortment of ruffled and beribboned petticoats with drawers, corset covers and nighties in matching sets. Some of the more intimate wear required hand embroidery, and I'm sure Mama must have feather-stitched forty miles.

I yearned to have a part in this trousseau making, but most of the time I was just in the way. I did get to run errands. Several times a day Mama sent me to town with samples of lace and ribbon and embroidery to buy another yard or spool or card of whatever was needed. White nainsook[24] was carried home by the bolt.[25] The floor was littered daily with the debris of the sewing spree. Never had I fallen heir to so many and such generous scraps for my dolls.

Sister held herself ready to dash away to the dressmaker's at all hours. Once she took the train to Paducah,[26] where the wedding gown was made. Everything had to be fitted and refitted. We wondered if it all could possibly be finished on time.

The whole family was treated to new clothes for the wedding. My dress was of white organdy[27] with rows and rows of fine tucks and lace insertion in fancy designs. The dressmaker had seen one like it on her last trip to St. Louis. She went to St. Louis twice a year to a tailoring institute and brought back new patterns and the latest word on styles. She made Mama's dress of a thin material over silk that rustled with every move.

Where did Papa get any money at all in a panic year, and where indeed did he ever find enough for the wedding extravagances? Sister's meager savings, of course, helped to pay for the trousseau. The rest, I suppose, was more of the providential magic. Somehow on faith, Papa came through. The family tradition was a solid one: Papa could always "manage."

Two weeks before the wedding Papa went back to his old home community[28] in Weakley County to help a fellow minister in a revival. He did this every year so he could spend a week with his mother. I had on previous occasions gone with him, and I looked forward to my summer frolic at Grandma's,[29] but this time I wanted to stay at home. There was too much going on that I didn't want to miss.

I was not consulted as to my desire. Before I knew it, Mama had the suitcase packed, not only one for me but for brother Joe as well.

"For a little I'd send the baby, too," she said.

Everyone apparently was anxious to get rid of us, and I didn't like it. However, we had a good time with Grandma, ripping about and running free on the tired old farm, with its rolling fields and wood lots and clear flowing stream with sandy bottom, just right for wading and splashing. Some of the other grandchildren were there to add to the fun. Grandma let us go barefooted all day long, which was a treat. Of course, we grumbled at bedtime because we had to pump cold water on the back porch and wash our bruised and stained feet before we could go to bed.

By the time we got back home we had so many cuts, scratches and abrasions from our barefooted romping we could scarcely put on our shoes. That was something else for poor Mama to worry about, but when the time came to march to church, I could wear my white slippers without a limp, and Joe could be shod without too much commotion, so all was well.

Mama's vexation over our sore feet was slight, however, compared with the anguish caused by the baby while we were away. Little lads were going through the era of Buster Brown clothes and Dutch haircuts.[30] The baby, neglected for a moment, got hold of the scissors and whacked off his bangs and as much of the sides of his hair as he could manage. Mama sat down and cried when she saw the mutilation.

Even Sister stopped what she was doing long enough to commiserate with her over the disaster.

But not Papa. He laughed when he saw the baby's handiwork.

"I've been waiting for someone to do it," he said. "Now everything is as it should be. No more tears, Mattie. This boy and I have some business to attend. Bring the scissors."

After a few minutes of back-porch barbering, Key emerged close cropped all over. But he was no longer our baby; now he was a little boy.

We didn't have time to ponder over this transformation, for something I hadn't thought of was happening. The wedding presents were starting to pour in.

It was before parcel post[31] and everything came by express. Two or three times a day we drove Old Dick to the depot to pick up packages. Occasionally, the depot agent would telephone and say that the parcel was small enough for the children to handle. Then Joe and I would pull our red wagon along the plank walk to town and bring it back. The parlor rapidly filled with cut glass, hand-painted china, silver bowls, bonbon dishes, card trays and all kinds of bric-a-brac. A full-size rug contributed by a generous well-wisher was pressed into immediate use. Sister spread it over our threadbare Brussels carpet.

It was like Christmas every day, I thought,

The out-of-town bridesmaids were the first guests to arrive. On the last day the relatives came. Everything had been planned to the last cot for bedding down the guests. The neighbors with spare bedrooms took care of the overflow, and with much of the food prepared in advance and the rest arranged for, Mama was about to relax when Ray brought in devasting [*sic* devastating] intelligence:

"Jim Henry is in town!"

Loud groans and exclamations of annoyance.

"He's on his way out here for the wedding!"

Mama's vision of clear sailing the rest of the way faded. She threatened to become hysterical.

Papa took charge. It was his cue to rise and say again: "Everybody will be right easy. It will all be taken care of."

"But Jim Henry Parsons," Mama wailed, "that—that tramp—that simpleton. I'll not have him in this house. I'll—I'll . . ."

"Jim Henry wouldn't harm a flea," said Papa soothingly. "Just let me handle it."

Jim Henry was a religious oddity, good natured and harmless, who had been known to our family for years. He ambled about the country attending revivals, camp meetings, homecomings, and church events of all kinds, and particularly any Methodist affair having the traditional dinner on the ground. He was a prodigious trencherman,[32] and a church dinner with its abundance of country cooking drew him from afar. All the Methodist pastors up and down the Conference[33] knew him as a pious crank, but they tolerated him and treated him with kindness.

Whenever he showed up in our community, Papa took him in for the night and made him comfortable. A tall, gaunt man of unusual appearance, he amused us with rambling accounts of his pilgrimages. That is, all of us but Mama were amused; she was kind to Jim Henry when he was our guest, but she was far from happy over the shambles he made of her spare room. A wanderer much of the time, he was not addicted to strict cleanliness or tidy habits.

For him to show up now was almost too much for Mama. In a few minutes he arrived. It was just at suppertime.

After Papa greeted him at the door, Jim Henry lumbered right in, waving airily to all present.

"Big doin's, I hear, Brother Hart," he said. "Howdy, everybody. Mighty fine to see you again, Sister Hart."

"Mmmmmmmh! Seems like I smell ham fryin'!"

"Have a seat, Jim Henry," Papa told him. "I think there's a plate for you."

So Jim Henry ate at a small table with the children while the other guests crowded the dining table. Mama was sorry about this, but the house was full of company, and unfortunately, she explained, she was going to be extremely busy.

She thought that this hint would send him on his way, but Jim Henry didn't hear. He was busy telling Papa about the Methodist quarterly Conference at Big Sandy.[34]

Later, Sister came out and spoke to the shabby itinerant. She had a kindly feeling for him. Once, some years before, she had invited him into the parlor and played hymns and some gay tunes for him on the piano. He had been bemused, and begged her to play again and again.

"When I get to Heaven," he had said, "the angels will be flutterin' around and there'll be music just like that."

This had pleased Sister. Afterward she pretended not to notice his unkept [*sic* unkempt] appearance when he came to our house.

Now it was the evening before she was to be wed. She was in a glow of happiness. I suppose she wanted to do a kind thing for Jim Henry to remember, for impulsively she had slipped away from the parlor and brought her violin to the porch.

"Jim Henry, I'm glad you heard about my wedding and came to see us," she said.

"Miss Eleanor, I was wishin' I could hear you play one more time."

There was a full moon that night, and the moonlight came just inside the porch. Back in the deep shadow, on a bench, Papa held me on his lap. From the trees at the edge of the yard came the buzz and murmur of katydids and crickets. All the magic of a midsummer's eve was in the air.

Sister stood where the moonlight caught her face and shoulders. I thought no fairy princess ever looked more beautiful. She was like the loveliest of the Gibson Girls,[35] whose pictures are treasured—slender, poised, radiant. Her hair was braided and coiled, and she wore the popular shirt-waist and skirt of the day with a tiny gold watch pinned to the waist front.

Nothing more was said. Sister played several melodies. The music was sweet and tender and beautiful. Papa hummed softly. Everyone was still, entranced by her playing because she was a good musician with a sure touch, and also because it was a tender moment for all. Mama came and stood in the door. Others of the wedding party slipped out and sat with us on the bench or stood in the shadows. How unforgettable—"angel music" for Jim Henry.

Afterward we urged Jim Henry to spend the night—we always did that when he came—but he had "to see a man down at the depot." Actually, he had been skittish of sleeping at the parsonage ever since Ray once almost closed him up in the folding bed. He didn't want to be assigned to "that contraption" again.

The wedding day started off at 5:30 o'clock in the morning. At that untimely hour, while the roosters were still crowing, the fast express that never stopped at our town unexpectedly stopped. It let off two cousins, also unexpected.

We were not up when they knocked at the door. In a few minutes everybody was up.

It was Cousin Irene and Cousin Lou[36] from among the Weakley County kith and kin. Two more didn't matter at that stage.

Mama had Aunt Lisa there early and Aunt Lisa had brought another kitchen helper with her. Breakfast was soon ready—first table. We ate in shifts. It was a wonderful breakfast. We had pork chops and cantaloupe.

We might have had country ham with red gravy if it had been an ordinary breakfast. We were putting on airs for Sister's guests, so had ordered fresh chops, and, by special arrangement, these had been delivered before daylight. We had an ice box, a homemade, sawdust-lined one, but it was too small to hold very much, and anyway, the daily block of ice might have melted overnight. Mama wasn't taking any chances.

With the sizzling chops, Aunt Lisa served up fried apples, scrambled eggs, hot biscuit and cherry preserves. The cantaloupe was sliced and served from a big platter in the center of the table. Yes, country ham would have been too common for this breakfast.

Throughout the remainder of the day, the entire house was jumping. Everywhere you looked, someone was preparing a bath or curling hair with irons heated over the chimney of a coal-oil lamp, or arranging in vases the flowers that neighbors brought. And somebody was getting ice-cream freezers ready or showing Aunt Sally and Uncle Church[37] the wedding presents or escorting Cousin Irene in to see the trousseau.

"Did you ever see the like!" gasped Cousin Irene.

She all but swooned over the lingerie—the "sets of underwear that all matched up"; and the wedding gown with "a train as long as from here to the woodbox"; and the going-away dress with "a slit skirt, slit all the way past her shoe tops!"

The bridegroom[38] came in on the three o'clock train. He was from Savannah,[39] over on the Tennessee River. A young lawyer, he was, I suppose, correctly turned out in every detail.

Mama had told us he was Sister's "Prince Charming." He didn't look like my idea of a Prince, but I did think he was imposing and handsome, Ray greeted him and his best man at the station and led them to our town's only hotel.

There the "Prince" discovered when he unpacked his bag that he had forgotten his wedding shoes. Ray took him to the best store where he bought a pair at a price that widened Ray's eyes when he came home and reported the transaction.

They went to the livery stable and arranged for carriages to take everybody to the church and to the train when the bridal party was ready to leave. The church was just a few doors away and the station only a few short blocks; but that was the custom.

The bridegroom had not forgotten the bridal bouquet. Ray brought it out to the house.

Sister's big new trunk, brass-bound and leather-strapped was finally packed and locked. It had been a wedding present. It had three trays and even a little secret drawer in it. They were going to the Jamestown Exposition[40] on their honeymoon, trunk and all.

As a special courtesy, the Mayor at mid-afternoon sent the street sprinkler to lay the dust on the dirt street between our house and the church. Mama and Papa were pleased.

After an early supper everyone got ready. Mama dressed us one by one, starting with me, and dared us to move out of her sight until she gave the word. Mama's dress fastened up the back and had a high lace collar. I stood on a chair and fastened the three gold beauty pins on that collar while she cautioned me to get them straight. Nobody else had time to fasten the pins for her and I felt very important because she called on me.

The event was finally over. There was nothing to it all to my way of thinking. Papa in his frock coat went through the same performance I had seen so many times before. Ray was one of the ushers, looking tall and handsome.

Sister was a beautiful bride, but she had always been beautiful to me. There were no bobbles.

I stared down at the bridegroom's shoes. I couldn't see why they were worth ten dollars.

Then we were all back home with a houseful of people standing around eating caramel ice cream and Lady Baltimore cake. In a little while we were climbing into surreys and driving to the station and waving good-bye; and the girls and boys were throwing rice; and there sat Papa and Mama alone in a phaeton. Mama was crying softly.

The next two weeks were busy ones but not very exciting for me. The entire house was cleaned again and everything put back in its usual place. The wedding presents were packed in barrels, and by the time Sister and her husband returned, life had eased back to normal. They were there just long enough for Sister to collect her belongings and then there was another gala leave-taking with plans for their return at Christmas.

Sister returned—before Christmas. Her husband brought her back. Again the parlor was filled with flowers and friends; but this time they moved softly and spoke in low tones. She wore a shroud and lay in a casket.

We children were awed and could scarcely understand it. We had never seen our father weep, nor had we seen Mama when the neighbors had to take charge.

My sister had been ill only a few days. Death struck suddenly.

It was the first shadow on our rosy world.

CHAPTER 6

"Oh Dem Golden Slippers"

THE PARLOR STAYED CLOSED, THE SHADES DRAWN. IN IT WERE THE objects we so closely associated with Sister.[1] The upright piano; the violin in its case on top of the piano; the guitar which had given us so much enjoyment as Sister strummed the popular ditties of the day and we gathered around her and sang. Everything in the room awoke poignant memories. Just to open the door brought a wave of sadness to Mama,[2] to all of us.

On the rare occasions now when Mama went into the parlor, she could not hold back the tears. Once I found her there, lost in reveries and weeping gently, her fingers touching the long, splintered crack that marred the piano's walnut top.

I had reached the age of two and Joe and Key were as yet unborn when Papa gave up his career as a rural teacher and entered the Methodist ministry. His first assignment as a full-fledged member of the Memphis Conference[3] was, in the words of the older and more experienced circuit riders, "the jumping off place"[4]—the old Shiloh Meeting house[5] on the Civil War battlefield near Pittsburgh [*sic* Pittsburg] Landing, Tennessee.[6]

It was then a remote place, far from a railroad in a poorly developed section of the Tennessee River country, and it was a testing ground for new preachers. If a parson could survive here, he was ripe for wider usefulness in the Methodist scheme of itinerant evangelism.

Shiloh was more than a hundred miles from Cottage Grove,[7] my birthplace, where the family had lived for a number of years. Since Cottage Grove was almost as far from a railroad as Shiloh, there was no thought of shipping our household goods by rail to our new home. Instead, Papa hired two wagons with teams of mules to transport our possessions over land. It was a miserable journey.

The parsonage at Shiloh was already provided with bedsteads, tables, and various other necessary articles; thus amount we were required to take was not great. Papa loaded the essential plunder in one wagon—trunks, bedding, kitchen equipment, books, etc.—and consigned the piano to the other. The piano was the big problem; it was solidly constructed and heavy. With its cumbersome shipping case, it made a load for one team to pull.

If it had been necessary to leave everything else behind, the family would have voted cheerfully to take the piano. It was our pride and joy.

Sister, just seventeen, loved it passionately and played it beautifully. Where a poor country schoolteacher such as Papa had ever found the money to pay for it, I don't know and can't imagine. But somehow he had raised the money and had ordered it from St. Louis, and no piano had ever been more cherished by a possessive family.

We started for Shiloh in late November, over dirt roads that were rutted and muddy, heading more or less toward the part of the state where the Tennessee River crosses the Tennessee-Mississippi line. There was no road map. It was a hard four-day trip, requiring many stops to inquire the way.

Mama, Sister and I rode in the family buggy pulled by Old Dick. Papa and Ray had places on the wagons. Ray[8] was fourteen. We changed around now and then, and Sister and Ray sang and frolicked and joked to while away the tedious, jolting hours. If Ray "cut up" too much when he was in the buggy, Mama would make him hustle back to the wagon.

The entire route was through rough country. There were no hotels—or towns—and when night fell we had to depend on a convenient farmhouse for lodging. The people, though backwoodsy and rough-hewn, were hospitable. Poverty was the rule, but when they learned Papa was a preacher, they made us welcome and there was no charge. The accommodations for the most part were crude.

At our first stop we had sausage for supper. It was strongly laced with red pepper. It burned my mouth and I cried. Dessert was a mushy sort of pudding, flavored with bits of dried orange peel. The taste was sharp and bitter. I wanted a piece of pie! Cherry pie—like grandmother's.[9]

Mama, Sister and I slept in one bed. There were no sheets, so we took off only our outside clothes. We were wearing union suits[10] with sleeved "bodies" and two petticoats under our dresses. We were quite warm.

Papa and Ray slept in a room with a boy that was "not right"; he had fits.

The next night we had sheets for our bed, but breakfast time brought a surprise. The women [*sic* woman] of the house called loudly to her slovenly daughter to hurry and get out of bed so she could have the sheet for a tablecloth. Somehow the vittles didn't taste just right that morning.

That day we made slow progress. It had rained all night, and the roads at times were hub deep with mud. The wagons slipped and slithered and finally bogged down. One of the drivers rode a mule away in search of help, returning after an interval with a farmer and a yoke of oxen. This auxiliary power plus our teams freed the wagons and nudged us over a long difficult hill. The owner of the oxen turned out to be a Campbellite.[11] He charged Papa a dollar.

The last day brought tragedy.

It had turned bitterly cold overnight. In trying to keep his wheels out of the frozen ruts, the driver of the leading wagon edged too close to a ditch; the wagon tipped over on its side, and the precious piano was dumped on the hard ground with a splintering crash.

"Merciful heavens," shrilled Mama. "The piano is ruined!"

"My piano! Oh, my piano!"

Sister let out an ear piercing wail, jumped out of the buggy, and ran to the wreckage. Mama and I followed as quickly as we could. The driver was fighting to get control of his mules, panicked by the overturn. Papa, his eyebrows very high, stood surveying the damage, his arm around two frantic and weeping women.

"It will be all right," he said. "Be calm, be right easy."

"How can you say that?" Sister asked furiously. "You know my beautiful, piano is ruined. I'll just die . . ." She was unable to control her tears.

I was crying, too.

Mama took me by the hand.

"Let's go back to the buggy," she said. "I can't stand to see it."

"Can't Sister play anymore?" I sobbed. "Is our piano gone?"

To the female side of the family, this was the ultimate in disaster. Ray stood speechless, looking at the battered packing case. His face was ashy. His eyes bulged. He loved the piano, too.

After the team quieted and the anguished cries abated, Papa took charge of the salvage operation. With Ray's help, he quickly pried the shipping case apart. The drivers gave a hand, and the four eased the piano to an upright position at the side of the road. The heavy lid was split with a gaping crack its full length. There was no other visible damage.

"What's all the weeping about?" Papa shouted, his voice exultant. "It's not hurt—just a little crack—and I can mend that."

He had spoken too soon.

With his forefinger he tapped an ivory key. No sound. He quickly ran his fingers over the keyboard. Not the slightest sound. He was crestfallen.

When Sister saw Papa striking the dead keys, she immediately fell into a second paroxysm of tears.

"I knew it! I knew it! Oh my piano, it's ruined!"

She buried her head in her arms on the keyboard and wept uncontrollably.

"All right," Papa said. "That's enough. I'll fix it."

I'm sure he had not the slightest notion of how to go about repairing a piano on the side of the road, forty miles from nowhere—but papa was never bashful about trying.

One of the drivers produced a screw driver, and Papa took out his Barlow knife. They raised the cracked lid, each as innocent of ideas on the inner workings of the instrument as the other, and began to poke about. Mama couldn't stand it in the buggy any longer. She and I came back, Mama put her arms around Sister who was still crying.

The "mechanics" poked away. From inside the piano came "pings" and "plunks."

"Over there," we heard Papa say. "Maybe you can tighten that screw."

Papa tried the keys. We got a feeble note or two.

"More," Papa told his helper. "Now, over on this side."

Talking to themselves, circling the wounded instrument, the men worked feverishly. The rest of us just stood and waited. Sister's sobbing subsided into a series of low moans. She refused to watch, pacing back and forth, and hugging herself convulsively. As Papa and his companion pried and wrenched and adjusted the jumbled parts inside the piano, the suspense grew. Mama was trembling as I clung to her skirt and whimpered.

"Don't cry anymore," she said. "Papa will make it play . . . I hope."

Then it happened: From within the piano we heard exclamations by both men. They straightened up, looking triumphant.

Suddenly, Papa was running his fingers along the keyboard, and the notes were loud and clear. All the keys were sounding. A miracle had happened. It seemed as good as new.

The piano was fixed!

"Whoopee!" yelled Ray.

He whirled and danced on the frozen road. Sister's tear-stained face instantly blossomed with a smile.

"Oh—oh—oh, thank goodness!" She cried delightedly. "It still plays. I can't believe it. I'm so happy!"

Papa already had the stool out of the wagon. He calmly placed it on the icy ground in front of the piano. He seated himself, rubbed his fingers together, and, grinning broadly, broke into a fast rendition of "Oh, Dem Golden Slippers."[12]

Ray jigged; Mama and Sister hugged each other and urged Papa on: I jumped up and down and shouted happily.

Then Mama picked me up and held me, and we gathered around Papa and sang as he played "When the Roll is Called up Yonder."[13]

The wagon drivers standing over at one side took off their hats and grinned sheepishly.

※

The rest of the trip was an anticlimax.

We arrived at our new parsonage home, unloaded, cleaned he [*sic* the] premises, and straightened up. While this was being done, Mama sent Ray to the village on Old Dick to get a bar of Big Deal soap. He came back with interesting intelligence. He had heard that the parishioners were coming the next night with a pounding.

A pounding was important to a new preacher. If the church folks were liberal, and they usually were with what they had, it could mean enough provisions to run the family for months.

Since this was Papa's first church, he and Mama wanted to do the correct thing. Refreshments must be ready. Back to the store went Ray to get chocolate and fresh coconut needed for baking cakes.

The pounding was a big one. We heard the crowd coming just before dark, and Papa went out to meet them. Sister held me up to the window to watch. They were marching two by two, led by a man in a coonskin cap, playing a fiddle. Every person had a sack or a box or a jar or a crock containing a gift for the preacher. One man had a live turkey. We ate that bird for Christmas. Two boys carried a pole on their shoulders; suspended from the pole was a dressed shoat.[14] We would have fresh sausage and backbones and spareribs and tenderloin from that carcass, to say nothing of a hog's jowl to go with the blackeyed peas for good luck on New Year's Day.

We had another visitation from the good church people in a few weeks. This time it was a gathering for a New Year's Eve watch party.

Before this event, there was a great deal of talk I couldn't comprehend. Since it was called a "watch party," perhaps everyone would bring Papa a watch. When I made inquiries on this point, I was assured that it was to be quite different from a pounding, that there would be no gifts. On New Year's Eve, soon after dark, I found myself the object of a discussion between Mama and Papa. Mama was insisting that it would be foolish to let me stay up or to awaken me. I didn't know why, but I begged to be allowed to stay up. A compromise ensued. Papa promised to wake me at midnight. Of course, I didn't want to miss anything, even if I didn't know or couldn't understand what it was.

(Years later I was able to find out. A new century was being born at midnight that night, January 1, 1900. At least, that was the popular conception; the 1800s were going out and the 1900s were coming in. Papa didn't want his baby girl to miss it.)

The group from Shiloh church gathered at our house sometime during the evening. How they carried out their program of watching, I don't know; I was sound asleep. At midnight I was awakened. I wasn't too happy about being taken away from slumberland, but as soon as I had rubbed my eyes open, I was ready for action—if any.

"Has it come yet?" I asked.

"Any minute now," Papa said. He took me in his lap. I sat there in my gown, shivering a little with excitement. The new century was coming, and it would be here any minute. I didn't know what a new century was. What if it came right in this room and grabbed us? I hugged Papa as tightly as I could.

All eyes were on the Seth Thomas clock[15] on the mantel. The hands were straight up, the room was still.

"When the clock strikes twelve," Papa said, "this old world will have lived out another hundred years.

"Let all the bitterness and troubles and hard times of the old century die with it, let old scores be forgiven, let—"

"Bong, bong . . ."

The clock was striking midnight . . . nobody spoke. I sat up and looked toward the door. In whatever manner the new century arrived, it didn't come through the door, I decided. ". . . bong, bong!"

The clock finished striking twelve. The roomful of people remained silent. "Let us pray," Papa said.

We knelt by our chairs, and Papa prayed long and earnestly. Afterward Sister played, and all joined in singing "Onward Christian Soldiers."[16] Then Mama and Ray passed apples and popcorn. There was no horn blowing or even loud talk. For us, the Twentieth Century came in on a low note.

Life at Shiloh was pleasant enough. Construction of the Shiloh National Military Park[17] was getting underway. Soon engineers and surveyors, army officers and official delegations were all about us. Some of the young men on this project found their way to the parsonage, calling on Sister that summer while she was home from Boarding School. Adding to the occasion, we had a house guest—a pretty girl from Nashville—who came to visit Sister. Song sessions around the cracked-top piano were very popular.

For my part, I had a wonderful time playing with the neighborhood children. A favorite pastime was gathering "minnie" balls[18] after heavy rains. Occasionally we found a rusted canteen in the woods near the house. Ray uncovered a sword, its leather scabbard rotted away, half buried in a thicket. In our imagination, we re-enacted the fierce skirmish in which it had been lost.

One of the excitements of the year was a two day celebration of the anniversary of the Battle of Shiloh, April 6th and 7th. Mama and Sister and her visitor were busy for days making dresses for the anniversary event. They wanted two complete outfits, one for each day. When the first of the great days arrived, we drove two miles to the bank of the Tennessee River, scene of the main festivities. It was a carnival time; thousands were there.

We "scattered around" and took in the sights, listened to the music by resplendent visiting bands, and gawked at intricate drill formations by crack companies of soldiers. From time to time we stopped at a lemonade stand and had all we could drink for a nickel. The lemonade was served from barrels. Each barrel contained a big block of ice. We drank from tin cups tied to the barrels.

At noon we spread a cloth for our basket dinner. Then came disaster—a sudden hard shower. Mama, Papa and I ran for the buggy, and Papa put up the top and fastened the side curtains as quickly as we could.

At that moment we saw Sister and her chum with their beaux flying in our direction. The girl's finery was soaked. Their wet clothes clung so tightly to their bodies that Mama gasped. We could see the corset prints! New hats were bedraggled and ruined; the colors of the gay flowers had run, leaving red and green streaks on the straw bonnets and down the lace on their dresses.

The girls piled in the buggy with us—their escorts had brought them in open, narrow-gauge buggies, the kind that throw the boy and girl close together—and Papa drove us home. I looked back and giggled at the damp young gentlemen trotting along in their unprotected buggies. Their straw hats and starched collars were limp. They were comical.

There was a great stir when we got home. Papa built a fire in the kitchen range so the young men could dry out their clothes, while the girls changed into fresh outfits.

We drove back to the river and re-spread our picnic. The ghosts of Nathan Bedford Forrest[19] and Albert Sidney Johnson[20] [*sic* Johnston] may have been around; I don't know, I was too busy with stuffed eggs and lemonade.

The celebration must have been a grand time for courting. That evening Papa married a corporal and his Shiloh sweetheart in our parlor; and within three days he united three more couples. The fees helped tide us over till the next Quarterly meeting.[21]

※

That fall Mama received a telegram. It came to Selmer,[22] the nearest railroad station, and was sent out to Shiloh by a messenger on muleback. It said Grandfather Kennedy[23] was "bad off sick" and asking for Mama to come home.

The message came at nightfall. Mama got ready immediately while Papa hitched up Old Dick. In less than an hour we were on our way to Selmer, a distance of eighteen miles.

It was on Monday, court day in Selmer, and the nearer we approached the town, the more drunken ruffians we passed.

Some were running their horses and swearing. Groups of men were dismounted, passing around jugs or shooting craps by the light of the fire. They yelled profanities at us. Papa ignored it all. Mama and I were frightened.

"Giddup!" Papa would say as we passed a boisterous party, and he would slap Old Dick with the lines and speed away.

Finally, we came to a wretch who had fallen off his horse. He was lying dead drunk in the middle of the road, his horse standing over him, snorting and pawing. The moon was out, and the man's plight was plain to see. Mama wrung her hands. She was afraid the horse would stomp the unfortunate man, but she also feared that if Papa got out to save him, he might rouse up and become violent.

What to do? Papa resolved it by pulling Old Dick off the road, up a bank, and around the fallen stranger without disturbing man or animal. Then Papa stopped and looked back.

"I can't go on," he said.

Quickly he stepped out of the buggy, walked back to the unconscious man and raised him to a sitting position.

"Are you hurt?" Papa asked loudly.

When the man's only response was a glazed look, Papa dragged him to the side of the road and propped him against a rail fence. Papa then hitched the man's horse to the fence and returned to the buggy where Mama and I sat trembling.

"Just rest easy now," Papa called back over his shoulder. "You'll be all right. Giddap [*sic* Giddup], Dick!"

We came to Selmer after midnight. I had been asleep but I became wide awake as Papa drew up to a small frame hotel and called loudly: "Hello!"

We heard someone stir, and a lamp was lighted. The front door opened. There stood a huge man in his cotton drawers, holding a light over his head.

When the innkeeper saw Mama, he jumped back behind the door.

"Excuse me, Sister," he called, "I didn't know you had a lady with you."

Next morning when the train rolled in, the snorting engine frightened me. Papa picked me up, carried me into the car with Mama and put our suitcase on the rack and kissed us both goodbye.

We had to change at Jackson,[24] and Mama thought we had missed our connection when another train pulled out just as we alighted there. We started to run toward the moving cars, but a kind conductor calmed us. The train was switching tracks. It came back.

Our last stop was Dresden.[25] Uncle Potter[26] was there to meet us. He drove us out to Little Zion.[27] Grandfather was still alive, but the end was near. Everybody began to cry when Mama walked in. Grandfather knew her and was comforted. He died that night.

I sat with Mama in the Little Zion Meeting House at the funeral. The weeping by so many people upset me. I told Mama out loud that if she didn't stop crying, I was going back home. She took me in her arms and didn't cry anymore.

I have one other vivid recollection of Shiloh.

On a bright, sunny afternoon Papa took me along on a pastoral call. As we drove home, it suddenly became as dark as night. I was astonished, unbelieving; but since Papa was there I knew no harm could befall me. What on earth could it be?

Papa put his arm around me and smiled.

"It's a total eclipse[28] of the sun," he said. "You may never see another."

I wasn't old enough to read the almanac; I wasn't sure what an eclipse was, but I accepted it as something natural and proper. As Papa explained it to me, it was evidence that all was well, that God was in heaven, and that the Almighty was operating the world on an exact schedule.

Not much of that sank in. I was really impressed though when we returned home and I learned that the chickens had gone to roost in the middle of the afternoon.

Our stay at Shiloh was coming to an end. Papa was rounding out a good year. Now he was a full-fledged circuit rider.[29]

In a few more weeks we departed. Again we piled our plunder in wagons, this time bound for the depot at Selmer. And again Sister's beloved piano was crated and loaded—but this time with more loving care than ever before.

❧

The cracked top of the piano was never replaced. Through the years it remained to remind us of an unforgettable trek to Shiloh, and of the time when tragedy on the road was turned to comedy.

Was it any wonder that Mama stood weeping as the unforgettable past came back to her and her heart ached with longing for that which could never be again?

CHAPTER 7

When Mama Laughed Again

THE WEEKS AND MONTHS THAT FOLLOWED SISTER'S[1] DEATH WERE difficult, though I knew—as children sense in times of family distress—that Mama and Papa were doing their best to bear up and make home-life as pleasant as possible.

Never did anyone have kinder friends and neighbors that autumn. Everybody tried in some way to be comforting. People called for short visits. Huge armfuls of chrysanthemums, still blooming in many yards, were brought to brighten the house. Many a fat pullet or jar of choice preserves found its way to our table as a gesture of sympathy from those living around us. It was the hunting season, and the men who went to Reelfoot Lake[2] remembered us when they returned with full game bags; we feasted on wild duck and quail.

But Mama was not the same gay, fun-loving Mama. I would come home from school and tell her everything amusing that had happened; I could only provoke sad smiles. I thought: If I could only make her laugh once more.

Christmas came and Santa Claus had never been so lavish. He outdid himself that year in filling our stockings. Church members from other places where we had lived remembered the entire family in many ways. The loving kindness of such a large circle of friends of friends must have helped to soften the blow for our parents, for our world gradually began to brighten.

There were weddings now and then in the year that followed, but they impressed me only because Mama, no longer caring to go, usually sent me. Before, I had never been considered for the role of wedding guest; but Mama now seemed to want me to take her place. She would decline an invitation and explain that she had to stay with the young children. I felt quite dignified to be among the chosen guests—and I always dressed in my very best and tried to "sit proper" and act "grownup."

Soon after Christmas, Mama expressed the wish to spend a week with her mother, as Papa had to be away for a church conference at that time. Grandmother[3] was very old—nearly ninety—but she lived in the rambling old farmhouse where she and Grandfather[4] had started married life seventy years before.[5] After Grandfather's death, she had rented the farm to a young couple who moved into the house and provided the meals and looked after her and Mama's oldest sister,[6] who had never left the home nest.

Papa was anxious for Mama to have a change, so the visit was arranged with the hope that the winter weather would turn mild. Usually when Mama went on such visits, the children were left at home with Papa, aided by our colored helper, Aunt Lisa; but this time, since Papa was to be away, too, we were all packed up with our schoolbooks—Joe[7] was now in school—and away we went.

The plan was for Papa to join us at the end of the week and come back with us on the train. We would have a three-hour layover at Hollow Rock Junction, a dreaded wait for a woman alone and trying to manage three small children. Papa could help her manage on the return trip.

❧

Hollow Rock[8] was the key to all travel to and from Weakley County,[9] home of all our kin—it was where the branch line veered off from the main Memphis-to-Nashville route. It was, if the stories told about it are to be credited, a station of nightmares.

I really believed, and perhaps it really was true, that passengers sometimes got off a train at Hollow Rock Junction and were swallowed up and never heard of again.

This exaggerated idea was attributable to the fact that the tiny station was completely isolated, "out in the middle of nowhere," and hopelessly dreary. All passengers dreaded the layover a [*sic* at] Hollow Rock. No trip was complete without a misadventure there.

Actually there was a Hollow Rock station—for the town called Hollow Rock—and a Hollow Rock Junction. They were a mile or two apart. The train stopped first at the town. The conductor, the flagman and the porter came through the cars and warned those who were changing at Hollow Rock Junction not to leave the train at Hollow Rock station. As passengers alighted at the station, they were buttonholed and interrogated by the conductor as to where they really wanted to get off, and warnings were repeated. Nevertheless, mothers with babies, old ladies clutching reticules, elderly Confederate veterans, and many others regularly managed to become stranded at the village depot, with the train pulling out and leaving them while harassed trainmen pleaded with them to get back aboard.

The name Hollow Rock was imprinted on their minds as the place where they were to change. No persuasion, no threats could save them. They fought off all representatives of the railroad and disembarked at [*sic* a] one-room depot away from everywhere in spite of all that could be done for them.

Did they ever get to the Junction? Nobody knows. If they did, it was by trudging down the track, or taking to a rugged dirt road. Possibly some never made it. Perhaps they are still wandering along the rusted tracks of a ghost line in a never-never land of forgotten railroads.

In the past, we had endured our share of the troubles at Hollow Rock.

For instance, we had tried as hard as anyone else to get off at the wrong stop, but the conductor always managed to get us back to our seats to wait for the Junction.

"You announced Hollow Rock," Mama had said firmly on such an occasion.

"This is the town of Hollow Rock," said the conductor patiently. "Your ticket says change at Hollow Rock Junction—that's the next stop."

"Aren't Hollow Rock and Hollow Rock Junction the same?"

"No, madam, they're two miles apart."

"Well, why don't you give them different names?" Mama reasoned with him. "It seems so confusing."

"Lady, I don't name the stations, I just run this train."

"It's a funny way to run it," Mama said, subsiding.

Of course she wasn't the first—or the last—to comment on the oddities encountered in the operation of a railroad.

Small boys sometimes met the train at the Junction and sold paper-sack lunches for twenty-five cents. One of these consisted of a piece of fried chicken, always a wing; one hardboiled egg, a wedge of corn pone, and a fried pie. The most charitable thing that could be said is that it wasn't lethal. We only tried it once. Luckily we recovered.

A drummer once got fresh with Sister at Hollow Rock Junction. She had dropped her parasol on the platform and the drummer, in pin-stripe suit and button-top shoes, murmered [*sic* murmured] "Oh, you kid" as he retrieved it and handed it to her with a smirk.

Sister blushed. Perhaps she was about to say something, but Mama nearby had overheard, and before this sort of thing could get out of hand, she had her daughter by the arm.

"Thank you," Mama said to the forward traveling man, and she whisked Sister inside the station. There they had a talk about what happened to girls who allowed themselves to be drawn into conversation with strange men.

The tedium of a layover at Hollow Rock Junction was devastating. The benches were hard. The possibilities of amusement were nil, whether the wait was one hour, two hours or half a day. If a freight train passed, I had to watch through the window; I was never permitted to go out on the platform. The only other diversion was when the porter came in and stoked the pot-bellied, tobacco-stained stove, and put fresh sawdust in the box in which it sat.

In one corner of the waiting room, on the wall, was a chewing-gum vending machine. Naturally, in the bleak circumstances of a train wait, this drew me like a magnate [*sic* magnet]. After the unnerving experience with the drummer, Mama kept us close under her wing; but finally I wheedled a penny from her, and headed for the machine.

The machine got my penny but it failed to produce the gum. It was out of whack.

Of course, I did what comes naturally—I stuck my finger in the opening to see why the gum didn't come out. Unluckily I probed too far, twisted my finger, and suddenly found it was stuck fast and I couldn't get it loose.

I was small and frightened, so I screamed.

Mama and Sister came running; the station agent came running; depot loafers, passengers, everybody came to help.

"Now you've done it," Mama said. "Pull hard and try to slip your finger out."

"It hurts," I whimpered.

Mama turned to the station agent.

"Can you please do something? She put a penny in and now she's caught her finger trying to get the gum out."

"Well, now,"—said the agent lamely. He obviously didn't know what to do.

"Please get the key and unlock the machine so I can get my child back," Mama urged.

"I've got a key somewhere," the agent said, "but I—now let's see—where did I put it?"

He was no help. So Mama, who had been trying to ease my finger loose all this time, turned to Sister. "You try, but don't hurt her."

I was crying all his time, as my finger was twisted in such a way that it was painful.

Then help came from an unexpected quarter. The colored porter, a shuffling old man wearing a battered trainman's cap, pushed his way through the spectators and looked at me with a chuckle.

"What's the matter, li'l girl? Don' got yo'se'f stuck?"

"Can you help us, please?" Mama asked.

"Ain' nothin'," he said. "Happen all the time. Ol' machine ain' no good nohow."

The porter had me stand a little to one side, then he gave the gum box a sudden vigorous cuff on top with his big fist.

It worked perfectly. The mechanism whirred and clicked. My finger was released, a piece of gum dropped out—and my penny was returned. I was instantly overjoyed and began to laugh. Everybody laughed. Everybody except Mama. She clucked her tongue and admonished me.

"Don't ever put your finger in a machine again."

It was good advice, and I followed it ever after.

※

There was another reason for Papa to join us at Grandmother's.

A distant cousin who was also a niece of the couple[10] living with Grandmother was to be married and had been invited to have the wedding in Grandmother's parlor. She had asked Papa to officiate, if he could be present.

Of course, a wedding in her old home was the last thing Mama wanted to see; but plans were made, and, as Papa pointed out, the event would give them an opportunity to visit with many of their friends of happier days.

This homecoming was especially sad for Mama. Grandmother had not been able to attend Sister's funeral, and it was the first time Mama had seen her since that time of sorrow. Sister had been born in that farmhouse—in the same room in which Mama was born—and had spent much of her childhood there visiting Grandmother. She had been a general favorite with the relatives and was well known to all in the community. So when the word went out that Mama was back home, the house was full of company, morning, noon and evening. Mama's two brothers, Uncle John[11] and Uncle Harris,[12] lived nearby. They came with their families along with other kin and friends, expressing sympathy and trying to be cheerful.

It was a time of delight for the small fry. We had our lessons right after breakfast, and then we were more or less footloose. The house itself had always been a great source of entertainment. Now we were free to play and explore from cellar to attic, and to run at large in the big yard outside.

My grandparents had arrived in West Tennessee as young children travelling across the mountains with their pioneer parents and relatives from the Carolinas and Virginia.[13] When Grandmother and Grandfather married,[14] they received from Grandfather's father[15] a section[16] of land that was part of the original patent.[17] With the aid of two slaves, who also were wedding gifts from their respective parents,[18] they cleared the land and built a log cabin with a lean-to at the back and a loft overhead. That log cabin was now the parlor of the old house in which we romped and played games.

As Grandfather became able, he had improved and enlarged the house through the years. He first dug a roomy cellar, still in use, then he built another log structure, with a "dog trot"[19] between it and the original cabin. This was a two-story addition with a good-size room upstairs. As the years passed and the family grew, the house continued to expand. Other additions included a long ell[20] with wide porches, a large kitchen, and a still larger dining room. A pantry was tacked on here, and a well house and shedroom there. Surely there was never a more intriguing place for children.

The best places of all were the loft over the parlor and the cellar underneath.

The steps to the loft were out in the hall. The room had two little windows that gave just enough light for reading, and we had a free hand in pulling out the old books and treasures of every kind that had been stored up there and forgotten for a half a century.

The cellar was sort o' creepy. It was the "dungeon cell" in our games. It was a fascinating place, too, in a way. We would grope around in the dark and feel the dampness of everything; then we'd light a candle and count the strange looking crocks, and rows and rows of jars filled with good things Grandmother had stored away. There were wooden tubs, buckets and churns[21]—most of these had not been used in years—and barrels that had held grape wine and sweet cider when Grandfather was alive and ran the farm.

Sometimes there would be a binful of apples, but most of the bins were empty now and belonged to the past.

The front porch was a wonderful place. We spent a lot of time on it that January week. It faced the south and usually was sunny and pleasant. It had wooden banisters all around. The whole house was painted white, including the porch and banisters, but the ceiling of the porch was bright blue. We called that the "sky." We would stand on the benches that ran along the walls and try to reach the sky. Running around the porch under the eaves was fancy "lacework." We called this "clouds."

Around the yard was a white picket fence with a front gate that was also very fancy and lacy. Just outside the gate was a wooden block—like the stump of a tree—called the horse block. Mama told us that when she was younger, she had stood on that block to mount a side saddle on Old Molly. When we drove up in a buggy we stepped out on the block, then to the ground.

Back of the big house was a vegetable garden, and behind that was the horse lot and barn. There were various other buildings—corn crib, wagon shed, granary, and a cow shed where the milking was done. That part of the place held no interest for me. I was wary of most farm animals.

We were twice blessed on trips like this, as Papa's mother—Grandma[22]—lived about a half mile away. We rotated from one place to the other, and stayed in high spirits all the time.

Grandma, too, was now a widow. Her youngest son—Uncle Potter[23]—not yet married—lived with her and managed the farm. She was a much younger woman than Grandmother, and would play games with us; and our young uncle was jovial and easy-going. Sometimes he let us play in the hayloft.

As soon as we got to Grandma's, we would start teasing to hear the grandfather clock strike.

"That old clock!" Grandma would say. "It's always run down."

She would call Uncle Potter and have him wind it.

"Now listen. This will be the last time."

And she would run the hands one complete time around so we could hear the mellow "bong" resound from one to twelve times. That was a special treat, it made Key clap his hands in delight.

Grandma knew what was coming next. We begged to see her operate the spinning wheel. So Uncle Potter would bring it down from the attic, and Grandma would produce some wool from a little store she kept on hand—sheared from a pair of Uncle Potter's old sheep, and washed and carded against her grandchildren's visits. In a few minutes she would spin enough yarn on the whirring spool for us to wind into a ball for our games.

The spinning process never ceased to entertain me, but though I tried and tried I never could get the hang of it.

"You'd have learned fast enough if you'd been here after the war," Grandma said a little grimly. "We had to spin and weave, too, if we wanted anything to wear. Your papa wouldn't have had any britches if I hadn't been for this old wheel."

Toward the end of this sunny week, things were in a general stir over the wedding that was to take place in Grandmother's parlor Saturday morning. Papa would be there Friday night, and we children were to ride into town in a surrey with Grandma and Uncle Potter to meet him at the train.

Getting the house ready for company was a ritual a [sic at] Grandmother's, and the grownups were glad to have the children kept out of the way. First, a big fire was made in the parlor fireplace. Grandmother knew the room was musty from the cellar underneath.

While the fire was blazing away and driving out any dampness, the room was thoroughly cleaned—though I never saw a speck of dirt in it in my life. To aid this operation, wisps of cedar were dipped in a basin of water and scattered over the floor. This kept the dust down when the carpet was swept, and also left a faint fragrance in the room. The carpet not long before had been taken up and beaten and aired in the yard; and before it was laid again, fresh wheat straw had been put on the floor. This made the carpet very soft to walk on.

We got back from town late in the afternoon, and by the time we had eaten supper it was dark. Then we all moved into the fresh, sweet-scented parlor, and sat around a roaring fire. Grandmother was in the center with Papa and Mama on each side and the others of the household grouped around. I had the footstool and Key and Joe were on the rug in front of the hearth. Old Watch, the family dog, had his regular place in the chimney corner.

We listened to Grandmother tell about the first year she was married, and how this room was the only home she and Grandfather had.

Joe could scarcely wait to ask the question he had asked many times before:

"Were there any Indians, Grandmother?"

There had been a few Indian scares[24] when Grandmother's folks brought her over the Wilderness Road[25] to Kentucky, and on into Tennessee and she remembered he [sic the] sentries they posted at night with loaded muskets against surprise raids. But most of the Indians had been moved west of the Mississippi River before the Obion and Forked Deer country[26] could be settled, and only a few fugitives were wandering about when our grandparents arrived in Weakley County.

"When the dog barked a certain way, we knew an Indian was nearby," Grandmother said. "Pa would take his rifle and look around to see that the horses were safe."

"Once he shot at a skulker he glimpsed in the corn patch back of the barn, but usually when the dog barked we could see an old Indian in a ragged blanket out by the fence begging for vittles. If his squaw was along, he's [*sic* he'd] send her in to get anything we offered like corn pone and a piece of side meat.[27]

"The dogs all growled and tore around like it was the Old Scratch[28] as long as the varmints[29] were on the place. They had to be tied up before a squaw could come inside the gate."

"Did they have tommyhawks?" Joe persisted.

"The only ones we saw were dirty and ragged—miserable looking critters, too old to be whacking around with tommyhawks."

"Didn't they take any scalps?"

"Nairy a scalp."

But if the Indians were mostly harmless objects of pity, there were other perils. Black bear still roamed the dense bottoms and howling timber wolves sent chills down the spine of the "young 'uns" back in the days Grandmother described.

In the winter when food was scarce, the wolves came right up to the barn lot and killed the stock," Grandmother recalled. "Pa set traps and caught a good many. There was a bounty and he took the scalps to the courthouse and got twelve and a half cents apiece for them."

"Then in the summertime, we had to watch out for rattlers. Your own Grandfather killed one with twelve rattlers in the cellar—right under where I'm sitting this minute!"

I shivered at that, and Papa changed the subject. He told about the days when he was courting Mama, and had to leave by nine o'clock. They were married in this room, standing right over there near the front window.

I looked at the lace curtains touching the floor by the window and wondered how they kept from stepping on them. They'll get stepped on tomorrow, I bet.

But Grandmother wasn't through reminiscing. She told us about the tall press[30] between the back windows.

"It belonged to your Grandfather's folks,"[31] she said. "They brought it from South Carolina over the Wilderness Road, in an ox wagon. Effie May's great-grandfather[32] drove that wagon." Effie May[33] was the cousin who was to be married the next morning.

"Your grandfather's people were in a big party—several families of kinfolks. They had to travel together for protection. They had plenty of corn meal and some other provisions along, but the menfolks had to go off into the woods and shoot game for fresh meat. By and by, one of your Grandfather's aunts[34] was taken bad sick and died on the side of the trail. It seemed like such an awful thing for them to go off and leave her buried in the middle of the wilderness."

The press had three drawers in the bottom part and above the drawers a shelf let down and made a desk. It had a lot of odd-shaped pigeonholes, but I never had a chance to look into those. The top part was a cupboard with shelves that went almost to the ceiling. This was where Grandfather kept his most prized books.

The mantel over the fireplace was draped with a silk lambrequin that had fancy embroidery and long fringe. It had been bought from a peddler who came around once or twice a year. Grandmother got her towels and linen tablecloths from him. A brass-trimmed clock was in the middle of the mantel and at the ends were matched vases with flowers painted on them. In one of the vases was a bunch of peacock feathers. "That's for good luck," Grandmother said.

Another thing on the mantle [sic mantel] fascinated me. It was a little lamb kneeling on a box made of milk glass.[35] The box was opened by lifting the lamb. It held cones of French chalk[36] and a mole skin. Grandmother spoke sometimes of "chalking" her face. How I wanted to get into that box and try out the moleskin and chalk.

When the fire had burned low and the red coals were just right, Mama popped some popcorn, which she poured into a crock on the hearth. We had to sit up close to eat it so none would be dropped on the carpet. We also roasted chestnuts—from trees down in the wood lot—and again we were not permitted to wander far from the hearth to eat them as he [sic the] room had to be kept clean for the next day.

At last we trooped across the hall into Grandmother's room and then up the funny steep steps that turned a sharp corner to the bedrooms above. The baby was already asleep, and Joe and I were almost too drowsy to say our prayers. The beds were high off the floor. When I was lifted onto mine I sank deep; into the soft feather mattress. It was made from goosedown, plucked from the hissing geese that waddled about in Grandmother's yard.

The next morning I felt the undercurrent of excitement that pervades any spot where a wedding is pending. Even Grandmother seemed worked up. By the time Mama had us bathed and dressed, people were beginning to roll in.

They were mostly in buggies and surreys, but a few men and boys were on horseback.

We sat on the benches in the warm sunshine of the front porch and watch [*sic* watched] them arrive. Everyone spoke to us and observed how much we had grown, or whether we looked like our mother or father, or some more distant forebear. We endured it with what patience we possessed; even so, I might have been tempted to get "smart" if Mama had not been within earshot most of the time.

The bridal party had driven up the lane and entered quietly through the side porch. All of the group was waiting in Grandmother's room.

If the entrance of Cousin Effie May and her betrothed was without "hoorah," the arrival of her grandfather a few minutes later made up for it. We were entranced by the commotion he caused. Most of the guests went out to the gate to help get him in.

This old man—we had been instructed to call him "Cousin Pigg"—had been in poor health for many years. He had finally suffered a near-fatal seizure and had lain near death for weeks; but he had rallied and could now sit up and be wheeled to the table three times a day.

Cousin Pigg had reared his granddaughter, and after his wife died the girl had nursed him and become his mainstay and chief comfort. When she reached marrying age, he was anxious to see her suitably matched, so he caused word to be spread that the farm and everything on it would go to her if she married and continued to live here and to take care of him.

It was rich bottom land, and before long a robust young farmer asked for Effie May's hand. So arrangements were made by Effie May's aunt, living with Grandmother, to have the wedding at Grandmother's and here we were with the ceremony about to begin.

Cousin Pigg had not been well enough even to attend church in several years; thus his coming to the wedding had focused as much interest on him as on the couple to be wed. Detailed preparations had to be made to get him there. It was decided that the easiest way to move him from his home to Grandmother's would be to lift him, wheelchair and all, into a wagon. So stout poles were placed under the sides of the chair, and the hands on the place loaded him up. Blankets were wrapped around him, stone jugs of hot water and heated bricks were placed at his feet. His head was swathed in a muffler and furlined cap.

Mama gasped when she saw the invalid drive up.

"Cousin Pigg would be better off at home," she said.

With the poles it was easy enough to lift Cousin Pigg and his wheelchair from the wagon and set him down on the porch. I had seen pictures in my storybook of kings and queens being carried in sedan chairs, but I decided the resemblance here was not too close. However, it sure was an interesting sight.

Papa left the poles in the hall and rolled Cousin Pigg through the crowd and fixed him a good place in the parlor where he could see the ceremony. Then everyone pressed into the room, leaving the center open for the couple and their attendants. Mama stayed in the hall, and, after the bridal party marched in, moved Grandmother's chair to the door. I took a post at the door with them.

The usual sort of reverent hush had settled on the crowd, and though I had my eye on Old Watch, who was sniffing at a cricket in the hallway, I could hear Papa's practiced voice saying "Dearly Beloved, we are gathered together . . ."

Suddenly his words were drowned by a loud cracking, crunching sound.

The bride toppled over backward. Papa grabbed for her, half fell, half slid into a tangled heap at her feet.

The floor had caved in over the cellar!

Women screamed, children howled, and a mighty scramble took place in the middle of the room where the floor had subsided to a depth of four or five feet. Everybody, except those with their backs to the walls, had been pitched headlong into the depression, or had instantly found themselves sliding forward feet first.

"Look out for the fire!" These were Papa's first words, and he had abandoned his preaching voice; he was speaking with authority born of alarm.

For the hearth had tilted forward and the burning logs in the fire threatened to roll into the catapulted heap of humanity. This was no time for Papa's usual "let everybody be easy." This was real danger.

Willing hands scrambled to hold back the logs and embers. From the porch rushed a frantic guest with a bucket of water. Some of it went on the fire, most of it on Papa.

"Effie May! Effie May! Are you all right?" This was from the bride's aunt, clawing to get to her poor niece who was sprawled in a heap of petticoats and ruffled drawers, amidst a jumble of arms, legs and frightened faces.

But where was the bridegroom? He had lurched to one side, grabbed the lace curtains and crushed his way through the nearest window. Now he was back at the window with the poles that had supported Cousin Pigg's chair. He thrust these downward to Papa and Effie May, who began to pull themselves upright and toward safety.

And where was Cousin Pigg? His wheelchair was there—empty.

Quickly the men on their feet pulled the fallen guests out of the hole and shifted the chairs and other pieces of furniture. Perhaps the old man was at the bottom of the pile and done for. But no Cousin Pigg.

And where was he when they did find him? Sitting outside the front gate on the horse block. He had sprung from his chair in terrified flight at the first sound of splintering timbers, and without human aid or mechanical device had reached his present perch.

"He ran past me like the Devil had his coattails," Grandmother told us. She was all a-tremble from the scare herself, and Mama was administering to her with the camphor bottle and smelling salts—but they both laughed and laughed when it was all over.

Miraculously, no one was hurt. So many people had crowded into the room that the tired old sleepers[37] under the floor had just given down. The strong flooring and carpet saved the room from a complete collapse and possible tragedy. Instead of being caught and held in a pocket, dozens of people might have plunged to the bottom of the cellar with all the furniture on top of them. When the party had reassembled on the porch, Papa offered a prayer of thanksgiving before going on with the ceremony.

I saw it all and was scared and thrilled, too. But everything else was as nothing compared with the joy I felt when I heard Mama laugh again. Her peals of laughter brought tears of joy to my eyes.

Hope Hart as a teen dressed for a high school dance. *Journey Into Yesterday Dresden, TN Sesquicentennial*, p. 60.

Hope Hart going to a congressional dinner in Washington, DC. Courtesy of the Hart family.

Hope Hart announced her retirement after thirty-six years of congressional service. She started in 1929. Courtesy of the Hart family.

MISS HOPE HART VISITED ENTERPRISE

Hope Hart visiting the *Dresden Enterprise*, a local newspaper office in Weakley County, in her home area. She is going over a ten-part series called Kilth [*sic* Kith] & Kin about her family. *McKenzie Banner,* Thursday May 12, 1966.

Hope Hart enjoying a donkey ride on vacation in Santorini, Greece. Courtesy of the Hart family.

Hope Hart's parents, Sterling and Matti, celebrating their sixtieth wedding anniversary. *Dresden Enterprise*, Friday, December 17, 1943.

Sterling Hart, Hope's father. From his obituary, *The Commercial Appeal*, Memphis, Saturday, August 11, 1956, p. 21.

THE REV. MR. HART DIES IN WASHINGTON

Former Circuit Riding Pastor Of Tennessee

The Rev. Sterling Reece Hart, former circuit-riding Methodist minister in West Tennessee, died at 1 p.m. yesterday in Washington. He was 94. Services will be held Monday at 2 p.m. at the Methodist Church in Dresden, Tenn. Burial will be in the church cemetery.

Born in Dardanelle, Ark., during the Civil War, the Rev. Mr. Hart grew up in Weakley County, Tenn. Several years he was a schoolteacher in that area.

His first church assignment was with the Methodist Chapel on Shiloh battlefield at Pittsburg Landing, Tenn. He later served in Pryorsburg, Wingo, Sedalia, and Murray, Ky., and at Obion, Ridgely, Dyersburg, Finley, Gleason, Mason, Trenton, Camp Ground, Covington, Curve and Atwood, Tenn.

After his retirement, the Rev. Mr. Hart lived in Dresden for several years before moving to Washington. His wife, the former Martha Nelson Kennedy, died in 1945, ending a marriage of 63 years.

He leaves three sons, R. K. Hart of Little Rock, N. K. Hart of Chevy Chase, Md., and Joe R. Hart of Beltsville, Md., one daughter, Miss Hope Hart of Washington, a half brother, Potter Moore of Dresden, two half sisters, Mrs. Annie Hodges of Cape Girardeau, Mo., and Mrs. Alice Killebrew of Memphis, three grandchildren and six great-grandchildren. Bowlin-Riggs Funeral Home of Dresden is in charge.

Gravestone of Eleanor Hart Harbert, Hope Hart's sister.
Courtesy of the Hart family.

CHAPTER 8

Grandma

Ninety-Five Pounds of Grit

AFTER OUR SATISFYING VISIT TO GRANDMOTHER'S[1] WE SOON WERE BACK home[2] and again settled in our routine of school and play, while Papa and Mama were finding new peace in the difficult task of keeping the family alive and going.

Before we were aware of it another summer was at hand. Its long days and lazy evenings were filled with the joys and occasional excitement of small-town life. It was a continuation of that wonderful time of indolence and innocence which we enjoy only during our swiftly drifting childhood.

Parental reins seemed to slacken a little. More than ever life was a frolic and adventure.

There were blackberries to pick . . .

One day Papa and Mama took the whole family berry-picking in the woods near the abandoned site of an old sawmill. The bushes were loaded with luscious fruit. We filled our pails and ate the ripe berries till our lips and faces were splotched with purple. Then Joe and Key and I frolicked awhile in the sawdust pile that had been left at the mill. After that we shucked our shoes and stockings and went wading in a clear branch that trickled through the woods.

That was the day Papa distinguished himself as a high hurdler. While we were wading and splashing in the branch, a bee disputed the right-of-way with Joe as he reached for an overhanging pawpaw blossom. The bee won. Stung on the arm Joe let out a shrill scream of pain—and Mama, who had just cautioned us to "watch out for snakes," instantly thought he had been struck by a copperhead.

She screamed even louder than Joe. Papa, still gathering berries, threw his pail in the air and heaved his two-hundred pound bulk toward the cries of distress at an incredible speed. He covered fifty yards in Olympic time, clearing six-feet clumps of berry brambles in great leaps. Joe's tears turned to chortles of glee at the sight of Papa coming through the briar patch.

And there were fishing trips to the Obion River bottom . . .[3]

Getting to the fishing place was a big part of the fun. Once Papa pulled the buggy off the road to take a short cut. In the dense woods and undergrowth we were hopelessly lost for hours.

"Well, we'll wind up in quicksand, or heaven knows where," Mama moaned.

"Everybody sit right still," Papa replied calmly. "I know where I am. The river is right over there." He gestured vaguely, a giveaway that he didn't know, really. "I'm an old hand in the woods. I'm travelling by the sun."

"I think the river's back that way," Mama persisted. She was uneasy.

"Oh no, you're turned around. That's the way to San Francisco; we want to bear east. Giddap [*sic* Giddup], Dick."

We had been scraped by bushes, entangled by overhanging vines, mired in sloughs, and unnerved by the gloomy, endless stretches of river bottom by the time Papa finally gave in and admitted that he was lost. He stopped by a sluggish bayou and announced: "Here's where we're going to fish."

It wasn't Papa's day. The bayou produced no fish—not even a nibble. We ate the picnic lunch that Mama had packed, and soon headed for home. Old Dick knew the way.

And so the summer continued. We watched the trains go by and played mumblety-peg[4] and swung in the hammock in our shady yard. There were buttered roasting ears to eat nearly every day, and fried chicken was a sure thing on Sunday. There were June apples in the neighbors' orchards, and Papa had a watermelon patch. We watched the watermelons as they got bigger and bigger, our mouths watering against the time when they would be ripe. There was a hayride for my Sunday School Class. Oh, there were many, many things to keep the parsonage children occupied.

And that was the summer I learned all about my spunky grandma, who was ninety-five pounds of sheer feminine grit, and Caesar, her watchdog, stopped a raid . . .

Ray[5] was home from college. His activities quickened the pace for the whole family, and my smaller brothers and I never tired of the grownup talk that swirled around him. Being a law student, he spent a good part of his vacation days at the courthouse listening to cases being tried before Judge Galloway and he made a great effort to overawe the family with judicious remarks on what he had heard. He played baseball with the town team. His home runs were epic in recital. He sang tenor in a quartet of young blades who went around at night serenading the girls. He and his fellow merry-makers sometimes did their crooning at our house. Mama let us stand in the window in our nightgowns and listen. Papa made lemonade, and Mama set the pitcher and a plate of tea cakes on the front porch to reward the boys.

So it went . . . games . . . every day a carefree romp . . . our big brother at home to liven things up.

But through all the pleasant little happenings that our family was enjoying, I became aware of something going on that I couldn't quite grasp. I detected an undertone to family conversation. When I entered a room, the talk sometimes trailed off into whispers, and knowing looks were exchanged. Something was amiss.

I imagined all sorts of things. Maybe Cousin Elroy, the one who drank and got into "scrapes," had really wound up on the gallows. Or perhaps the "panic" that everybody talked about had broken loose. I visualized the "panic" as a monster with bloodshot eyes and long tusks, whacking around, laying waste to crops and towns, and "ruining the country."

Finally, by diligently listening and piecing together bits and scraps of talk I gathered that the thing I wasn't supposed to hear was something about Grandma; that Grandma was going through some kind of crisis, and that it involved the affairs of one of her sons, our Uncle Charlie.[6] It had been Uncle Charlie's misfortune to be kicked by a horse in the spring of that year, and he had died from the injury.

Papa had made a hurried trip to Grandma's when Uncle Charlie died, and the veiled conversation at our house had been going on ever since. It was to be months before my young mind could puzzle it out—in fact, it was not until that autumn when Grandma came and spent two weeks with us. Then the mystery was dispelled and I could breathe easy again.

Uncle Charlie, to get things straight, was Papa's half brother. Grandma[7] had been married twice. Her first husband, our real grandfather,[8] died as a young man while serving in the Confederate Army, leaving her with a two-year-old son and Papa, a tiny baby.[9] Six years later, she married a neighboring farmer, a widower who himself had two children.[10] This kindly and hardworking old gentleman was the grandparent we knew as Grandpa.

Grandma and Grandpa by their union had six more children of whom Uncle Charlie was the oldest. Charlie was past thirty[11] when the accident occurred that was to prove fatal. At that time he was still making his home with his parents, although he owned a small farm a few miles away. In the spring and early summer when crop work was heaviest, he occupied a shack on this farm, where he "kept batch" and lived to himself.

Uncle Charlie had a good saddle horse named Prince. He was fond of Prince and valued him highly, but Prince was a vicious kicker.

"He was always a mean horse," Grandma said, with a positive bob of her head. "I told Charlie never to trust him."

Grandma looked away sadly.

"Just a high-spirited critter," she said. "I warned Charlie, but he got careless."

The accident that saddened the family, and set off a curious train of events, happened one Sunday morning.

Uncle Charlie had saddled Prince and tied the fidgety animal to the fence in front of his shack while he spruced up to go to meeting at Little Zion.[12] He would see his folks there at the church and, he probably thought, one of the girls whom he sparked from time to time might invite him to dinner. His grub while he was batching was pretty tedious.

As he prepared to mount Prince, Uncle Charlie indeed did get careless. Setting a foot on the low fence, he leaned over to flick a bit of dust from his boot. In that instant Prince lashed out with his iron-shod heel. The blow caught Charlie in the side and crushed his ribs.

It was a painful injury. Lige, a colored field hand from the next farm, passed along the lane an hour later and found Uncle Charlie barely conscious. The colored man managed to get him inside the shack and on the straw bunk. Then Lige rode his mule bareback the six miles over to Little Zion and called Grandpa out of the meeting house to give him the news.

Grandpa—with Grandma hastily summoned—whipped his buggy horse all the way to Uncle Charlie's. One of Grandpa's boys arrived with Doctor Busby[13] from Elm Grove a few minutes later. They found Charlie delirious.

After the elderly doctor had administered to Uncle Charlie and made him a little easier he called Grandpa outside.

"This is bad," he said gravely. "His ribs are caved in. I can't tell yet whether the lung is punctured. He will have to have mighty good care if he pulls through."

The doctor told Grandpa that Uncle Charlie was not to be moved. Grandma sent home for what she needed, and settled down to nurse her boy.

Uncle Charlie was a favorite with Grandma.

He was the steady one. No nonsense, no alibis—just good old dependable Charlie. On top of it all, he was as handsome a man as you'd find on all three forks of the Forked Deer[14]—tall, fair and blue-eyed, with black curly hair, and he had Grandma's nice manners and gentle ways.

As soon as he reached twenty-one, Charlie had started operating on his own. By hard work and shrewd trading he soon accumulated some property; the creekbottom [*sic* creek bottom] farm where he batched in summer and raised tobacco, cotton, corn and hay; a wagon and team of good mules; and the fast-gaited Prince; with a tidy sum in the bank.

Being a busy man, Charlie didn't have much time for the girls, but that's not to say that he was immune to them. He took time out now and then to squire a beribboned and many-petticoated belle to a picnic or to a church social at Little Zion or Ore's Spring;[15] but he passed these attentions around cautiously among the young ladies who were "on the carpet," avoiding commitments.

Of course, every dimpled miss for miles around knew Charlie, and all about his "prospects"; and each had her hook out. But Charlie wasn't taking the bait. He continued to play the field—when he could take the time from his farming and trading—while wishful mothers with marriageable daughters clacked their tongues and kept appraising eyes on him.

This spring, however, there had been a slight change. While as busy as ever with his crops, Charlie had made several Sunday excursions on Prince to see the daughter of a prosperous storekeeper and cattle buyer,[16] some ten miles away. Once he brought her home to Grandma's for dinner, and stopped for an all-day singing at Little Zion. Not much was known about Caroline Griggs[17]—called Carrie—when these visits started. But the grapevine soon carried full details. She was the eldest of Squire Griggs' five girls, and by neighborhood standards, she was a little advanced in age for a suitable bride. She was reliably estimated to be "over twenty-five," and there were some who said she was "pushing thirty."[18]

All the excitement about Carrie Griggs seemed to be wasted though. Two Sundays hadn't passed until Charlie showed up at Little Zion with Prince hitched to a glittering new buggy brought on from Paducah, squiring persnickety Eloise Futrell, daughter of the school-master of Hickory Grove. That eased the minds of Grandma and the rest of the family. He wasn't serious about Carrie after all, they thought.

It relieved Grandma to feel that Charlie wasn't to fall into the grasp of "that woman from way off over there." That was her way of saying she didn't know how far she could trust people who lived ten miles away and across the line in the next county.

"She was just to [sic too] ficety [sic feisty] for age." Grandma said later—"always flouncing around and never still long enough to tell whether she had any bringing up."

"I always had a notion Charlie would pick a quiet, serious-minded girl—if he ever picked one. This one though—Lord-a-mercy!" Grandma shrugged in bafflement.

Grandpa was blunt about it.

"Chatter. Nothing but chatter. That girl's chin wags up and down like a churn dasher. You've heard of perpetual motion? That's it."

But what Grandpa and Grandma didn't know was that Squire Griggs, a widower[19] with a houseful of daughters on his hands, had taken a liking to Charlie. Since Carrie was his oldest,[20] he was ready to see her hitched to a man, and since Charlie had sparked her a little, he saw no reason why that man shouldn't be Charlie. At least that's what Grandma and Grandpa later were to think.

When the news of Charlie's accident reached Squire Griggs, he didn't hesitate. He mounted his fastest horse and rode over to see what he could do.

The next day he returned in a buggy with Carrie, and a basket of fried chicken, corn lightbread, [sic light bread] strawberry preserves and chess pie. Charlie weak and feverish and suffering agonies from his bashed-in ribs scarcely knew they were there and could eat nothing. Grandma had been with him every minute, day and night. He had been able to take a little broth she made, nothing else.

Carrie and her father paid a second and a third visit as a week passed. Each time Carrie brought something—flowers, a bottle of homemade wine, pound cake. Once the squire sent a wagon with a cake of ice covered with sawdust on the long trip to Charlie's farm so the patient could have cool water and lemonade. Carrie and the Squire remained attentive and solicitous. Grandma wasn't altogether taken in by the effusive Carrie, but she was gracious and appreciative.

A few more days went by and Charlie seemed to mend a little. He appeared to be stronger. He took some milk toast one morning and Grandma was encouraged. That noon when Grandpa drove over, she decided to return home with him to get needed supplies and a good night's rest. She told Charlie she would be back early the next day, and left him in the care of a neighbor woman who promised to "sit up" that night.

Then came the real tragedy. That afternoon Charlie became feverish, and had a painful coughing spell. When Dr. Busby got there he examined Charlie, and walked out of the sickroom looking very solemn.

"It's pneumonia," he told Mrs. Travelyn, the neighbor. "The broken ribs are pressing against his right lung and congestion has set in. It is very serious."

Mrs. Trevelyn shuddered. Pneumonia was a killer everybody feared.

"Should I send right off for the folks to come back?" she asked.

"No," Dr. Busby decided; "His mother is badly in need of rest. If she's not back by noon tomorrow though, send someone to get her here as fast as you can. The crisis should come by evening, and his folks ought to be here then."

The doctor's directions were meager. There really wasn't much he could do. The only drug he left was a sedative.

"He must be covered lightly and whatever you do keep him absolutely quiet."

The doctor took his pill bag and left. He had seen a lot of pneumonia. He wasn't optimistic.

A few minutes later Squire Griggs drove up in his buggy. He was on his way to a stock sale in a nearby community, he said, and just wanted to see how the patient was doing. Mrs. Trevelyn walked out to the fence and told him the news. The Squire pushed back his straw hat, scratched his head, and gave a short whistle.

"That's bad, ain't it?" he asked. "Mighty bad."

Unconsciously Mrs. Trevelyn lowered her voice as she gave the details.

"It's them busted ribs," she said. "Pore man, and he was doing right well up to dinner time today. I told his ma . . ."

The Squire wasn't listening. He went right on in and pulled a split-bottom chair up to Charlie's bunkside.

"How you feelin, boy?"

"Mighty poorly, Squire," Charlie said. "I'm glad you came by—wanted to thank you and Miss Carrie . . ." his voice faded and he went into a deep throaty spell of coughing.

Squire Griggs waited a moment for the coughing to subside.

"Now don't you worry yourself, Charlie," he said. "Carrie wanted to come over with me today, but I had to tend to some business over here a ways, and I wasn't aimin' to go back tonight. If she'd known you wasn't feelin' so peart she'd a-come sure."

Charlie didn't appear to hear what the Squire was saying. He groaned, and turned his face to the wall. He was hot with fever now, and past any desire to talk.

The sick man was in great pain.

Squire Griggs again tried to make some conversation. Wouldn't Charlie like to have a pretty girl there to wait on him? Charlie roused up a little, and said he guessed that "would be all right."

"Charlie," the Squire continued, "why don't you and Carrie go ahead and get married so she could really take good care of you and get you well again? Wouldn't you like that, boy?"

Charlie didn't turn his head. His eyes were half glazed. His hand was twitching back and forth across his chest. He finally answered: "Oh I guess so."

Griggs and Mrs. Trevelyn exchanged a long look. Nothing more was said. In a few moments Squire Griggs quietly rose, walked out to his buggy and drove away.

That was about 4 o'clock in the afternoon. By midnight he was back in a two-horse surrey with Carrie, a marriage license,[21] and Brother Bob Corey,[22] a local preacher. Carrie had barely taken time to slip into her Sunday dress and velvet-topped button shoes.

She wore a straw sailor on her head with a veil tied under her chin. She and her father had roused an early-retiring County Clerk out of his bed and driven him to the courthouse to get the license. They had gathered Brother Corey into the surrey as they drove out of the county seat. The horses were well lathered and blowing hard when the Squire yelled "Whoa" at Charlie's place.

And so Uncle Charlie was married—in the dead of night without any of his family being aware of the event and only old Mrs. Trevelyn and her husband for witnesses.

The Trevelyns had feebly protested that Grandma and Grandpa "ought to be there." Squire Griggs quickly talked them down.

"You heer'd his wish, didn't you?" he insisted. "He said he wanted to get hitched, and I'm goin' to see that he gets his last wish."

"Well, he may pull through after all"; Mrs. Trevelyn had been left in the position of trust by Grandma and she "didn't feel right about such goin's on."

With the old lady shushed, the Squire had propped the fever-ridden, glassy-eyed Charlie up on his pillow and told the Parson to "knot 'em."

Before daylight Mrs. Trevelyn hurried off a Negro boy on a mule to summon my grandparents. They came as fast as they could in a light spring wagon. When they arrived there wasn't anything else they could do about the amazing turn of events. Bride Carrie had taken over and was running the show, her tongue clacking and rattling. Poor Charlie had worsened, and now was barely conscious. He wasn't able to speak to Grandma.

Grandpa was a man of strong temper when aroused, and he felt outraged.

"Griggs is a rascal," he fumed. "I got a great mind to go over there and hosswhip [*sic* hoss whip] him."

But Charlie's life was in the balance and Grandma prevailed on him to quiet down. "We'll have to see what can be done later," she said.

Her first suggestion was to send for Papa. "Reece will know what to do."

Uncle Charlie died that afternoon. His death and the implications of the midnight wedding crushed Grandma and the family. To add to their bitter tea, Uncle Charlie was scarcely cold in his grave when Squire Griggs and the widow Carrie began winding up Charlie's estate. As soon as the courthouse arrangements could be made, they sold the farm, stock, Prince, tools and fixtures; arranged for collection of amounts outstanding that had been owed Charlie in connection with his trading and took over his bank account.

Grandma and Grandpa saw their successful son's possessions taken with great sadness. If the money and property had been inherited by the family, it would have added to their comfort and security. As it was, they felt that the unfortunate Charlie and the family had been tricked, that the widow did not justly deserve anything. Outspoken relatives and friends suggested taking the matter to court. But Grandpa's pride was hurt and he finally decided he didn't want the affair aired anymore.

It was about all of these events that I had been hearing so much veiled talk at home. Mama and Papa thought at first that perhaps it was a "shotgun" type wedding, but when they got it all straightened out they were sure it was just a case of a schemer and his daughter taking advantage of an unusual situation. When Grandma came in to visit us, she gave us the final dramatic chapter of the story.

After everything had been sold by Charlie's widow—even the crops growing around the shack when Charlie died—the family believed they had seen the last of Carrie, Grandma related, but that was not to be.

One day in the early fall Grandma glanced out of her front window and saw Carrie and Squire Griggs drive up in a wagon.

Carrie was swathed in her widow's weeds[23] which she had worn on all public appearances since Uncle Charlie's death. A black veil covered her face. The Squire was in work clothes with a black slouch hat pushed back on his head. He cracked a black snake whip over his mules as he swung the wagon around in front of the gate and boomed, "Whoa, thar!"

Grandma didn't have to be told what they were after—Charlie's personal belongings. Grandpa had driven to the county seat that day and she was alone, except for Ca'line, the colored woman whose family lived on the farm. Ca'line cooked and washed for Grandma. Growling in the front yard was Caesar, part shepherd and part something else.

Grandma opened the front door and called Caesar. The dog whined and trotted to her. She fastened a leash to his brass studded collar. Then holding the quivering animal closely, the frail little lady, her wispy hair tucked under a crocheted cap, her skirt lifted slightly to avoid sweeping he [sic the] brick walk, strolled out to the gate.

She had not seen Carrie and the Squire since the funeral. She had a lot that she was holding in.

"Howdy, Paralee," Griggs said briskly.

Grandma said nothing. She rested one hand on top of the plank fence and looked at the avaricious father and daughter. There was a glint in her eyes.

Griggs eased his bulky frame down from the wagon, still holding his loosely coiled whip, and took a step toward the gate.

"Now, Paralee, there ain't no use for you to get yourself worked up about this," he said, "What's done, is done. Pore Charlie's gone, and I reckon we can' do nuthin' about that."

Grandma still said nothin. Carrie hadn't moved.

Griggs stopped two feet short of the gate.

"We come to get Charlie's feather bed and clothes and such stuff," he said. "We want the bedstead, too, and his bureau and linen press."[24]

Carrie came to life. She swept back her veil and fixed cold and greedy eyes on Grandma.

"I want his watch, his guitar and hat [sic that] enlarged picture of him and Prince he had made in Paducah."

Grandma, calm till now, suddenly seethed with righteous anger. If she had had Grandpa's loaded musket, she confided to her bulging-eyed grandchildren, she would have blasted the Squire right then. As she told the story, her eyes snapped angrily, and we believed implicitly that she was capable of doing it.

Mild-mannered, kindly and compassionate though she was, Grandma had plenty of spirit when pushed. She was famous for her courage in the face of danger.

She married my Grandfather Hart, a Confederate lieutenant,[25] when she was sixteen. Before she was twenty,[26] she had been left a widow with two babies, stranded far from home, and had been beset by the dangers of guerrilla fighting, blockade running, and a Mississippi River flood. She needed the courage of a dozen fighting men to survive—and survive she did.

Her Confederate husband was in a regimen that was sent to fight under General Sterling Price at the disastrous battle of Pea Ridge, Arkansas.[27] He lived through that sharp and bloody engagement, and then, on furlough, he returned to his Tennessee home for his bride and their infant son, Loesco.[28] At that time there was great fear that all of West Tennessee would soon be engulfed in the fighting, so Grandfather Hart decided to move his family to Arkansas where his uncle had a plantation and a commissary. They would be safe there, and he would have a job in the commissary after the War.

On the rough journey, dodging Yankee patrol boats on the Mississippi and traveling by night and oftentimes hiding out by day, they were so delayed that Grandfather's furlough was running out and he had to leave his family with strangers in the outpost settlement of Dardenelle [sic Dardanelle], Arkansas.[29] Here Papa[30] was born about six months later, in May 1862. And here his father came home on another furlough to die of typhus fever.[31] Grandma was left with a two-and-a-half year-old son and a three-months-old baby[32] to depend upon the mercy of anyone who might help her.

Grandma's only money was Confederate currency. This was all but worthless and soon gone. Her mules and most of the plunder they had carried in the wagon were stolen. In desperation, she appealed to a woman who also had lost her husband in the war, and the good woman took the Tennessee refugee and the two babies into her one-room cabin and shared its rude comforts.

That fall Grandma decided on a risky step. She sold the last thing she had, the wagon and took passage on a small boat down the Arkansas River. The boat was to run the Mississippi River blockade at the mouth of the Arkansas, and try to get a cargo of supplies to Confederate forces based in Tennessee.[33]

Grandma and her babies were the only passengers. The Captain was

"Mudcat" Buckner, a rough river man, heavily bearded, a "chaw" of tobacco stuck in his cheek most of the time. He was a "mighty careless type of man," Grandma recalled. He didn't always bother to spit with the wind. Otherwise he treated his passengers with great solicitude and respect. The crew consisted of a pilot, who was another gnarled and bearded man of the river; a young boy, who served as cook, and as Grandma put it, "did the best he knew how," and five Negro roustabouts.[34]

For his passenger's comfort, Captain Buckner boarded up a tiny space next to the wheelhouse and draped it with an old coverlet to give them a sleeping space and a minimum of privacy.

The trip down the murky, winding Arkansas took several days, and was without incident. Captain Buchner tied up a few miles from the junction of the Arkansas and White Rivers,[35] and not far from where he [sic the] Arkansas empties into the Mississippi. His intention was to make a run past any Yankee gunboats that happened to be in the vicinity sometime during the night. He was grim when he told Grandma the plan, but he tried not to frighten her.

"Now, Miz Hart," he said, "there may be some shootin' if the Yankee boats happen to be around and they hear us. It's the dark o' the moon, and they ain't likely to sight us at all. If we get past the patrols safe and sound, I'm a mind to make a run downstream close to yonder shore, and I'll put you off at Sawyer's Landing[36] first daylight."

"If I ever set foot on dry land again . . ." Grandma began, but the Captain shushed her and putting a protective arm around her shoulder, showed her a nook among the packing cases and barrels piled on the deck where she would be safe from any gunfire.

There among the freight Grandma crouched, shawl drawn around herself and two sleeping children while the chuffing little sternwheeler tried to run the blockade.

The moment Captain Buckner nosed past the mouth of the White River, the jig was up. The Yankee gunboats were there all right, and they had the mouth of the Arkansas neatly stoppered. It was inky dark, but a spark from the smokestack gave the blockade runner away. From dead ahead, a hundred yards or so, came a sudden yell and a burst of rifle fire. Then a small cannon boomed. It was aimed at random and did no damage. However, it had the effect of stopping the contraband boat instantly.

Captain Buckner had tested the blockade before; he knew he was a sitting duck if he didn't get out of there. The paddlewheel was reversed. The pilot, steering by instinct, quickly guided the little boat astern until it was in more sheltered waters where the heavier gunboats couldn't follow.

"Damn Yankee devils! Damn, y'u to hell!"

Captain Buckner shouted into the darkness as the gunfire died down. He spat tobacco juice in the direction of the Federal boats like a rattlesnake's spewing venom.

"Excuse me, ma'm," the Captain added. He couldn't see grandma, but he knew she was there somewhere among the boxes and barrels.

Buchner made three more runs at the blockade before he finally gave up. Once he tried it just before dawn on the chance he might catch the patrols asleep. It didn't work, nor did it succeed when he hugged the shallow water near the shore, and tried to sneak into the Mississippi just after dusk. After that he bided his time and waited for a rainy night; finally, he made his run at the height of a thunderstorm.

It was a bold try, but the lightning flashes betrayed him, and this time his boat had a really narrow squeak. On the previous attempts, by edging close to the willow-lined bank, he had been able to stay at a fairly safe distance from the Yankees. With the storm going, he had boldly tried to give the patrol boats the slip, and break out into the Mississippi. Once there, his aim was to make a run for the shoal water on the opposite side.

Two patrol boats spotted him in the lurid flashes of lightning and closed in, one on each side. Shot from the Yankee cannon tore a hole in the wheelhouse, scattering boxes and barrels of cargo. At the last possible instant, the pilot swung around and ran for the protection of the shore, and eventually he was able to nose back into the safety of Arkansas. That was Captain Buchner's last skirmish with the blockade. The only remaining roustabout, stoking the boiler when the cannon firing started—his companions had melted away after the first attempt to break out—had been convulsed with fright when a cannon ball smashed through the planking of the boiler room. He dived overboard to an unknown fate.

Grandma, huddled with little Leoso [*sic* Leosco] and Papa,[37] had crooned to her babies and prayed.

The adventures on the river covered about six weeks in all. The Captain found a new stoker and steamed back up the Arkansas to their starting point. Grandma returned to the lady who had taken her in before.

The war was over before she had another chance to go home.

Life for Grandma and her babies during the intervening period was harsh indeed. Even if she had possessed gold with which to pay, there were no supplies to be bought. Her benefactor had a lean cow that provided them with a scant supply of milk. They planted a garden to get fresh food. Grandma plaited wheat straw to make hats for her boys. Their shoes were moccasins. Grandma herself at times was laid low with chills and fever. There was no quinine, but eventually she managed to get back on her feet.

When the war was over and the chance finally came to go home—Although the countryside was still infested with bush-whackers,[38] and there was a great fear of harm by roving bands of ex-slaves—. Grandma was ready. Her plight had come to the attention of the Masonic lodge in the county where she was stranded. The fraternal order, of which my Grandfather had been a dues-paying member,[39] raised a purse for her stagecoach and steamboat fare. The trip took two weeks and was memorable for axle-deep mud, ruffians encountered along the roadside, and a high-water crossing of the Mississippi River.

Then, too, there was a leering stagecoach driver. The first leg of the journey was in a covered wagon, called a stagecoach by courtesy only. It had no springs or upholstered seats and it was piled high with odds and ends of freight for the crossroad stores. There was a plank seat for Grandma and her children.

After the first day the only other passenger, a pack peddler, dropped off. Suddenly at a lonely spot in a creek bottom, the driver yelled his four-mule team to a halt. He was a bleary eyed, unshaven man, dressed in dirty homespuns and rawhide boots. His shirt was open at the neck, exposing a hairy chest. He had hardly spoken to Grandma up to this point. Now he walked to the side of the wagon—the canvas cover had been tied back for coolness—put a foot on the brake beam and squirted a stream of tobacco juice off to one side. Then he leaned nearer, and put a grimy hand on Grandma's knee.

"Well, little lady," he said, with a snaggled grin and a broad wink, "It's powerful lonesome out here, now ain't it!"

"Git!" Grandma spat the words at him, shrinking back.

"Now, hold on thar," he said, "ain't no reason why we can't be friendly-like."

Then he reached for her with both hands.

By that time Grandma was thoroughly aroused—and scared. But she wasn't hysterical or helpless. As the ruffian came over the side of the wagon, she reached down and grasped an iron wagon wrench. She was slight of frame but she had a pioneer girl's strength. She swung the wrench mightily, catching the intruder squarely on the noggin. The little Harts set up a loud squalling.

The driver picked himself up from the ditch water at the side of the wagon ruts. He was a little dazed.

"Great God, woman!"

Grandma stood there with her weapon upraised, ready for the next onslaught if it came.

"Put down that damn wrench," he said. "It's all right. My mistake, I reckon. I just wanted to see what kind you was."

With that he remounted his lead mule, cracked his whip and drove on. There wasn't any more trouble.

A few days later, Grandma and the little ones had made their way to the shore of the Mississippi opposite Hickman, Kentucky.[40] At Hickman, just north of the Tennessee border, they would be nearly home, but danger still lay ahead. It was June flood time; the river was high. The swift current almost capsized the ferry boat, and it was swept downstream. It finally made a landing below the town. The ferry passengers were shuttled into Hickman by skiff and farm wagon, and then Grandma and her youngsters spent the night in a cheap hotel. Gambling and roistering parties were all around the hotel, and Grandma not only didn't sleep a wink, she didn't undress. While the little Harts dreamed peacefully, Grandma sat up, grimly counting the pistol shots in the street outside her window.

Next morning she didn't lose any time. Soon she found more Masonic friends, and with their help engaged transportation to Tennessee and her old home. They had to ride on top of a wagon loaded with corn, but a gold-plated chariot could not have been finer, no cushion of velvet any softer to the homeward-bound family. Two days, two nights, almost without stopping, and there she was piling into the courthouse square in Dresden.[41] More than three years had gone by since the young bride had left to make a new life with her soldier-husband in the West. Not one word of news from home had reached her during that time.

Weeping, shouting, Grandma jumped down from the corn wagon and flew straight into the arms of her brother,[42] who was standing in front of the courthouse. He had come home from the war that same week.

Their reunion was immediately touched by sadness as they exchanged their tragic news—her husband dead in Arkansas; their brother,[43] a Confederate captain killed at Chickamauga.

Old Caesar stiffened and growled as Grandma's hand tightened on the leash. Grandma's anger was flaming now.

"Turn these mules around and leave here!"

She spoke slowly and distinctly and her words were as sharp as a steel edge. Squire Griggs flushed. "Hold on, Paralee . . ." he flared.

"Now" Grandma's cold gaze never wavered. "Get in that wagon and travel. Now!"

"I'm damned if . . ."

The Squire got no further. At that instant, Grandma's hand flicked the snap on Caesar's leash.

"Get him Caesar!" Grandma raised her voice for the first time.

"Sic 'im!"

Caesar was over the fence at a bound, and with a deep growl leaped for Griggs' throat. The astonished Squire took a step back, raised his arm, and brought his heavy whipstock [*sic* whip stock] down on Caesar's snout. The dog missed the jugular, but his weight and the suddenness of his leap knocked the Squire sprawling. Carrie in the wagon let go a panther scream.

"In the wagon, Pa— quick, in the wagon!" The widow's strident voice could scarcely be heard in the din.

Whacking furiously with his whip, the Squire scrambled to his feet. Again Caesar sprang. The Squire aimed a vicious kick at the dog, but he had had enough.

With Caesar nipping at his coattail, he turned and vaulted into the wagon. Quickly he lashed his mules, swung the wagon around on two wheels, and made off down the lane, Caesar pursuing in full cry.

"I'll have the law on y'u!" Squire Griggs yelled over his shoulder. Carrie, black veil flying, clung to the jouncing wagon seat and didn't look back.

That was the last Grandma was to see or hear of her beloved son's deathbed bride.

CHAPTER 9

The Mail-Order Bride

IN A SMALL TOWN[1] LIKE OURS, WHERE EVERYBODY NOT ONLY KNEW everybody else, but also knew everything about everybody else's business, a nuptial affair, even a pokey[2] little one in the minister's parlor, was sure to create a flutter of interest.

If there chanced to be anything unusual about the bride or bridegroom—say the bride had a wart on her nose, or the groom had a peg leg, or either had an ex-spouse in some faraway place like Texas or Ohio—the flutter could develop into a tongue-clacking sensation.

And if the State Militia were to arrive during the ceremony and bivouac on the public square, it could be overwhelming.

It happened to us in the next town to which Papa was assigned. A mail-order bride stepped off the train one day to claim a well-to-do widower, and before they were hitched . . .

Well, again, Papa was in the midst of things as the officiating person and I was there with him, pop-eyed. Who says this was a creep-along era beset by boredom? In twenty-four hours, the tedium of our town was shattered by twin strokes.

It had all started when a respectable businessman, bereft of his good wife, answered a letter in the lovelorn column of the Chicago "Saturday Blade."[3] He soon found himself in a warm correspondence with an Illinois lady who was matrimonially inclined, and their exchange of sentiments soon blossomed into a proposal, which the lady accepted.

John Humberfield's plan was to meet the woman he had courted sight unseen—and now was to marry—at Gibbs Junction[4] and bring her to town on the noon local. The ceremony would take place immediately in the parlor of the Commercial Hotel across the street from the depot. He made all the arrangements in advance.

The news slipped out at once, and it sent conversation swirling in every direction, up and down the streets, through the café and poolroom, across back fences, into the shacks where the colored folks lived; everywhere. Everybody was talking about "old man Humberfield," and the bride he had "ordered from Chicago."

The things I heard about "that woman" caused me to wonder whether Mr. Humberfield had lost his mind. All the neighbors gave him the benefit of their views, and nothing that was said was kind. "That woman" was bound to be "trash."

Even Elizabeth, my closest chum, passed harsh judgment.

"I'll bet she wears a wig."

I heard Mr. Britton telling a customer in front of his hardware store: "He's buying a pig in a poke; he'd better look out."

Mama didn't want the matter discussed where the children could hear. I caught the word "disgraceful" in the comments she was making to Papa. She wouldn't say anything bad about the "poor woman," but she considered the "principle" all wrong.

"It's like going to the store for a sack of potatoes," she said. "It's sacrilegious."

"Let's just wait and see," was all Papa said.

Mr. Humberfield, generally called "Old Humberfield," wasn't so old really, but he had a beard and looked elderly. He ran a substantial feed and produce business and was prominent in local affairs, yet he was regarded as a "character." He especially enjoyed being in the limelight. That's how the story of his odd romance became known—he leaked it to his close friends.

His first wife had been buried only five months before. Her death had been a devasting [*sic* devastating] blow to Mr. Humberfield. Never had the local people seen such an outpouring of grief. He grew drastic at the funeral and cast himself on the grave. Later he went to the cemetery every day, sometimes more than once. After the tombstone was placed, he kept it dusted and polished. Once after a driving rainstorm had left it spattered and soiled, he sent the cleaning woman to scrub it with Bon Ami.[5] He placed a memorial poem in the paper on her birthday, and several times he stood up in church and bemoaned his loss.

So when the word got out that "Old Humberfield" was taking a second wife—a lady from "way up North" who he had never seen—it rocked the town. I was listening in the kitchen, my mouth full of bread and jam, when Mama told Aunt Liddy about it. The colored woman sniffed, the way she sniffed her disdain for any of the astonishing ways of white pople, [sic people] and went on with her cooking. She was not surprised to learn that Mr. Humberfield's grief had vanished.

"Bawlin' calf soon fergit his mammy," she said.

I went with Papa to greet the bearded Mr. Humberfield and his bride-to-be at the train. To my surprise, a big crowd was there—all the depot loafers who met all trains, plus everybody else who could think up an excuse, and many more who came for the fun. The genteel ladies of the town, of course, would never have permitted themselves to be seen at such a gathering, but they were represented, and lines of communication were ready to carry the full details. The bank was closed. The cashier found it necessary to meet the train for an important shipment of currency—he said. At the livery stable a lone Negro boy was left of the usual dozen employes [sic employees] and hangers on.

In all, including hilarious boys and girls having a lark, and the smaller fry swarming over the station platform, it seemed that half the town was there in the reception party. A cheer went up when the local came bustling around the bend in the distance; and again as a plume of white from the engine was followed by a mellow whistle.

As the train crunched to a stop, Mr. Humberfield and the conductor immediately came out on the platform between the cars. Mr. Humberfield, in a grey-striped suit and a broad-brimmed Panama hat, was in jovial conversation with the conductor. They shook hands.

The crowd was holding back for the big moment, the appearance of the bride.

"Where is she?" somebody yelled. "Bring her out!"

For the first time Mr. Humberfield turned to find the station full of people staring him in the face. His jaw dropped; he was startled. Obviously he hadn't expected any such an ogling turnout.

"Oh, you kid, Humberfield!" called another. "Let's see what you drew."

Mr. Humberfield reached back in the coach and plucked out a big suitcase—a bulging and scuffed affair of straw matting with a light cord around its middle to reinforce the clasp. Following the suitcase came a plainly dressed, fairly plump woman of about forty. She wore a sailor hat pinned on top of her tightly combed hair which was slightly grey. Her face was set and white. She was scared.

Mr. Humberfield looked around wildly, then he half turned as if considering an escape down the steps on the other side of the train. He thought better of any such idea, squared his shoulders, and started to alight in front of the massed spectators. In doing so, he gave the suitcase a vigorous heave, the cord broke and it flopped open, spilling the bride's trousseau, such as it was, and her other personal belongings at the feet of the conductor, Papa and a couple of hundred goggle-eyed witnesses.

Papa took charge.

"All right, all right," he said. "Let everyone be right easy." But he was quickly drowned out by a blast of guffaws, whistles and hoots.

Ignoring the hubbub, Papa shook hands gravely with Mr. Humberfield, and gave a warm hand clasp and greeting to the woman in the straw sailor who now was very red-faced. I thought she was going to cry.

Papa took the open suitcase from the hands of the benumbed Mr. Humberfield and laid it on the cinder platform. With two rakes of his long arms and a couple of grabs, he had recovered everything—clothes, nightgowns, curling irons, a pair of shoes, a Bible, toilet articles and other odds and ends—and somehow had stuffed all back in the battered old bag and retied the string in a few seconds.

With great composure, Papa handed the bag to Mr. Humberfield. Then he raised his hat and gallantly offered his arm to that gentleman's uncomfortable lady friend, at the same time taking a firm grip on my hand. As the crowd parted for us to pass we started for the hotel. Mr. Humberfield by now seemed to be enjoying his role, as the crowd tagged along cheering every step.

On the short walk to the hotel, I heard Papa telling the couple not to worry about the little mishap with the suitcase. When people are getting married, they are always nervous, he told them; anything could happen.

"On my wedding day," Papa said, "I was so excited I forgot the ring and had to send back home, a mile away, to get it. The wedding was held up half an hour."

We entered the hotel parlor with many of the people from the depot crowding in right behind us. Others pressed around the door and windows.

There was a short wait. The best man hadn't arrived. Mr. Humberfield's joviality began to fade a little; he fidgeted and looked at his watch, which he carried on a heavy gold chain looped across his vest. The lady plainly was ill at ease. I was sure she wished she were back in Illinois. Papa was still talking to them, but they weren't listening.

Finally the best man came in. He had the ring and the license. Papa told the couple to take their places with their backs to a big bay window. Against the glass window we could see dozens of curious onlookers stretching their necks and trying to catch a glimpse of what was going on. The ceremony began.

Just at that moment something else began on the outside.

We had heard the train arriving and the switching some cars on a nearby siding. Suddenly a cry went up from somebody at the window:

"It's the soldiers! Come on!"

It was a special train carrying a contingent of the State Militia[6]—sent by the Governor[7] to put down the "night riders"[8] who had been on a marauding and killing rampage in the wild country around Reelfoot Lake.[9] There had been rumors that the guardsmen would be called out, but nobody had known when or where. The announcement that they had arrived electrified the town.

In an instant Mr. Humberfield was playing second fiddle. The knot-tying show and the mail-order bride faded into insignificance. The crowds of spectators in the parlor and at the windows melted away, and all at once Papa was standing there reading the marriage lines to an uneasy couple and an empty house—empty of witnesses that is, except for the best man and me, and the best man kept glancing over his shoulder.

As for me, I didn't look back as I shot out of the room.

The Humberfield nuptials were completed all right, down to the last "amen," but Papa said later it was his fastest job. He almost forgot about his fee—a five dollar bill—as he hurried forth to save us from the cannon's mouth.

There had never been such a commotion at the depot. People were running from every direction. I tried to find something to stand on so I could see what the soldiers were doing. Then, suddenly, there was Papa holding me up. I could now see a line of soldiers standing at attention with guns on their shoulders; I could hear men shouting orders.

"Hurry," I told Papa, "we have to go home quick and get Joe and Key.[10] They'll miss everything. Hurry, Papa, hurry."

I wanted to be the first to tell. I ran on ahead and was already at home and was giving Mama a firsthand account of the soldiers and guns when Papa got there.

But Mama had something else on her mind, and it wasn't militia or night riders.

"What did she look like?" was the question she asked.

"I didn't notice," Papa said. "I really think the governor means it this time."

"What was she wearing?" Mama persisted.

"Two full companies—rifles and complete field equipment. It's war all right."

Mama stamped her feet.

"Tell me," she said in the greatest exasperation. "Did Mr. Humberfield's bride get here, and did you or did you not marry them?"

"Oh, that. I believe we had some sort of ceremony at the Hotel. Yes, come to think of it, I'm sure we did, but right now get the children ready. I'll hitch up Old Dick and take all of you to see the militia."

"Whoopee! Whoopee!" Little brother Joe was eager to start.

And away we went—the whole family crowded into the buggy—to see the spectacle. I was impatient to get back to the "Invasion." Old Dick was too slow. I longed for my often promised bicycle, so I could ride on ahead.

I had been hearing a lot about the night riders. They had taken the law into their own hands and gone on a rampage of thrashing innocent people, and even committing murder. It was some kind of trouble over fishing rights on the lake, and it had become so bad the Sheriff[11] had called on the Governor for help. The Governor had finally acted. The militia had been ordered out and was now camped in our town.

It was as good as a carnival. The soldiers pitched their tents right on the square.[12] They would march off to Reelfoot the next morning. They brought wagons and mules with them and the mules were braying and making an awful racket. Loads of equipment were being rolled off the flatcars. A cook tent was going up. Papa said that was where the soldiers would eat.

Joe was tremendously impressed. He thought they might fight a battle right there where we could watch—something like Shiloh,[13] where our Grandpa Moore[14] rode Old Calico and had his elbow shot off.[15]

But most of the grown-ups looked very serious. There was real trouble in the air. There might be fighting and bloodshed before the ring leaders were caught.

The next morning as we were finishing breakfast we heard them coming right up the street. We pressed against the palings[16] and watched the line of marching troops go by, followed by wagons loaded with provisions and equipment. The guardsmen were in high glee, whistling at dogs and shouting jibes at the people along the way. The wagon drivers were showing off, too—cracking the long machine whips and yelling at the mules.

The night-rider trouble was quickly put down, and the militiamen, a little subdued from marching through swamps, came dragging back in about a week. That was another thrill for us—but not quite as exciting as before.

What had become of Mr. Humberfield and his bride? In the excitement over the militia they had departed unnoticed on the evening train for a short honeymoon in Paducah.[17] Soon they were back and established in the Humberfield house, two streets over from us. Now the town could turn its thoughts again to the phenomenon of the wedding.

Mrs. Humberfield, it turned out, was a stem-winder,[18] a Yankee lady with a lot of know-how. After her first embarrassment over the incidents of her arrival had subsided, she quickly settled down to the business of remaking Mr. Humberfield and remodeling his home.

The first step in the process of redoing Mr. Humberfield was simple and effective—she had him shave off his beard. The town passed at that. But that was as nothing compared with her assault on the house. Lightning rods went up, and a balcony came down; a bay window blossomed on one side, a new porch on the other.

And that wasn't all. Only the courthouse and the school building had steam heat. She had Mr. Humberfield install a furnace and put radiators[19] in all the rooms upstairs and down. It was unheard of. Some people said it was "unhealthy," and all agreed that poor Mr. Humberfield would be bankrupt right away.

But Mr. Humberfield, with his shining new face, seemed to like it. When cold weather came, he invited people in from all around to enjoy the warmth of their nest.

"That woman"—the town used the expression a long time—didn't have a parlor in her home. She fixed up her best room, and used it every day for a sitting room.

And her carpets—they weren't really carpets at all. They were rugs that were almost big enough to cover the floors. Furthermore, she had some kind of odd covering on her kitchen floor—called it linoleum.[20] Mr. Humberfield had ordered it from St. Louis. Aunt Liddy was contemptuous of this "improvement."

"Now [*sic* How] you goin' to scrub you' floor ever' Sat'day if you got somethin' on top of it?"

It was a ritual with Aunt Liddy to scour the bare kitchen floor on Saturday afternoon with hot water and lye soap.[21] She kept it white and clean without a grease spot, and it was capital punishment if you tracked up her floor before it got dry.

The first time I was permitted to go to Mrs. Humberfield's on an errand for Mama, my eyes popped out. She was washing clothes on the back porch—herself. I didn't know what all of our good colored laundresses would think about that. I stayed around awhile to listen to a little Swiss music box she had.

Mama had been the first to call on the newcomer. They seemed to "hit it off" fine, and soon became good friends. When Mrs. Humberfield joined the women's [*sic* Woman's] Christian Temperance Union,[22] which had just organized a local chapter, the friendship was confirmed. She not only turned out to be a good neighbor, but she was a woman of character. She had been through some kind of personal tragedy—Mama knew what it was but would not give me a hint—and risen above it. Mama seemed to find comfort in exchanging kindnesses with her.

The whole town soon accepted her and took her to its bosom as if she had been born right there; and eventually the people stopped calling her "that woman" and forgot that she was a "damn Yankee."[23]

CHAPTER 10

A Gambol[1] on the Mississippi

NOVEMBER CAME NOT LONG AFTER THE MEMORABLE VISIT OF THE militia to our town, and again it was Conference time.[2]

That was a momentous occasion for parsonage children. It meant that Papa and the other Methodist ministers were going away to make their annual reports to the Bishop,[3] and, far more important to us, the ministers would receive their appointments for the next year's work.

Would Papa stay another year in the little town we had grown to love and where we had so many chums, or would we move to another town and start all over again?

It was an annual experience that we approached with both a touch of sadness and tingling eagerness. We were not dissatisfied with things as they were; but somehow moving was a lark—at least for the youngsters of the family—and we just couldn't resist the prospect of something new and different.

To us, this suspenseful time held a mystical kinship with such delights as those of Christmas morning or a birthday surprise or a circus.

The return from Conference each year was a grand happening in two ways. First, for Papa's answer to our shrill greeting: "Do we move, Papa? Do we move?"; and, second, for the precious store of books he brought us.

The publishers had their stalls at the Conference, with their agents buttonholing the country preachers. Papa never failed to respond to their blandishments. He brought home theological works and encyclopedias, song books and world histories, compendiums of home cures and books and world histories, compendium of horse cures and weighty tomes of the world's great orations. Those were in the name of culture. He didn't forget entertainment. Never did Papa come home from Conference without a valise full of story books and fiction for the whole family.

It was tradition of the family that Papa was a "sucker" for book agents, but in addition to the lemons he drew, he brought away many prizes at bargain prices. He had managed to acquire a serviceable encyclopedia; John C. Ridpath's "Library of Universal Literature,"[4] a twenty-five volume work with leather and cloth binding; another glorious set, also handsomely bound, called "Hero Tales of All Nations,"[5] and eventually a popular-priced edition of the Harvard Classics.[6] There were short-story collections, poetic works, essays and weighty volumes of sermons and religious reference books. There were children's books galore. When we moved, a big part of the freight bill was for Papa's books. He never left any behind.

The parcels of books after each Conference kept trickling in for weeks. Orgies of reading were to follow during the long winter evenings.

With his wealth of books that Papa gave us it was our destiny, of course, to be a reading family. We devoured everything that came our way. Each one developed his own favorites, but all of us often united in the choice of a popular story to be read aloud in our family reading circle.

Papa and Mama were the readers for such occasions. The place was our living room and the best time was a winter's evening when we all gathered in front of an open fire of hickory logs. The logs spewed fragrant juice as they snapped and sizzled and gave off sparks. The room was softly lighted by coal-oil lamps.

On one side of a table at the center of the circle sat Mama, a shawl usually around her frail shoulders against the chill that crept into the back of the room away from the fire. The old cliché was true—in severe weather our shins baked while our backs were icy cold. Mama was busy with mending or other needle work except when she was called upon to read.

Papa was on the other side of the table in a rocking chair, usually scanning his Testament, his feet stretched toward the fire as he waited for the reading to begin. Sometimes during such waits he would nod over his book then come to himself with a gasp and a snort—and that would bring forth a peal of laughter from the rest of us.

As the youngest, Key was privileged to a special place on a footstool directly in front of the fire. Joe and I sat on chairs, one near Papa and the other near Mama, neatly balancing the circle. Curled on the rag rug near Key—but just out of his immediate reach—was Whiskers, purring softly.

Thus was the stage set on any of the occasions when we had a good book for family reading. The material might be either a short story or a full-length book. If a book, the reading might extend over several evenings.

Our only requirement was that the story or book be entertaining. A dry or tedious book or one in which the story line and action were slow in developing rarely survived beyond the second or third chapter. We were ruthless in turning thumbs down. The condemned books usually were silently read through to the end by Papa; but Mama was ready to quit with the rest of us at the first outcry of disfavor.

Lessons were done at lightning speed on nights when family reading was planned. All problems were worked, all exercises written, all spelling words memorized long before the supper things were put away. As we impatiently waited, Mama finally adjusted the lamps and settled back in her rocker. Mama was the chief reader, Papa the auxiliary reader. Mama was faster.

The joys that followed were unalloyed. Such surefire classics as "David Copperfield,"[7] "Oliver Twist,"[8] "Tom Sawyer"[9] and "Huckleberry Finn,"[10] "The Last of the Mohicians,"[11] "Mrs. Wiggs of the Cabbage Patch,"[12] "David Harum,"[13] and "Ben Hur"[14] held us all spellbound night after night. The ten o'clock deadline was forgotten as the whole family abandoned itself to the delights of these and many more tales.

Mama, reading rapidly in a clear voice, was good for four or five chapters without stopping. When she tired, she would ask Papa to take over, but he was inclined to dawdle and to pause often to consider the turn of a phrase, which we quickly protested. After a rest, Mama would start again.

When a story took a sad turn, Mama sometimes faltered, with a catch in her throat. She always made a clear distinction in her side comments between the "good" characters and the "bad" or "mean" ones. The untimely death of a good character could bring a tear to her eye. She would try to hold it back and to keep her voice at an even tone, but finally the tear would roll down her cheek and she would choke up a bit. We were watching, of course, and if we were impatient for the story to continue we might chuckle at this show of feeling, but not always. Sometimes I cried too—for example, over Little Well [sic Nell] in "Old Curiosity Shop"[15] or the touching story of Peggotty and Little Em'ly in "David Copperfierld." Most of the time, though, we were ruthless. We would laugh out loud at Mama's tears; then she would laugh, too.

Mama's expressive reading cued us, of course, to the play and counterplay of good and evil forces in our stories. We tended to be sad when she was sad and to burst into laughter as her voice brightened over the gay and humorous passages. We went so far as to hiss the villains and applaude [*sic* applaud] the virtuous and courageous, especially when the latter were triumphant—and they always were in contrived popular stories of the time.

Mama sometimes ran down. Perhaps the deadline had been passed and she was growing drowsy. Her words began to trail off. Her voice blurred and soon there was nothing but a mumble and drone as her eyes gradually closed. Finally she would nod and come awake with a jerk and that was the signal for the gayest laughter of the evening—the fun of listening to Mama run down.

There was almost no end to the variety of our stories. We were completely catholic in our choosing. Mama liked both the popular novels of the day and the tried and true favorites of the past, with a leaning to Biblical narratives and the sentimental. A relative had a complete set of the works of E. P. Roe,[16] a Civil War chaplain and prolific writer of romantic best sellers in the nineteenth century, and Mama had read them all. She had enjoyed them very much. Our reading circle in due course was treated to Mr. Roe's "Barriers Burned Away,"[17] based on the Chicago fire of 1871.

Mama had read and reread silently the famous best seller, "In His Steps,"[18] by Charles W. Sheldon—a story of the development of Christian character. And she was fond of "My Loving Tent,"[19] a touching story by the widow of a Methodist minister, a Mrs. Mooney. These held little interest for my brothers and me. Another of Mama's favorite novels was a book of great popularity during her girlhood, "St. Elmo," by Augusta Evans Wilson.[20] Only by the narrowest margin did I escape being named for "St. Elmo's" heroine, Edna Earl, Mama often told me. Mama also was greatly moved by another of the prolific Mrs. Wilson's stories, "At the Mercy of Tiberius,"[21] a florid tale with a Biblical setting.

In Mama's mind were a number of reservations about her melodramatic "Les Miserables"[22]—it excited and moved her profoundly, but the experience of the unfortunate Fantine and the gruesome episodes such as the flight through the sewers of Paris[23] caused her to shudder and doubt the wisdom of exposing the story to children. Nevertheless it was one of our all-time favorites in the reading circle.

Mama was not happy about the stories of Jack London[24] that were sweeping the country; but we managed to work "the Call of the Wild"[25] and "The Sea-Wolf"[26] into our circle. She objected to the "coarse characters."

She also was reluctant to include "Vanity Fair"[27] among the reading choices, and she balked completely at "The Scarlett Letter."[28]

It was books such as these that Mama sometimes tried to skip. If passages became too lurid and the details too rare for younger ears, she turned several pages at a time and resumed the reading at a more sedate part of the story, hoping we would not notice. Of course we always detected such deception immediately and demanded that she go back. If she thought the part in question was too offensive she would call a halt.

Then we would raise a clamor and Papa would be drawn into the discussion. He quite often ruled in favor of the unexpurgated version, overcoming Mama's objections by pointing out the moral side of the story and he [sic the] lesson to be drawn. He might even take charge of the reading for awhile; at least until the going got better. Papa's attitude was simply that almost any book finding its way into the parsonage was likely to have something good in it. He read "The Scarlett Letter" silently, then decreed it was a moral book notwithstanding poor Hester's misstep and gave it his blessing for a reading to the family.

And so it went: "Treasure Island,"[29] the absorbing stories of George Eliot,[30] "Ivanhoe,"[31] "Tess of the D'Urbervilles,"[32] "The Light that Failed,"[33] "Tom Brown's Schooldays,"[34] "The Vicar of Wakefield,"[35] passed as in a procession of delight. Key, just starting to school, selected "The Little Shepherd of Kingdom Come,"[36] a Civil War story by John Fox, Jr., for his first attempt at reading a grownup book. He tired halfway and had to give up. Mama went back to the start and read all of it to the entire circle and on the final night Key was permitted to stay up past the deadline to hear the end.

In our varied reading excursions, Mama and I shuddered at such things as the scalping of the Hurons by the Chingachgook and Uncas in "The Last of the Mohicians."[37] My brothers were thrilled. They yawned over "The House of Seven Gables,"[38] but cheered "The Count of Monte Cristo,"[39] and all of us were carried away by Sherlock Holmes.[40] Our favorites among the A. Conan Doyle[41] stories were "The Hound of the Baskervilles"[42] and "The Sign of the Four."[43]

An especial delight was provided by one of our own Tennessee authors, John Trotwood Moore.[44] His story, "The Bishop of Cottontown,"[45] captured our fancy because the characters were like folks we knew. We were jumping with excitement at the climactic scene in which the Bishop, a backwoods preacher, entered his old buggy horse, named Ben Butler, in a trotting race against the thoroughbreds of some sporting gentlemen—and amazingly won. The old horse collapsed at the finish, but our joy was complete when he revived and ran away with the Bishop before he got home. We rolled with glee.

The prize money was to pay for restoring the health of the Bishop's small granddaughter, Shiloh, victim of child labor in a cotton mill. We stayed up long past eleven o'clock as the thrilling characters unfolded.

There was one other part to the reading circle. Nearly always after the book was closed Papa reached for his Testament. It was a long, thin volume of the all-purpose variety—well worn from daily reading and from occasional use over the years for spanking this one or that one of the children. Opening the tattered book before we scampered away to bed, Papa would read a chapter, after which all of us knelt at our places as he prayed. The prayer was of medium length, quiet, earnest. It made us feel very solemn.

Now Papa was ready for his annual pilgrimage to the Conference, and, as usual, his cuffs were a little frayed, his suit a little threadbare. This was mortifying to Mama, Conference was being held in Memphis in a fashionable church. Mama didn't want Papa to look seedy.

"You'll just have to get a new suit," she told him. "You can't go into that fine church looking like a hayseed."[46]

"Oh, I'll make out . . . somehow."

Papa meant he would be careful not to be conspicuous; that he would conserve the few dollars he had scraped together and spend them with his "cousins"; the book agents.

Mama could only shake her head. She liked books too—but still it was a touchy point. Literature was expensive by many standards of the times, but by parsonage standards[47] the cost was usually fantastic. She thought it was simply disgraceful that Papa would prefer a fifteen-volume set of "Cozy Journeys to Faraway Lands"[48] to a respectable new suit and a dignified new derby.

Somehow Papa got to Conference that year with his well-worn clothes, and not being there ourselves we were spared whatever humiliation we might have felt. But we knew that all alone from a forward pew he stood straight and tall and in his deep, resonant voice reported on the modest doings of his rural circuit.[49] Perhaps after all the presiding Bishop saw beneath the shiny suit the heart of a man who had labored diligently in the Lord's vineyard.

And so Papa came home with good news. We were going to move.

The new appointment was in an adjoining county not too far away; and it was a promotion[50] for Papa.

The town to which we were going was on a newly completed spur-line railroad.[51] This line was opening up a corner of the state that had previously been to a great extent inaccessible and slow to develop. Now a lumber and agricultural boom was under way. Business was prospering. The church was growing. A new sanctuary had been finished the year before and a new parsonage was already in the works. The pastor's salary was to be well above Papa's past salaries. He might even get some actual money instead of sausage and stove wood.

We arrived at our new home on Thanksgiving Day. That evening we enjoyed a bountiful supper at the home of a leading Methodist and before we left our hosts on that first evening a spruced-up couple drove by in a rubber-tired buggy[52] drawn by a spirited horse and asked for the new preacher. Yes, they had a notion to get married.

The ceremony was performed in our host's parlor after the customary preliminaries. It was like scores of impromptu weddings Papa had solemnized before, but in one way it was different. When he opened the envelope containing the license, he found a twenty-dollar bill and a pair of kid gloves.[53]

Papa didn't show the money to Mama until we got back to the parsonage. Then he handed it to her. "My stars!" Such a windfall was indeed astonishing to Mama. Quickly she tried to make the most of it.

"This time I mean it," she said firmly. "You simply must have a new frock coat. You can't afford to show yourself in the pulpit in the old one. It's too shabby."

In less than a month Papa was measured for a new "preaching suit" in the local clothing store. It was ordered from a tailor in Memphis. It was of fine broadcloth and was paid for in cash from the generous quarterage, augmented by wedding fees that had been rolling in. A Methodist doctor peeled ten dollars from a huge roll of bills and bought Papa a black felt hat. A Methodist ginner,[54] flush with cotton money, provided an overcoat. Even Mama had a new cloak, ordered from a department store in Memphis.

The whole family emerged from its rather threadbare appearance, and caught step with Papa's well heeled parishioners. I had a new silk dress for Sunday School. Key and Joe blossomed out in button shoes with red tassles [sic tassels]. It was all beyond our dreams.

It wasn't long before we had our new parsonage. Lumber was cheap and abundant, the church members generous and enthusiastic. Papa did a lot of sawing and hammering himself. It was the nicest parsonage we ever had.

Life was sweet as our new home was going up until Key, now at school age, stepped on a rusty nail in the debris of planks and shingles left by the carpenters. There were no antitetanus shots to take. The foot swelled ominously; there was a lot of praying. It probably was a close thing but he was all right after a bit.

After the parsonage was finished, Papa set to work on another project. There had been friction and dissention in the congregation and the Bishop had selected Papa for this assignment because Papa was known to be an expert at promoting good will among quarreling church members. It was to take time, but Papa's efforts were not unrewarded. In the next two years he drew the people together and restored peace and brotherly love to the congregation.

(Papa may not have been one of the great pulpit orators of the Conference; but he was always beloved by those he served and he had a knack of bringing peace and harmony wherever he was sent. A remarkable tribute to him, I think, was a simple thing at his funeral. When, at the grand age of ninety-four, he passed to his reward, a rural church where he had been pastor more than fifty years before sent a wreath for his grave. Older members of the congregation had read the notice of his death. They remembered and loved him.)

Our life, as before, continued to be enlivened by the vagaries of Papa's parishioners. For example, there was an eccentric church member who wanted to be baptized by immersion[55] in the middle of the night; and a bride and bridegroom who barely made it to the altar in time . . .

Mr. Frampton[56]—or some such name—was the man with a yearning to have sins washed away by moonlight. This middle-aged gentleman, proprietor of a variety store,[57] was well known in the community as an odd character. His merchandising methods were most unusual: In the fall, for example, he might fill his shelves with straw hats and sell them at ridiculously low prices; or he might stock up to overflowing with coal scuttles or chamber pots or feather dusters. He had a hilarious time at his sales of such items and farmers from "out yonder" always dropped into his little store to josh with the queer[58] Mr. Frampton when they came to town on Saturdays.

While Mr. Frampton was a member of Papa's church and attended Sunday preaching and Wednesday evening prayer services regularly, It seemed he had a little problem—he was fighting a long-time losing battle with John Barleycorn.[59] In fact, about twice a year he went on prodigious sprees during which his store remained closed and he wallowed in a filthy back room where he batched and slept, kept company only by a jug. After an interval of some days, the constable would finally force his way into Mr. Frampton's quarters and cart the numb and jabbering man away to the calaboose,[60] where he would be looked after to some extent until he sobered up.

Following such a spree, Mr. Frampton usually came by and had a talk with Papa. Then he would resume his churchgoing habits for another period.

One night just after Mr. Frampton had been reported on a prolonged alcoholic flight, we were awakened by a loud pounding on the front door.

"Reece,[61] get up—someone's at the door," I heard Mama say.

"What time is it?"

"It's past two o'clock. I just heard the clock strike."

The pounding continued, reverberating through the parsonage.

"All right, all right, I'm coming," Papa said loudly. I heard his feet hit the floor and the scuffing of his slippers as he groped his way to the front of the house. Then he [sic the] latch clicked as Papa opened the door.

"Who's there?" Papa asked.

"Brother Hart, it's me, Jim Frampton. I want you to help me, Brother Hart. I need help bad."

"Why Brother Frampton, are you all right? What can be troubling you at this late hour? You'r not . . ."

"Sober as a judge, Brother Hart. I want to be baptized."

"Baptized?" Papa's voice was incredulous. "At two o'clock in the morning? I'm afraid we'll have to wait until daylight . . . until we can make proper arrangements.

"No, I've got to be baptized now, all the way under. I've been talking to the Holy Ghost.[62] He came into my bedroom and we had a conversation. He told me my time was nearly up and to get my sins washed away before it was too late. I've got to do it. I've got to be baptized right away. The Lord told me."

Mr. Frampton was almost hysterical. He grasped Papa's arm and, his voice high and quavering, began to plead.

"Please, Brother Hart, please come and baptize me. The Holy Ghost is after me. I've got to come clean and wash away my guilt before it's too late. Oh, Lord, help me. Please, Brother Hart . . ."

Then I heard Mama's voice:

"Reece, tell him to come back in the morning. You can't stand there talking—you'll catch cold. Tell him you can't do it now."

It was early March and quite cold. Frost was in the night air.

Papa hesitated as Mr. Frampton clung to him and began to moan.

"No, Mattie," Papa said, "I can't refuse to do as he asks. Just stay in bed and I'll take care of this."

Papa was rummaging for some old clothes while Mr. Frampton continued to moan and pray on the front porch.

"All right Brother Frampton, let's go." Papa had dressed in less than 5 minutes. I heard his clunk, clunk down the steps and the sound of Mr. Frampton's still shrill voice as they left the house.

Papa's reasoning was simple and in keeping with what he conceived to be his duty as a minister: He was there in his pastoral role to help the people who were troubled, to comfort them and to administer the rites of religion that they craved.

So Papa led the weeping Mr. Frampton a few blocks to the edge of town. He untied the gate to a pasture and without hesitating marched Mr. Frampton straight into the horse pond, breaking a film of ice around the edge. There Papa took a stand in water that was a little more than knee deep. He quickly telescoped the words of the baptismal rite, grabbed Mr. Frampton by the nape of the neck and thrust him to the bottom of the murky pond.

"... In the name of the Father, of the Son, and of the Holy Ghost. Amen ... Are you all right, Brother Frampton?"

"Gurgle, gurgle, glub . . ."

Mr. Frampton sputtered and gasped, then sneezed mightily.

"Hallelujah!" Mr. Frampton said hoarsely.

With that he wrenched himself free of Papa's protecting grasp and floundered toward the shore. The last Papa saw of him he was still croaking "Hallelujah" and streaking for home.

Papa filled in the details for Mama the next day.

"I know he had been baptized three times before," he said. "That's not the point. He said he had been talking to the Holy Ghost. Who am I to say he had or had not seen and spoken to the Holy Ghost. My job was clear—here was a man in deep trouble with his own conscience. Somehow he craved the comfort and assurance that goes with the practice of his religion. I couldn't deny him that comfort."

"Well, Mama said, "I hope you don't catch pneumonia."

"I thought of that possibility," Papa said. "That's why I wore my high rubber boots."

Papa's philosophy of reluctance to deny aid and comfort to those in need was imprinted in our home life. When a pair of Mormon missionaries[63] passed through and the constable was about to run them out of town, Papa intervened, invited them to our house for supper, listened to them talk for hours, and gave them beds for the night. Hoboes[64] who came for a handout were never turned away. Papa had scriptures[65] to quote justifying his actions. While Mama yielded to Christian duty, nevertheless she lived in fear of bubonic plague from vermin that might be brought into the house by a wayfarer.

Next door to us lived a young doctor who afforded us our first close up view of that new marvel of the age, an automobile. It wasn't much of an automobile really—just sort of buggy with an engine underneath and a tiller for steering. It made a great clatter and excited all the children, dogs, poultry, cows and horses wherever it went.

The doctor still used a horse and buggy for his rounds. The auto was for sport.

For instance, one Sunday he drove the little runabout with a lady friend as a passenger over to the next town, five or six miles away. While there visiting friends he made the mistake of getting drunk. So drunk, in fact, that when he started home he couldn't see the road, much less guide the runabout. His lady companion took the tiller, but she was perhaps the original woman driver about whom men like to joke. In the dirt road, she left a serpentine tire track that advertised their difficulties. The erratic tire marks remained for all to see until they washed away by the next rain.

The alcoholic episode and the wild trip might not have attracted more than passing gossip but for the fact that the doctor's lady companion happened to be another man's wife. That was indeed a juicy bit of scandal.

I was permitted to hear comments only on the fringes of this episode. I would have been astonished had I known that our doctor friend called on Papa a few days later in the greatest agitation. He wasn't a member of the church but he was in big trouble. He looked to Papa as a friend for help. He had, he said, just received word that the husband of his girlfriend on the Sunday ride was on the way to town with a gun and had sworn that he was going to kill the doctor.

Papa's eyebrows were very high and his eyes wide when he heard this.

"It does look bad," he told the doctor, "but I'll see what I can do."

Papa had he [sic the] doctor leave the parsonage by the back door. "Get out of town right now and stay until you hear from me."

It was true. The irate husband was in town at that moment and he was broadcasting his homicidal intentions. Papa sent a friend to invite the wrathy gentleman to come to the parsonage. In a half hour, with the upset physician already aboard the afternoon train and on his way to a safer climate, Papa received his visitor. Their conference was long and earnest, at times bringing a heated reaction from the aggrieved husband. But, at the end, his anger was abated and he joined Papa in prayer. When the visitor left, his pistol stayed with Papa for temporary safekeeping, and the visitor had agreed in principle to forgive and forget. Papa vouched for the doctor's future conduct.

The story had a happy sequel. Some years later in another town to which Papa was assigned, the same doctor came to take over a practice. He and Papa recalled the stirring incidents of the past. Papa found the doctor had grown in character and judgment and soon invited him to come into the church. He accepted and became the teacher of a man's Bible class and had an influence for good in the community.

As commonplace as weddings were in parsonage life, I was to find our new location that the possibilities for the sensational and bizarre had not been exhausted for me. We had been in town only a few weeks when a man came by to ask Papa to perform the marriage ceremony for his eldest daughter and a young man from Ohio.

They wished to be married at six o'clock that evening and planned to take the nine o'clock train on their way to Cincinnati where they were to live. The good gentleman, a member of Papa's church, was in an expansive mood. He invited Papa to "bring the whole family," for the wedding and reception.

It seemed to me when we arrived that it was just another run-of-the-mill affair, and after doing what scouting I could—under Mama's watchful eye—I concluded there would be no ice cream. A large punch bowl was on the dining-room table but I didn't like punch. I began to lose interest.

Something was in the air though. The "happy feeling" of most weddings somehow wasn't there. I wondered what was up.

After a somewhat gloomy rendition of "Love's old Sweet Song"[66] by a local girl, the wedding party marched in and stood in front of banked ferns and cut flowers in one corner of the room. The bride, plump and rosy, was quite pretty, I thought, in her lacy white dress and long white veil; but the groom looked as if he needed a good dose of calomel.[67] The ceremony was without hitch. Then everyone trooped into the dining-room for a go at the punch bowl. The spirit and tempo of the occasion picked up at this point.

"Brother Hart, you and Sister Hart[68] come right in and have some punch," the father of the bride said jovially. "I can assure you it's not spiked."

"I'm sure it's not," Papa said in good humor. "Your friends tell me you took the pledge many years ago." This brought a general round of laughter.

The mother of the bride, who had been weepy around the eyes when we arrived, joined in the light conversation.

"He took it, all right," she said, with a wan smile. "If I can just keep him on the wagon, . . ." Her voice betrayed a little skepticism.

Everybody laughed again and the punch, unspiked or not, disappeared rapidly.

We left early and on the way home I heard Mama tell Papa in an aside that she felt something is wrong, but she couldn't imagine what it was. The next day we knew.

The story was this: Right after the guests departed, the bride suddenly "collapsed." Her father sent for a doctor. By midnight the old gentleman had a new grandson. The bride's "condition" had been a well-kept secret. She had gambled on getting the knot tied and leaving town before the facts were known—and had lost.

The whole affair was a liberal education for me. I heard the details at school the next day, the bare facts stripped down to the chassis. Even in that distant era, we received sex education in the schools, but not from the teacher or a book. We got it by word of mouth from child to child. So on that day, after the wedding of the night before, I had my first lesson in the Facts of Life.

That wasn't the only sensation of the search for me. A new and undreamed of treat was coming my way.

Our little town was only three miles from Cottonwood Landing[69] on the Mississippi River. In late summer and early fall when cotton began moving to the market and everybody had spending money, the showboats[70] often tied up a [*sic* at] Cottonwood for two or three-night stands. How did we know a showboat was around? The calliope.[71] On a still evening we could hear it nearly three miles off—pulse—quickening, stirring, marching tunes that made us want to drop everything else and fly to the Pied Piper's strain that promised bright lights and theatre magic.

Did we ever get to do that, to rush off to see the showboat; The answer is "No."

Showboats were "dens of iniquity."[72] They were beyond the pale of respectable society, we thought. They drew idlers and crap shooters and whiskey drinkers. Self-respecting persons should avoid them as they would yellow fever or the Old Scratch.[73]

The performances were disgraceful, we had heard: showgirls in tights, and singing and dancing like that in the lowest dives on Beale Street.[74] Such were the dire stories that greeted every inquiry I made about the showboat, and every such warning whetted my desire to go and see one of the "cesspools" with my own eyes.

Imagine then my astonishment one day when the proprietor of the general store at Cottonwood Landing drove up to our gate in a surrey and asked Papa apologetically whether he would consider going over to marry a couple who were members of the showboat troupe. He hurriedly explained that the boat had been stopping at the landing several sessions, that the couple were "the nicest kind of young folks," no matter what the "bluenoses"[75] had to say about show people. Here he apologized again and added that he "didn't mean anything personal" by his remark, and that they wanted to be "hitched" by a regular parson, not a Justice of the Peace.

"Well, Brother Kirby," Papa said, "I know you and your good reputation, if you vouch for them and say they are respectable young people, that's good enough for me. If they need my services, I'll be glad to go."

"Thank you, Brother Hart. I know they'll appreciate it they're just two people that want to get married the same as anybody else. I happen to know the girl's father. He lives in Cairo[76] and he's a Methodist. I guess that is why they wanted a Methodist preacher to tie the knot."

Papa took his watch out of his vest pocket, pressed a spring to open the case and glanced at the time. "It's twelve o'clock now," he said, "and we're just about to eat dinner. Come in and have some dinner with us, and then we can drive over to the Landing."

Mr. Kirby took off his black broad-brimmed hat, scratched his head and thought a moment.

"Now that's real kind of you, Brother Hart," he said. "Matter of fact the matinee is not starting until two-thirty, and that will give us plenty of time to get there before they go on. You can meet them and make the arrangements.

If you're sure I'm not imposing on Sister Hart, I-er-don't care if I do stop for a bite."

"Fine," Papa said; "Just hitch your horses under that tree and I believe dinner is ready."

While Mr. Kirby hitched his team a quick back-of-the-scenes drama was taking place in our kitchen. I had overheard all of the conversation and I was wild to see the showboat. Mama was aghast.

"Lord a-mercy," she exclaimed to Papa, "Take a child to"—she shuddered—"a showboat? Are you out of your mind?"

Papa smiled broadly. "I've never seen a showboat either," he told Mama. "I've heard a lot about them. Maybe this is my big chance."

"Reece, do you mean to stand here and tell me you are actually going . . . ?"

"Of course," Papa said, "We're all going!"

We ate dinner in a daze. We had fried chicken and peach cobbler with cream but it could have been sawdust and feathers. I ate but didn't taste a thing. I was dancing on a pink cloud to calliope music.

Mama, secretly pleased, though still protesting, bundled us into Mr. Kirby's surrey and away we went right after the dinner table was cleared.

In the daytime, without lights, the showboat Belle of Memphis[77] wasn't very glamorous, but as we drove down to the Landing, the calliope was going full steam and the neighbors from miles around were trickling in for the Saturday matinee.

"Now, Brother Hart," Mr. Kirby said, "I'll just have the young couple come up to the store where you can meet them. Then we can have the ceremony at my house or anywhere you . . ."

Mr. Kirby hesitated.

"Of course," he continued, "if you and Sister Hart care to go aboard and see the show, I'm sure they would be glad to have you, and the wedding could be taken care of after the performance. That way you could get in on the . . ."

"Well," Mama said with starch in her voice, "I'm sure we're not here to 'get in on' anything."

"Hold on Mattie," Papa said, "Brother Kirby may have a very sensible idea."

"You mean, Reece Hart, that you would . . ."

"Exactly," Papa said. "Look at that show bill over there. It says they're playing 'The Shepherd of the Hills'[78]—remember the book?—and I'd like to see that."

The play was a dramatization of a popular book—a best seller of that time—about Ozark Mountain people, a highly moral tale in which Virtue triumphed over Evil in spectacular fashion. We had read the book in our family circle.

"Well, it was a fine story," Mama said, "I suppose . . ."

Seeing which way the wind was blowing, Mr. Kirby broke in:

"I'm sure Captain Jack"—Captain Bill Jack was the proprietor of the Belle of Memphis—"will be tickled to have you folks as his guests. Now, I'll find the bride and groom and let them know what's coming."

Mr. Kirby hurried aboard the boat and in five minutes returned with Larry LaTrue and Eva Gaye, leading man and ingenue of the Belle of Memphis troupe. The introductions were a little reserved on both sides, the betrothed couple seeming a little abashed in the presence of a minister of the gospel. They stared at us and without a doubt we stared back.

The prospective bridegroom, Mr. LaTrue, was a little short for my idea of a dashing leading man, and his eyebrows met over her bridge of his nose. Otherwise he was handsome enough and he was quite flashily dressed—in pin-striped suit, spats and a jaunty hat with brim turned down on one side. In his cravat sparkled a "diamond" stickpin. Miss Gaye, clinging to his arm and dimpling prettily, was a blonde type, petite and saucy. She had a turned up nose and was a little freckled. She spoke with a slight lisp.

When the ice had been broken, Mr. LaTrue addressed Papa.

"Reverend Hart," he said, "while Miss Gaye and I are only temporarily engaged in theatrical work in a company of this type, we have truly become very attached to the Belle of Memphis and to Captain Jack and the entire company. Would you—could you possibly have our little ceremony on the stage with our fellow Thespians as witnesses?"

"Well, sir," Papa said, "it is perfectly all right as far as I am concerned to have the rites after the performance, but of course I do not believe it would be seemly or is "or is [sic in] keeping"[79] with the sanctity of the of the occasion to have the ceremony as a theatrical spectacle."

"Of course," Mr. LaTrue said quickly, "I understand. I didn't mean to have the ceremony in any way connected with the performance. Miss Gaye and I were hoping to have the ceremony after the audience had gone and the stage setting is cleared away. It's just a sentimental wish to be married on the stage to which we are dedicated."

Miss Gaye still clinging to Mr. LaTrue gave Papa the treat of her most dazzling smile.

"It would make uth both tho happy," she said.

Papa, now in the showboat deal beyond the hope of escape, succumbed.

"In that case," he said, "I think we can work it out without any difficulty. Our altar will be on the stage and you may have your friends of the company as witnesses. We can have a dignified service, quite in keeping with the solemn nature of the marriage vows."

With that, there was a quick round of "thank you's" and handshaking and the couple took their cue for a quick exit.

Papa glanced at the license Mr. LaTrue had left with him. The couple's real names were Lawrence Cooger and Evelyn Hodstetter.

Our eyes were wide with wonder as we crossed the gangplank and entered the floating theatre. The seats inside were red plush. The aisles had thick plush carpets. Overhead were crystal chandeliers that tinkled slightly with the swaying of the boat. The drop curtains, footlights and draperies were to me the last word in refinement. We were, so to speak, knee deep in elegance. And if he Philharmonic had been there, it could have sounded no grander to me than the Belle of Memphis orchestra—three colored musicians—piano, fiddle and drum—playing ragtime by ear.

"The Shepherd of the Hills" turned out to be a melodramatic rouser. Mr. LaTrue was a homespun hero of the Ozarks, Miss Gaye the mountain girl who went away to finishing school but eventually returned to her sweetheart in the hills. The big fight scene in the second act was almost the troupe's undoing. The hero and the villain slugged it out across the stage in front of a set representing the interior of a grist mill. The hero finally bested his plug-ugly enemy and with a mighty blow intended to knock him out of the mill through a closed door.

It was a trick door, I learned later, designed to fall apart with a crash of boards when the villain sailed into it. Somehow the property man had nailed it too tightly. When the villain's body crushed into the door, the boards held fast, but the entire stage set of lashed-together flats toppled over backward, exposing the cluttered space backstage and several embarrassed actors in various stages of costume changes.

The friendly audience howled at this disaster—including Papa and Mama.

I kept sending sidelong glances at Papa and as the show unfolded. To my wonderment, after all Mama had heard about the depravity of the showboat, they were enjoying it. Actually, as it turned out, the Belle of Memphis unlike some of the other showboats of ill repute, was one that came to the same landings every season catered to the family trade. There was nothing rowdy about the show, no objectionable material, no high-kicking or low-cut chorus girls; in fact, it was all strictly, as the show bill stated, "for refined people."

My parents and I were especially delighted with the entertainment between acts; a one-legged banjo player who danced on his peg leg while whanging away at "Turkey in the Straw";[80] a trio composed of Miss Gaye and two character actors in juvenile costumes singing "silly kid" ditties; and a comedian in a ludicrous tramp outfit who, in a whirlwind finish, brought the house down with an eccentric dance in which he cut the pigeon wing[81] while scraping out "Dixie"[82] on a cigar box fiddle.

It was all but too much for Mama. She finally abandoned her minister's-wife reserve, sat back and enjoyed everything. Papa kept his dignity but he "hee-hawed" now and then and patted his foot to the music.

At the end, the audience soon filed out and suddenly we were alone in an all-but-empty-house. Then the ornate curtain rolled up again and the show folks were all on the stage in a jolly, bantering mood. The wedding itself was an anticlimax to the lively proceedings we had just witnessed. Papa read the usual service and he managed to make it solemn and within the bounds of dignity, despite the tinseled surroundings and he [*sic* the] odd assortment of actors still in their show costumes and grease paint.

To me the entire afternoon had been a delirium of delight. I was in Fairyland where I had just landed from the tail of a comet. Sleeping Beauty had awakened and the Prince was leading her into the courtyard. Next the King's musicians would play a gay tune and the fairies would dance in their little red shoes.

Now it was all over. Suddenly I was walking up on the stage with Mama and we were shaking hands with the hero and heroine—that is, the bride and bridegroom.

Then I got a good look through the wings and behind the scenes and I realized the show was really over. It wasn't Cinderella's palace at all—it was more like an old barn, except well-kept barns weren't nearly so cluttered and musty.

Mr. Kirby took us back to his store and we all had soda pop with cheese and crackers. Then we piled into the surrey and, as I dreamed of the wonderful world of make-believe behind the footlights, jogged our way home.

Mr. LaTrue's "diamond" stickpin must not have been a true clue to the degree of his affluence. He gave Papa two dollars. There was an unexpected windfall from another source, however. Mr. Kirby generously presented us with a twenty-pound ham.

CHAPTER II

Our Thanks to God

KEY[1] WAS NOW IN SCHOOL. HOW PROUD HE HAD BEEN WHEN HE TRUDGED to the schoolhouse that first day, holding my hand and carrying a satchel with his slate and primer. Joe[2] was in the third grade. He usually had the most head marks in spelling and the most stars opposite his name on the honor roll and never took his nose out of a book when he was at home.

I[3] had so many outside projects going that my lessons would never have disturbed me too much except for the heavy guiding hands of my parents, who were unrelenting when it came to homework. Along with everything else, I had piano lessons and also elocution—spelled with a capital E—taught by a formidable lady who came from a nearby town twice a week. I memorized long poems and recitations which she taught me to deliver with complicated gestures and footwork.

An occasional excursion to the banks of the Mississippi River was among the experiences we enjoyed. To me there was something about standing and watching the river's swirling, muddy waters that was almost frightening, and when the waters poured over the banks after a long rainy season, it was a fearful thing. All of my life we had lived on the smaller tributaries of this mighty stream.[4] I could remember when half of the town where we happened to be living was covered for weeks by the "back water." When the Father of Waters rolled out of its bed, it was a cause for concern.

That spring we had the highest flood water[5] since the levees in that area had been built, and our town filled with the refugees from the river bottoms. They were billeted in the courthouse and even in the churches, and their presence made a field day for the school children.

As a result of fraternizing with the refugees, many children in our school broke out with the itch. Joe and Key and I didn't catch it, although some of our playmates did. But life wasn't at all easy for a few weeks. Mama scrubbed us and scraped us and practically boiled us twice a day and we were about as raw as those who had to scratch where they itched.

Summer and fair weather finally came and the river subsided. Then school was out and we breathed freely once again. During the summer months, after the cotton was "laid by,"[6] there was a season of revival meetings[7] which kept Papa very busy. Often he would be called upon by the ministers in adjoining towns to assist them. He would go and stay from Monday morning until Saturday night, and it was great fun for some of us to go with him.

Joe usually didn't want to go. He preferred to stay at home with Mama and read his books—but Key and I were always ready. We would have suitcases filled with enough clothes to last us the entire time and Papa would be charged by Mama to put us into clean outfits twice a day so we would always be presentable at each church service. He would forget about it after the first day or two and then about Friday morning he would look into one of the suitcases and say, "We had better start wearing some of these fresh clothes your mother sent. She's not going to like it if they're still clean when we get home."

One memorable occasion, Papa spent a week helping a young minister who had been sent by the Bishop[8] to preach to the people living along a twenty-five mile strip of river bottom near us. These people didn't have a church, but in winter, or in rainy weather, they worshipped in a schoolhouse or perhaps a store or even in the home of some good brother. Now the weather was very warm and a brush arbor had been built for revival services right on the bank of the river. The construction of this temple was primitive. Posts were set in the ground and rough beams nailed across to support the thatch or brush that made the roof. Rude benches were made from slabs of wood from a nearby sawmill. A pulpit or preaching stand was an upright box of rough boards.

Crowds of worshippers came every day and night and it was delightfully cool with a fresh breeze blowing off the river. We could see long barges and occasionally a river steamer going by, which added to the interest of the occasion for me. The river-boat pilots often saluted us with a mellow whistle.

We were invited to a different home for dinner every day and ate fried chicken and custard pie until our eyes were glazed. It was watermelon season, too, and peaches were ripe and plentiful. So, in addition to the pleasures of the stirring revival services under an arbor, we had a long week of feasting. The mosquitoes were our only annoyance. Key had a long spell of malaria[9] soon after we got home.

One family that attended that brush-arbor revival became our fast friends. They lived on an island in the river. The Mississippi is a meandering stream full of small islands, but this was one of the larger ones. It was six or eight miles long and two miles wide and stood high up out of the water. People had lived there and cultivated the island ever since this part of the country was settled. They had a school and a post office and a store or two, and on their rich soil grew fine crops. They were prosperous.

However, because of their isolated situation, these island residents were perhaps a little less polished than friends on the mainland.

We were taken across to the island by rowboat several times during that week and each trip was a lark for us. There was a great deal of conversation about the current of the river changing since the spring overflow. The current was now on the Tennessee side and the Government light—to guide the boats at night—had only recently been changed to a point just opposite the island on our side of the river. The islanders were greatly concerned because the current had become so swift that it was difficult to operate the ferry.[10] They belonged to the State of Tennessee and necessarily must attend to their legal affairs in the county to which they were attached.

The family whom we visited had a young daughter who was to be married that fall, and her father made arrangements for Papa to come back and perform the ceremony. They would write him when to come. They also gave me a very pressing invitation and I told them I would be there. Of course it would be another gay excursion for me.

We had a long rainy spell just before the word came for Papa to make the trip to the island for the wedding. The roads were soft and rutted deeply by cotton wagons carrying their heavy loads to the river barges. We had a slow trip, driving Old Dick from home to the boat landing where our host was to meet us and row us across to the island. He was waiting for us, but he explained the current was too swift to get across at that point and he had arranged for a wagon and team to take us about a mile farther down to a more favorable spot.

The road followed closely the high bluff next to the river and I was having the time of my life. Perched high up on the wagon seat I could see away across the river in the mid afternoon sun. The Arkansas bank was very clear, past the point of the island.

Suddenly there was a jolt that almost caused me to fall off the seat. A wheel of the wagon had dropped down into a deep hole. We had to unload.

The mules didn't seem to be able to pull the wagon out. The wheel was in mud up to the hub. Since we were in sight of the boat, we walked the rest of the way and left the driver to get the wagon out and meet us there later.

The bride's home was a frame house with a wide porch and big chimneys. The ell[11] of the house had a long side porch with a shelf where the water bucket and dipper and a large tin wash pan were kept. On the wall was a little mirror about three or four inches square. Under the mirror was a tin comb case with a comb. Alongside was a roller towel. There was also a crisscross hat rack on the wall. The well at the end of the porch had a wooden bucket that was operated by a long rope on a windlass. On a high post by the well was a farm bell that could be rung by a wire reaching over to the porch. In the backyard I could see an ash hopper and everywhere I looked I could see evidences of the use of homemade lye soap,[12] the lye being a product of the ash hopper. The entire house inside and out was scrubbed and cleaned.

A big crowd had gathered—just about everybody who lived on the island and people from both banks of the river.

The kitchen was full of women admiring a new cookstove, [*sic* cook stove,] a wood-burning range.[13] It was so new, it smelled new—like stove polish. They were exclaiming over the big oven; the six eyes; the commodious warming closets; the ten-gallon reservoir and the nickel trimming. It was to the islanders a "thing of beauty and joy forever," but I couldn't work up much interest in it. I never had done any cooking, but I had to dry dishes at home and they were an end result of a cookstove [*sic* cook stove].

I went quickly to the parlor for I had heard Papa say that he was anxious to get back across the river before dark and I wanted to get that wedding over with. Besides, I was hungry and I saw every promise of an old fashioned wedding supper, the kind I had heard Mama and Papa talk about but had never seen.

As I looked around I passed a bedroom door and heard the bride, her mother father and a young cousin of the bride in an earnest conversation. The bride and her folks wanted the cousin to play something on the piano as a wedding march. The young girl said she couldn't do it—that she didn't know but one piece.

"Go on in there and play anything you know," the bride's mother said impatiently.

It had turned very warm and the father wanted to take his coat off. As I left they were debating that question.

I took my seat and looked around. I had never seen people in such a happy mood—or dressed as most of them were.

Everybody was painfully neat and obviously felt "dressed up."[14] Women in new gingham[15] and calico[16] dresses. Women in dressing saques[17] over silk skirts. Some island ladies had come with sun bonnets on their heads. Their "fine bonnets" made of black silk. There were women in stiffly starched Mother Hubbards[18] with white aprons trimmed in white crocheted lace. There were men in cotton jeans. Boys in fresh blue overalls. Some men wore bandannas around their necks. Most, however, wore neckties or at least collars.

There were saucer-eyed babies and subdued toddlers on every hand. It obviously was a great occasion for the people on that remote island and they were here to get the most possible enjoyment out of it.

Soon the reluctant young cousin came in and seated herself self-consciously on the piano stool and began the only piece she knew. It turned out to be "Pass Me Not O Gentle Savior"[19]—Instrumental Solo With Variations. As she warmed to her task and Papa could recognize what she was playing, I saw him raise his eyebrows. He didn't look in my direction though.

The piano was a large, square rosewood instrument. It must have been landed on the island before the Civil War—and I am sure it had not been tuned since then.

But there sat a red-faced girl playing the variations of an old religious hymn for a wedding march and in came the bride on the arm of her father. The bride looked sweet and demure, but the dress she wore was fearfully though lovingly made. It was in the style of clothes worn long before my time. Her father reminded me of a character in the funny paper.[20] He had a game leg[21] and had to use a cane. He walked with a hippity-hop. He had won out in the argument about his coat and gave the bride away in his shirt sleeves with red galluses[22] crossed over his back.

The couple having been joined in wedlock, the first group was invited out to supper. This included the bride and groom, the father, four "waiters," or attendants, the musical cousin and Papa and me.

The house had a large kitchen but no dining room. The table seated ten and it was loaded. In the center were three large cakes on glass stands. The cakes were frosted and decorated with pieces of candy. Later, for dessert, the cakes were sliced and served with home-canned peaches. The ladies assisting with the supper passed platters of boiled ham, baked hen and dressing, roast beef and a variety of vegetables. Among the delicacies was a bowl of navy beans!

Papa and I laughed later about the bride with a few beans rolling around her plate and nothing else. In addition to the peaches and cake, the spread included a tall stack of half-moon fried peach pies.

The bride was too timid to eat—she merely toyed with her navy beans—but the bridegroom took on a square meal washed down by two glasses of buttermilk.[23]

All the time we were eating there was a running conversation among the women waiting on the table about the new stove. I concluded that it was really the lion of the occasion.

We finally got away as the second table was filling up for the feast. We were safely back across the river an hour before sundown. The driver was there with the wagon and team but he was greatly upset.

He told us this story: After we left him, he had scarcely gotten the wagon out of the rut and moving again when he heard a noise, a great roaring noise, behind him. He looked around in time to see the road where he had been working slide into the river. The bluff for a distance of several hundred feet had caved in. That hole in which the wagon wheels had stuck was a crack in the ground where the landslide started.

We had had a narrow brush with death.

"Thank God for bringing us through safely," Papa said with his eyes closed.

He was very quiet all the way home and so was I.

CHAPTER 12

You Learned or Else

OUR HOME NEAR THE MISSISSIPPI RIVER[1] PRODUCED A CONTINUING FLOW of interests, excitements, joys and childhood tragedies.

It was here that I encountered the fiercest schoolteacher of my career—or, I feel safe in saying, almost anybody's career. He was an old-time, terrible tempered, iron-fisted, no-nonsense type of schoolmaster and he kept the youngsters in hand by virtually setting up a reign of terror.

This town, like most of the others we knew, was swarming with ornery youngsters and the assumption that most of us needed firmer guidance was beyond question. Before school opened in the late summer, we were more or less at large on the town, seeking diversion where we could find it; and at the start of the year's bout with learning the adult population looked upon us as a wild and hard-to-control passel of little imps.

I don't mean we were always on the lookout for mischief. Not quite. When there was nothing more tempting to do, my brothers and I, before we moved from the old parsonage to the new, could go down the street a few doors to Blakemore's blacksmith shop and watch old Mr. Blakemore shoe horses. This was capital fun for awhile. If he happened to be in a good humor Mr. Blakemore might let me pump the bellows;[2] then Joe and Key[3] would squeal with delight at the glowing coals and flying sparks; but a fractious horse almost stepped on Key one day and Mr. Blakemore shooed us away after that.

What we really liked to do was to go to the school-house across the street where there was a large playground. We gathered there with dozens of other moppets and made the neighborhood ring with our shrill games of bean ball,[4] jump the rope,[5] red light,[6] wolf-over-the-river,[7] and run sheep run.[8] Inevitably, free-for-alls[9] soon followed when the bully boys arrived and chased the little kids.

These exercises helped us to work off excess energy, and in doing so we permitted our high spirits to thrust into the background a certain foreboding. School was about to start and the word had come down to us that we were to have a strict new principal. He was a "tiger" for discipline, the grown-ups reported. Dire threats hung over us.

"Have your fun while you can," a sour-faced neighbor lady told us. "When school takes up, that new principal will make you toe the mark."

The school must have been in a bad way before we came to town. The year before, we were told, it had a "fine young man" for principal, but he was just out of Normal School[10] and too inexperienced to discipline the bad-acting "ye'rlin's"[11] who sprinkled the enrollment. Some of the big boys got completely out of hand. The timid principal lived in fear of being thrashed by one of his own pupils.

The year we arrived the School Board had "taken steps." It had canvassed the surrounding territory for a man of tougher fiber. The one they found and hired filled their bill.

Mr. Tigrett—immediately nicknamed "Tiger"—came from one of the hard-scrabble[12] counties over near the Tennessee River. He was redheaded, tall, gaunt and gimlet-eyed. He boasted of no college degrees but he was grounded in the fundamentals and his record for discipline was gilt-edged. He had never been ridden on a rail or locked in the outhouse by his pupils. It was the other way around.

At his last school he had ducked the biggest boy in the horse trough when he became obstreperous and had trounced the boy's irate father to boot, and had made it stick.

Mr. Tigrett's fierce reputation preceded him to our town. The small fry were afraid of him before he arrived, and the day school opened we trembled at our battered desks when we had our first look at his fiery thatch and his piercing eyes.

The School Board gave him a free hand. Before classwork had been underway a week, every lad from ten years up had been flogged at least once. Some of the older and tougher ones lasted through a second lashing, but I never heard of a boy getting a third.

Mr. Tigrett had strict rules not only for school hours; he regulated conduct during after-school hours as well. His ironclad code prescribed the number of times a pupil could go to town and how late he could stay. The evening mail train was at 7:00 o'clock. The larger boys and girls who had permission to go to the post office after that train were under orders to be home by 7:30. That allowed about fifteen minutes for the postmaster[13] to sort the sack of mail and gave the youngsters around ten minutes to scoot home.

The new principal's far-seeing eyes followed us home from school each afternoon. He knew how long the homeward trip required and he had a fantastic checking system on loiterers. Dallying on the way home—even long enough to watch two Domineck[14] roosters fight in the vacant lot back of the barbershop—drew a strapping for the boys and the writing of a wise saying such as "Waste not, want not" or "Procrastination is the thief of time" a hundred times on the blackboard for the girls.

The opening day of classes was a black day for me. Our last town had afforded a much better school than this one and I was farther along in most studies than the others of my age. To my horror, after a few questions as to "how far over in the book" I had been in grammar, Mr. Tigrett assigned me to the main study room. There I was to sit at a desk directly under his eye, and at least part of my instruction was to be under him.

I know now he was a good and efficient instructor but I wonder how some of us lived through it.

His desk was on a platform from which he glared down at the hapless pupils. Sometimes his manner was momentarily disarming. He might even smile and even pass a pleasantry with an overgrown boy on the recitation bench. That was part of his cat-and-mouse approach. He [sic The] next instant he thundered a question and if the victim was unprepared, the "Tiger" would pounce.

"You, Sir!" he roared. "You dare to come to class without preparing the lesson. Stand up, Sir!"

Then followed a caning or a rap over the noggin with a ruler—or worst of all—an eyeball-to-eyeball tongue lashing in a high-pitched, rasping voice in which the stupidity of the boy was delineated and dissected in detail and his fate in the world was predicted in the direst terms.

If the victim happened to be a girl she was spared corporal punishment. We supposed this was because of some defect in the code rather than any chivalrous inclination on the part of Mr. Tigrett, but the harangue was pressed in rising fury until the flaming-cheeked young lady burst into tears. Whereupon she was required to shake out her sobs while standing with her face to the wall until the carnage among that particular class ended.

Mr. Tigrett's pet subject, the one the "Tiger" really liked to get his teeth into, was grammar. "Rigdon's English Grammar for the Common School"[15] was the title of the torture instrument he used in thrusting syntax, sentence forms and punctuation from the throats of the pupils.

Grammarian Rigdon had rules in his textbook to meet every conceivable occasion in the use of the English language. He not only split hairs, he quartered them and then shredded each segment into microscopic fragments. With every fragment was a rule. In this class—and, although I was younger than the others, I had the profound misfortune to be in it—we had to learn every one of those rules. He thundered and cajoled; he pleaded and commanded; he gave "head marks"[16] daily to the one who "turned down"[17] the others on the recitation bench. Five head marks were good for a silver star; and, if any would-be genius in the class with an overdose of dogged determination desired to flagellate his brain into memorizing enough rules to win three silver stars, he got a gold star to paste in his tattered grammar book and a half-pound box of chocolate creams—priced thirty-five cents at Pennybacker's Drugstore—as an added prize.

At one time Gladys Graves, my bosom friend, and I determined to pool our talents and win that box of chocolates. In furtherance of this resolve, Gladys came over at night to study with me by the parlor lamp. Papa worked with us as we struggled to get the best of parsing and participles, but somehow it didn't work out. We soon decided midnight oil was too expensive to squander on the chance of winning a box of candy, and anyway, chocolate made Gladys break out. So we dropped the idea and fell back into the rut of learning a rule or two for each recitation and hoping that Mr. Tigrett would call on somebody else until he got to the rules we knew.

Partly responsible for our new disinterest in syntax was an unexpected outside diversion. Almost too good to be true, but we were going to see the President of the United States with our own eyes! Teddy Roosevelt.[18]

Gladys' father, Mr. Graves, was Postmaster in our little town. He had been appointed with the change in the Administration,[19] following President Cleveland,[20] and he had continued to serve under President Roosevelt.[21] Mr. Graves was the only Republican in the entire village.

The Memphis "Commercial Appeal"[22] carried the news that President Theodore Roosevelt would speak in that city while on the tour[23] he was making through the South. The Postmasters and the few members of the Republican Party who lived in our solidly Democratic section of Tennessee were given special invitations to be in Memphis for the event. Mr. Graves invited me to go along with him and Gladys. He was a widower and Gladys was his only child. Papa and Mama gave their consent and I was in a state of delirium over this unbelievable windfall.

As a member of the School Board, Mr. Graves had no trouble in getting Gladys and me excused from our afternoon classes in order to catch the three o'clock train. He told Mr. Tigrett that we would be back the next morning in time for school.

During the week before his impending event, Gladys and I had spent every minute of our time outside the schoolroom entertaining the other girls with the details of our forthcoming trip to Memphis. I am sure we were unbearably superior.

In the meantime, Mr. Tigrett seemed harder on us than ever and the game of head marks in grammar had palled,[24] for we had reached the grand finale of our fierce textbook—the Lord High Executioner of all grammar lessons: diagramming.

This ordeal started with little innocent three-word sentences and in a few days worked up to long double jointed, mid-Victorian[25] circumlocutions that ran to as much as 50 to 75 words. To diagram such a sentence required a whole blackboard and the drafting skill of an architect. Our unrelenting teacher seemed happiest when he had us at our battle stations tracing our tortured way through such drills.

The day of our return from Memphis, Gladys and I were the center of attention at the first recess, painting word pictures of our excursion amid a chorus of gasps and giggles from our bug-eyed young audience.

We left nothing untold from our arrival at the Gayoso Hotel[26] by way of horse-drawn cab, to our triumphal breakfast in the dining car that morning.

We told first of being at the Station when the President's Special train[27] rolled in. I was almost unconscious when we reached our places in the cheering, noisy crowd. As Gladys and I stood holding hands, we both shivered from excitement and the chill of that late October evening. The people were yelling and roaring greetings when Roosevelt came out on the rear platform of his coach. He had planned to speak from there.

But there was a misunderstanding. A large wagon truck had been prepared with a stand, just a few hundred yards from the railroad track. It was thought that those who came to see the President could get a better view and would be able to hear much better. The Presidential party seemed opposed to the change and when the crowd began to grow restless, Bishop Gailor[28]—Mr.

Graves told us his name—made his way to President Roosevelt and prevailed upon him to change his plan.

Teddy moved quickly to the improvised stand—decorated with red, white and blue bunting and a great bouquet of American Beauty roses and chrysanthemums—and flashing one of his big, toothy grins, began his speech with, "I can't refuse a Bishop!"

He spoke for nearly thirty minutes, then stood bowing and tipping his hat. The people clapped wildly and there were shouts of, "You'r[29] all right, Mr. President." And "You'll do, Teddy."

As he stepped down from the stand he raised the big bouquet of flowers and waved it at the crowd. He had difficulty getting back to his coach, but he pushed through the throng of well-wishers, talking and joking and shaking hands as he went.

"Did he shake hands with you?" asked a little girl in an awed voice. "No," Gladys and I said in unison, "but we could have touched him." Mr. Graves had managed a handshake.

The President finally reached the rear platform of his train and stood there waving and bowing. As the train began to move, a spectator shouted, "Hello Colonel!"

"Hello," responded Mr. Roosevelt. "I like for you to call me President, but I like more to be called 'Colonel' by men from my own regiment!" Mr. Graves then had reminded us about President Roosevelt's command of the "Rough Riders"[30] in the Spanish-American War. We watched the train with the Presidential party, bound for New Orleans, until it was swallowed up in the darkness. Then it had been all over—so soon!

Back in the Gayoso—the lobby now ablaze with the sparkling, dazzling chandeliers—we were to learn of the wild exploits of General Nathan Bedford Forrest[31] when he stole into Memphis early one Sunday morning, and with a handful of his picked scouts scared the Yankee soldiers, who were holding the city under siege, right out of their beds.

"Was there fighting?" several voices among our schoolmates queried.

"Yes, General Forrest sent one band of his cavalry straight to the Gayoso to capture the Yankee Generals quartered there. The party slipped along the streets through the fog and did not take time to light and hitch,[32] but rode their horses right through the big front doors of the hotel and into the lobby! Captain Bill Forrest, brother of General Forrest, was the leader. He threw his reins over the stairway banisters and told the startled night clerk to take him to the room of the General."³³

"Did he catch the Yankee General?" came from a chorus of listeners.

"No, a sentinel managed to warn him, but the General didn't have time to dress. He jumped out of bed and fled in nothing but his nightshirt."

"I'd be afraid to stay at the Gayoso," cheeped one timid little miss.

"Oh, that all happened over forty years ago! Way back in the summer of 1864. But it is kind o' scary to hear the old people talk about it,'" I admitted.

And so the talk went. First Gladys and then I told some incident of the wonderful twenty-four hours, just past. There was our trip home . . .

We left the hotel Gayoso quite early—before sunup, in fact—in order to catch the "fas train" that would get us back in time for school. His [*sic* This] train ordinarily did not stop in our town, but Mr. Graves had "made arrangements" with the station agent. That in itself was an eye-popping event.

It took an hour and a half to travel from Memphis back home. This gave us time for breakfast in the diner. When Gladys' father announced this plan, I was so overwhelmed that I scarcely had strength to walk through the several coaches ahead and into the dining car. I had never had his [*sic* this] pleasure before. I had only dreamed of it when long trains swept through town and I watched passengers, seated at tables, eating as they sped along.

My refreshments, whenever I had been on a train at mealtime, had consisted of fried chicken and deviled eggs packed in a shoe box.

And now what bliss! To be seated in such elegant surroundings, with a waiter in white jacket at my elbow and eating my oatmeal and drinking hot chocolate as I looked out on the whizzing landscape—well, I described it to my listening schoolmates with the arrogance of one who had been present at a Bacchanal.³⁴

But our colorful recital all too soon was drawing to a close. The bell rang and we were pulled back to reality—the very startling reality that we had been on the school porch during the entire recess and had not even been to the pump for a drink of water! Well, it was too late then.

After an uneasy study period, Mr. Tigrett called us up to the "torture bench" as we called our recitation place. There was a moment of portentous silence. We cringed and squirmed as we waited for the first turn of the screw. Satisfied with the effect he had produced, Mr. Tigrett fixed his steel gaze on Gladys and me and opened the proceedings:

"Now if Queen Victoria[35] and Queen Isabella[36] have recovered from holding court I will ask their royal highnesses to step up to the blackboard," he said with mock solicitude.

We scarcely had strength to make it to the board and take our places, chalk and erasers at the ready. Our fears of impending disaster were promptly redoubled when Mr. Tigrett cut loose with a sentence for us to diagram that exceeded anything even Rigdon's text had produced. Whether he was quoting from a book he had read or was making up this monstrosity of a sentence as he went along, I don't know, but it was to stay imprinted in my memory.

The gist of the sentence, leaving aside its tortuous phrases and syntactical excursions, was that "Charlotte Corday killed Marat."[37] To round the thought, as he gave it to us, she had "done in" her revolutionist friend[38] in his bathtub and thereby created quite a stir in French political circles.

As Mr. Tigrett proceeded to roll out the sentence with its compound and complex danglers, parenthetical expressions to be perched on stools, and a whole procession of wandering modifiers, I was numb with fright. I was sure Gladys would get it worked out some way as she was better than most at diagramming. I just knew I would never get it right and would be executed alone.

I was mistaken about my chum. When I finally dared to turn my eyes in her direction, she was standing rigidly at the board not making a move. She had copied only a few words of the sentence and her eyes were staring. I kept drawing lines and segregating subjects and predicates, at the same time watching her from the corner of my eye. She made a few feeble efforts to continue writing, dropped her chalk and remained frozen on the spot.

"Well, Gladys, are you going to stand there like a block of wood?" Mr. Tigrett railed at her. He was enraged at her inaction. His voice had risen and was menacing in tone.

Poor Gladys. I was scared, but she was petrified.

Then the tension broke.

When I looked again at my upset friend, the color was drained from her face, and she was standing in the center of a slowly expanding puddle on the floor.

Queen Victoria had wet her pants.

I was horrified. Everybody in the room was horrified and if the truth could be known, I'm sure Mr. Tigrett was horrified, too. But the "Tiger" played out his demon role. He looked at Gladys pityingly as she stood trembling and sobbing, and then said in a stern voice:

"Go home and put on some dry clothes."

With that he dismissed the class and rang the noon bell, a quarter of an hour early.

As the other girls and I led Gladys to the door, Mr. Tigrett fired a parting blast:

"And don't loiter on the way!"

❦

To our utter astonishment Mr. Tigrett got married that year! Fortyish, a glum bachelor, he regularly shunned all social affairs. Nevertheless, he had a weakness, and beneath his tough exterior was a soft heart that palpitated warmly in the presence of members of the gentle sex. It was no trouble at all for him to fall in love with pretty Miss May, the first grade teacher.

Miss May was blonde, vivacious, and ready. She had rejected various beaux over the years as she waited for something perhaps a little better than the local crop, and there were signs that she might have to settle down to a permanent career of single felicity with the first-graders.

But, Mr. Tigrett solved her problem—if she had one—and she quickly let him know she was willing. They set their wedding date in the late Spring, for the day after school was to be out.

The town was amused by the thought of the ogerish [sic ogreish][39] principal and the cuddlesome Miss May, and pleased, too, for Miss May was liked by everybody, and many had wondered whether she would ever be claimed.

As planned, it was to be a simple, uncomplicated, home wedding, and that's the way it turned out. But—- the community had to get involved in some way and this time it was over the bride's outfit!

The mail-order houses were in their heyday at that time. Parcel Post[40] had brought the glamorous big cities to every hamlet. The village dressmakers and tailors were passing from the scene. The fad was to order clothes readymade. The catalogues that came out each season were as eagerly awaited as Santa Claus. THE NATIONAL CLOAK & SUIT COMPANY, and BELLAS-HESS[41] were among the most popular firms for our area—one in New York, and the other in Chicago—and their labels were our marks of prestige. To be able to get dresses and suits, and even hats, right out of the fashion centers of the country by return mail was the marvel of the age.

Of course, many women still bought gingham and calico by the yard and made up their own everyday garments and their children's school clothes, but everybody who could sell enough butter and eggs to the general store, or pick enough cotton in the fall at fifty cents a hundred pounds, had a Sunday outfit from the mail-order house.

Miss May, fluttering about with her wedding plans, decided she and her tamed "Tiger" would go to the station to take a train for their honeymoon trip—to Memphis and back—immediately after the ceremony. She would be wed in her going-away suit and hat, instead of a white dress and veil. The spring catalog of BELLA-HESS was just out and she sent her measurements for one of their nicest, modestly priced suits.

One day while still busy with her duties for the closing exercises of school as well as her wedding plans, Miss May realized that the time was growing short and her suit had not arrived. She hurriedly sent off a note to the company explaining her urgent need and imploring them not to spare the horses. Soon it was barely a week before she was to go to the altar and she still had not heard from her order. That's when the entire population became really involved.

"Will, or will not Miss May's wedding suit be delivered on time?" became the town's leading topic. Every morning as housewives swept their front walks they called to each other:

"Has it come?"

Their husbands discussed the matter at the Post Office after each mail train. Some thought the company "ought to be sued!"

"How much do you reckon the blame thing cost?" one good burgher asked another. When the questioner's friend replied that his wife "had it straight from Miss May's sister" that the suit cost $19.95. Mayor Sparks pushed his hat back of his head and gave a long whistle.

"All I can say is them fellers in Chicago must be gittin' rich powerful fast."

Expensive or no, the suit was still missing when the wedding day arrived. Mr. Tigrett said he didn't see what all the fuss was about—he'd buy her a coat suit in Memphis when they got there.

"Tell everybody to hush about it," he said. "It's not important."

Typical words for a bachelor without too much experience with fashion-mad women. It was important indeed to Miss May—and from the way they carried on, to every man, woman and child in town.

When the last mail train before the wedding hour came, the people gathered in heads-together groups along the street breathlessly awaiting the news:

Did it come? Half of the population seemed to be at the post office when the station hack brought in the day's mail sacks.

Shivers and groans—the suit still hadn't come.

Sorrowfully the people went back home or to their work while a messenger took the sad tidings to Miss May. Everybody was sorry for her. It seemed more like an impending funeral than a wedding.

At three o'clock that afternoon, an hour before the ceremony, a local freight came through and the conductor handed the depot agent a sack of mail. The mail train that morning, through an error, had failed to throw off one sack and that sack had been entrusted to the freight conductor, when the mail train passed the freight train farther along the line. The depot agent hustled the bag to the post office.

The Postmaster sent a Negro boy on the run to the home of the bride with a package that contained her coat-suit. It had been in that errant bag of mail.

Miss May was already dressed—in her last season's suit—but her sister quickly took the new suit out of its box and pressed the wrinkles. It fit perfectly.

A few minutes later, resplendent in the latest fashion from Chicago and blushing the blush that only goes with all's well that ends at the altar, Miss May became the wedded wife of Mr. Tigrett.

The news of the suit had spread throughout the town by the time the happy bride and bridegroom drove to the station. People stood on their porches and on the street corners and cheered.

The cheers were for a bachelor who many thought was too mean ever to get married, and for the bride who tamed him—but mainly for the beautifully tailored spring suit that Miss May happily wore.

CHAPTER 13

The One That Got Away

WE GREW OLDER BUT THE ANTICS OF OUR ELDERS REMAINED UNFATHomable. Even as our years unfolded we were more than ever puzzled and amused by the fuss and bother usually generated among adults when a boy and girl fell in love, passed through a period of courtship and finally were married. Take one case of Georgianna and Bob Lee, for example . . .

Our next home town was a county seat, this time a little nearer to the "Old Country" and our neck of the Tennessee woods than the other places where we had lived in the past few years.[1] Some of our relatives were there, and it didn't take us long to get acquainted with just about everybody else. We hadn't been settled in the parsonage a week before we knew who was who, what was going on—both good and bad—and all about the impending marriage of Georgianna Johnson and Bob Lee Carter.

What we didn't know was that we were right then heading into a community-wide prenuptial whoop-te-do. It was to involve sensation upon small-town sensation; comedy, pathos and near tragedy were coming our way; and after it was all over, the town was going to have a good hearty laugh at its own expense.

The wedding of Georgianna Johnson and Bob Lee Carter actually was of such consuming interest that it was still to be remembered and to furnish material for conversation forty years later. Time came to be reckoned by this momentous event.

A few years ago I met a couple in Grenada[2] who turned out to be Tennesseeans [*sic* Tennesseans]. As people do when they come together on a foreign soil, we talked of the familiar places and people we knew back home. Presently, the town of the Georgianna-Bob Lee episode was mentioned.

"Have I ever been there?" the man replied to my question. "Certainly I have. I was there the day after Georgianna Johnson married!"

That dated and classified him.

Long after my brothers and I were grown and had scattered to distant States, when we visited our parents and sat around the family hearth recalling incidents of our childhood, perhaps in the midst of our reminiscences one of us would ask, "Mama, how old is Jessie Blanche Sarton?" She would think a bit and then say, "Well, I believe she is right close to forty. She was a good-sized child when Georgiana Johnson married. I remember she was old enough to run when her mother heard the news that morning. I can see her now, flying down the street to tell her grandmother."

Georgianna Johnson and Bob Lee Carter had been sweethearts since childhood. Not only were they young and attractive, they were liked by everybody, and everybody took it for granted they would be marching down the aisle sooner or later. But when Georgianna said "Yes" to Bob Lee, and finally started plans for their wedding, nobody remotely dreamed of the course her fortune was about to take or of the train of events that would ensue.

Georgianna really was just a normal, sweet young girl about to be married to a promising home town boy who owned a modest coal-and-ice business. Her mother had died when she was about three years old and she had been reared by her grandfather and his second wife.

Georgianna's lot had not been hard, but the neighbors felt that she had not always been given the love and devotion she might have had under different circumstances. Her father had been a ne'er-do-well, and soon after the death of her mother he had drifted away. Often several years passed without any word from him. He had come from somewhere "up North" originally. Now he seemed to gravitate around Chicago. Georgianna sometimes heard from him at Christmas and a few times he had sent her a five dollar bill, but that was about all he had ever done for her.

So it was grist for the conversation mill when Georgianna received from him a handsome gold locket set with diamonds on her eighteenth birthday. Her grandfather had it appraised immediately by the local jeweler to be sure that it was all that it appeared to be. It was genuine all right, and a short time later they learned that her father had remarried and was "doing well" in a Chicago firm. In fact, it was reported that he was now, by virtue of his second wife's wealth, on easy street.

It was about this time that Georgianna announced to her grandfather that she and Bob Lee were going to be married during the coming summer. Her grandfather's wife—known to everybody as Miss Maude—had always chafed a little under the burden of an extra child to feed and clothe and send to school. So now that the elusive father was showing signs of prosperity Miss Maude promptly wrote him of his daughter's coming marriage and suggested rather boldly that he might want to buy her a wedding dress.

By return mail Georgianna received the money for a railroad ticket and an invitation to come to Chicago for a few weeks so she could buy her entire trousseau in the best shops in the city. And, furthermore, her father's new wife—Georgianna's stepmother—added a cordial note stating that she would gladly help in the selection of the wedding outfit. This news spread quickly through channels familiar to all small towns, and interest began to mount.

The bride-to-be had three dazzling weeks with her father and stepmother and under their care and attention she blossomed like a sunflower.

A few days after Georgianna returned from Chicago, the boxes and packages of finery began to arrive. At once stories went the rounds about her father and his obvious new wealth. Georgianna said that he was a grain broker. Her grandfather said on the side that he was using his wife's money to deal in futures[3] (whatever that meant), and that he was, in the old gentleman's opinion, nothing better than a tin-horn gambler. Every woman in town was breathless with excitement and anywhere that two met—on the street, over the back fence, or the Entre Nous Rook Club[4]—they compared notes on the latest items of Georgianna Johnson's trousseau.

"Did you hear . . . pure silk crepe de Chine[5] teddies."[6]

"Pink? . . . well, I never!"

"Real lace brought on from France!"

"Yes . . . whole sets that match . . . princess slips . . . everything, I tell you. And all pure SILK!"

"Camisoles?[7] What's that?" . . . "With Persian ribbon and lace" . . . "Well, why don't they call them corset covers?"

"You never saw the like of her silk stockings."

"Donie saw then with her own eyes—and counted them. Twelve pairs!"

"Annie Sue said there wasn't any tellin' how many pairs of umbrella drawers and extra underskirts she had . . . ruffled and all prettied up . . . real point lace . . ."

But nothing in the whole collection, which included all of the beautiful frocks Georgianna had brought from Chicago—well, not even the wedding dress—caused as much running comment and head bobbing as two little corsets—but such corsets! They topped everything else. When Miss Angela, the little milliner who originally came from Cincinnati, heard about them, she turned pale and instantly crossed herself.

To begin with, almost none of the good women in that town had personally experienced a satin and lace-trimmed corset. There was something vaguely immoral about the thought of such a thing. Now, Georgianna had two of these intricate and alluring garments, made of the richest silk and finest quality whalebone, with heavy satin ribbon to lace up the back. Her waist measured only twenty inches or so, but the styles still demanded tight lacing. And there they lay, the boxes opened up for everyone to see. Visitors marched around them like they were viewing a corpse.

Most of the matrons in the community—especially those who were classified as "stout"—had to make out with what the regular drygoods [*sic* dry goods] store had to offer at one or two dollars.

It would have been sacrilege in Mrs. Aydlotte's ears to call a Spirella Garment[8] a corset. She was particular and used the correct terms of the trade. These "foundation garments" were well reinforced and made of such heavy material that jokesters said it took a fairly husky woman to carry one around. Uncle Billy once told Aunt Alice[9] that if he were to saddle Old Kate in a Spirella, the poor old mare wouldn't be able to trot around the courthouse square without stopping to blow at the water trough. So the women who had their figures galvanized with such heavy stays, tossed their heads and sniffed, perhaps wistfully, over the satin and lace "pretties" of Georgianna's trousseau.

With so much gossip in the air, my ears stayed straight out so I wouldn't miss anything. When I heard that Georgianna had a pair of pink mules[10] to match her lounging robe, I didn't question it for a single moment. I had never seen pink mules, but neither had I ever seen a lounging robe. When I finally learned that ladies' mules were just house slippers without heel stays, I was just about as puzzled as ever. However, it was a relief to know that she was not going to ride or drive a pair of mules—dyed pink—and that the lounging robe was nothing but a fancy kimono or wrapper, as Mama called it.

As the days went by, the whole town got caught up in the excitement. The tempo of the day-to-day activities increased until nobody walked at all—they ran. If they didn't hurry, they might miss something.

Ten days before the wedding, Georgianna's father and stepmother, Mr. and Mrs. Johnson, made their appearance. They took the best rooms at the hotel, and the stepmother took charge of everything and everybody as soon as she unpacked.

I had not been at the station when the Chicago visitors came on the four o'clock train, but goodness knows I heard enough about it. By nightfall the word had traveled from Depot Street to Whiskey Chute, and from College Hill to Black Bottom, that they had arrived. Mr. Johnson, the broker, was at once pushed into the background. He could have had two heads, and nobody would have noticed. All eyes were on her.

There were many versions, but basically the story was that she arrived in a blue serge suit—in the hot summertime, mind you—made in the latest fashion. The skirt was slit halfway to the knee, allowing a green taffeta silk underskirt to show when she stepped off the train. Her Milan straw hat was all but swallowed by long willow plume that, we learned later from Georgianna, cost nearly twenty-five dollars alone.

That was simply incredible. That was as much as Georgianna's grandfather paid his delivery boy at the grocery store for two month's wages.

It was also reported that her button shoes, with pearl grey suede tops, had cost twelve dollars and fifty cents! When Papa heard that, his eyebrows went up, and he exclaimed, "The dog's foot!" He sometimes used that expression when he heard something outlandish. That was the strongest language he ever used.

As it turned out, the stepmother was gracious and friendly, and only a short time had elapsed before nearly everybody could see that, for a Northerner,[11] she was as "clever a body as you'd ever need to know." Of course, her name was on every lip and, whenever groups came together, they discussed her pro and con—usually pro.

Even our Cindy, who toiled in the kitchen, had a comment:

"Miss Mattie," she said, "I don't believe Mr. Johnson's new wife looks none too stout."

"Why Cindy": Mama asked in surprise. "She appeared healthy enough to me."

Cindy replied, "Ain't you see how green she looks around the eyeballs? That's bad—mighty bad. I always hear it's a sign of ja'nders."[12]

The young girls and sometimes a frisky widow used a little rouge on the sly, but eye-shadow make-up was a novelty. Cindy was not the only one in our little town who was somewhat startled by Mrs. Johnson's "touch up."

Full of bounce and energy, the second Mrs. Johnson bustled around faster than the pace to which we were accustomed. She also had the knack of getting everyone around her busy, too. Before we knew it, the town was sown down with engraved invitations, not only to the wedding, but to a supper and dance to follow in honor of their daughter, the bride. Furthermore, Woodmen's Hall[13] had been rented, the floor had been scrubbed and waxed, and a ragtime band from Memphis had been engaged.

This immediately set up a new flurry of comment. Dancing was still somewhat frowned upon by the churches in the town, even though most parents of the younger fry knew there was dancing behind closed parlor doors.[14] And when parties went on camping trips to Reelfoot Lake[15] it was no secret that Pea Eye, Roscoe and High Pockets were usually along, not only as roustabouts, but to furnish music on the slide horn, French harp and box for those who wanted to try out the one-step and Turkey Trot. "Box" was the sporting set's term for the guitar.

Still up to that time, we had not been treated to a wedding reception with supper and dancing. People shook their heads in amazement over this.

For a few days after the invitations were issued, there was much discussion of the wedding ball among the parents, some siding for it and others speaking out against it. In the end, it promised to be too much to miss and women and girls were thrown into a state of agitation as they went about the task of preparing appropriate dresses. Sewing machines whirred and ribbon was bought by the bolt for sashes and for tying up the sleeves so bear [*sic* bare] arms might show.

I was not invited, but I begged and teased to be allowed to go and wear my new piano-recital dress. I wanted to watch. My pleas to Mama fell on deaf ears. However, Papa wore an amused smile over the whole business and said he saw no harm in the young folks enjoying themselves at Georgianna's wedding, and that maybe we could "look in" on the affair for a little while. But Mama was adamant and I was afraid I would be hustled straight home from the church, if she had her way.

Mama decided that Papa's Prince Albert[16] was a little seedy for such an outstanding affair. Papa didn't think so, but he got a new one, and I'm sure he hoped that the big wedding would net him enough in the way of a fee to pay for it—and of course, I always hoped for a fee that would pay for a bicycle.

Most of those on the invitation list spent either hard cash or a lot of time and energy getting ready for this unusual occasion. The whole town seemed to take on a general sprucing up. Lawns were mowed so many times and so close that Uncle Gabe, who kept the churchyard, got worried. "If Miss Georgianna and Mister Bob Lee don't hurry up and jump the broomstick,[17] won't be a blade of grass left in this town," he said.

That was the day the marquee was put up from the church door to the street. It arrived, along with the potted palms, on the early morning Accommodation from Memphis. The trouble was, nobody knew how to put it up. Mr. Johnson hired several Negro men and after a prolonged, knuckle-grinding, back-wrenching session, there she was, striped and fringed, a little droopy here and there, but another first for the bemused community.

This innovation furnished the material for a full round of curiosity-laden talk. Because its installation took place on Wednesday, the congregation at Prayer meeting that night was triple its normal size. Georgianna wasn't there to play the organ, but that didn't matter. Nobody expected her. All wanted to see the marquee. Most of those who attended felt safer to walk on the outside and not under it, and they scrambled over the guy ropes and up the steps, looking a little abashed as they entered the vestibule of the church. As they went to their pews, the worshipers, I'm sure, made an honest effort to lay aside thoughts of what was happening and to meditate and pray together as they had done through the years.

However, poor old Mr. Yarbrough slipped a little when, in an earnest supplication, he said, ". . . and O Lord, if you knew just half of the things that are going on in this town right now, you'd be surprised."

That was almost too much for Papa. He had difficulty rising from his knees with a sober face. Mama had to hide behind her fan several times during the remainder of the service.

The day finally came. Hot and a little overcast.

When Cindy shuffled into the kitchen that morning, she wore the masklike, non-communicative expression peculiar to many of her race. The air was so "close" we might get some fallin' weather, she told Mama. After a long interval, she added that a strange houn' dog was "howlin' on the church steps"[18] the night before.

"Sure sign, somethin's goin' to happen," Cindy warned.

Papa overheard his. He drily remarked: "Maybe there's going to be a wedding."

"Ain't goin' to be a weddin' in that church this day."

Mama's interest in what Cindy was saying perked up. She sensed that Cindy knew something and was waiting for the right moment to yield the information to us, but Cindy lost her big chance for at that moment, Miss Mamie Williams, a close neighbor, crashed through the door to the side porch, wheezing and shouting to know whether we had "heard the news."

"News, Miss Mamie?" Mama quickly asked, "What news?"

"Georgianna and Bob Lee have disappeared."

"What on earth . . . ?" Mama was startled.

"It's the Lord's truth."

"Well," Mama said weakly, "Aren't . . . aren't they getting married? After all . . ." Mama's voice faded uncertainly.

Miss Mamie wheezed, fanned herself with her apron to restore breathing and sat down.

"All I know," she said, "Is that they're gone—cleared out early this morning before daylight."

At that moment, Miss Mamie was followed into the house by her niece, a crippled girl. The child was out of breath and almost incoherent. She had been running, in spite of her leg braces.

"Now then," Miss Mamie said, "for Heaven's sake, calm yourself. What did you say?"

"Aunt Callie called—(puff, puff)—and said, (puff)—"

"Go on!"

"Aunt Callie said, tell you they think they went to Fulton[19] in a hack."

Miss Mamie and her niece left. They had other bases to touch with the latest bit of news. Mama at the same time threw aside her apron and hurried to the front porch. Across the way in front of our next-door neighbor's house was a knot of women, all talking.

"Dear me," Mama said. "I guess we'll have to wait until somebody else comes in with the details. What on earth will they do, after all the preparations?"

I ran to the fence. I could hear the neighbor ladies as they chatted excitedly.

". . . Yesterday afternoon? Then it was Bob Lee who balked . . ."

". . . Eloped? Who with? . . ."

"With each other, you dunce!"

"Lord help us!"

"Well, it does beat all . . ."

"Her father said what?"

"New Orleans? . . . Somebody said Memphis!"

"Does anybody know what she wore?"

". . . Run, honey, and tell Grandma. She's making damson preserves back in the kitchen and won't know anything a'tall about it."Doctor Tinsley? . . . What's the matter with Mr. Johnson?"

"All that brick ice cream at the depot . . . Lord a mercy! It's a pretty how-de-do[20] all right."

"You say Lula went in to see her—the stepmama? How's she takin' it?"

"Just sitin' at the breakfast like nothin' happened?"

"Well!" . . . "she's a queer[21] one . . . I like her though . . . Some ways she's as plain as an old boot . . . didn't put on any airs with me."

"Say, has anybody been down to the greenhouse to tell Jeff and Dovie? . . . They'll have every blossom in town cut and ready by now . . . Get Junie to run down to the church to see if they've started . . ."

"And so it went. I sat with Mama in the swing on the front porch and traveled back and forth to the gate as the town's swiftest and knowingest tale bearer paraded along and we listened to the clack—clack—clack of busy tongues and excited voices.

After a while, Papa went to the post office and when he returned, Mama met him expectantly, eager to get the latest developments. He handed her a letter or two, then calmly seated himself and opened the "The Commercial Appeal"[22] to read the day's news just as he did every morning. Mama exploded.

"Reece Hart, if you sit there with your nose buried in that old Governor's race as if nothing has happened, I'll . . . I'll . . ."

Cindy stuck her head in the door and, with a few tinkles of the tea bell, said, "Dinner's ready, Miss Mattie."

My brothers and I were sent to wash our hands, and this time we moved with dispatch.

We dipped fingers quickly in the basin, flapped them dry against a towel, and flew to the dining room, knowing that Mama would be too preoccupied to make inspection.

Papa said grace and served our plates. Then he turned to Mama, but before he could say a word, she burst out laughing and said, "I know you don't know a thing! You could have stepped over two dead bodies and still wouldn't know a thing!"

Cindy came in and passed the hot corn sticks, and suddenly Mama stopped in midair, so to speak. She remembered something.

"Cindy, you knew about this when you came this morning, didn't you?"

"Yes'm. Miss Mattie, I knew all about it. You see, I lives with Floss—my sister—and her boy Clabe. He works at the icehouse for Mister Bob Lee. Yes'day evenin' about quittin' time he told Clabe to get a rig at the liver' stable and bring it 'round to his house. Clabe thought they was goin' for a drive after supper but after he go there Mister Bob Lee had him bring out two valises and h'ist 'em in the back, and then Miss Georgianna come feistin' out all dressed up with her hat on, an' they got in an' tol' Clabe to drive to Fulton—an' to hurry, 'cause they had to catch a train. By then it was about dark an' nobody saw 'em leave."

"Mister Bob Lee left Zack with his Papa and tol' him not to say nothin' or go away until they got back."

Old Mr. Carter was crippled with rheumatism and Zack, who worked on the place, took care of him.

Cindy continued with great gusto.

"Clabe says Mr. Bob Lee's been grumblin' for a week or more about such a stampede over one little weddin'. He wanted to get it over with. He just blowed up an' put his foot down when they brought it up about rehearsin' or somethin'. He said he'd been to suppers an' all till he was tired—an' there wasn't no sense in practicin' a weddin' an' he wasn't goin' to do it. So he finally said he couldn't waste no more time an' begged Miss Georgianna to slip off."

"Then she say she'd have to ask her pa 'cause he'd been so good to her, but she dreaded namin' it to her stepma."

"But right here Miss Georgianna, she got fooled!"

"After she talk to her pa, he just laugh and laugh—leastwise he laughed when he wasn't holdin' his stomach. He's been right po'ly the last day or two. He told Mister Bob Lee he didn't blame him none—to take her an' run, but he hated to think what people were goin' to say when they heard about it, an' then he slapped his sides and laughed some more."

"The stepma, she laughed, too, an' tole 'em to go ahead; that her an' Mister Johnson would keep their mouths shut till the news got out. She say she already had her money's worth."

"Before they crossed the county line, Clabe say they stopped at Squire Hudson's an' had the marryin' done. Then they drove as hard as they could go till they got to the depot at Fulton. They didn't have no time to spare, but Mister Bob Lee got the tickets an' they 'loped on the train."

"Mister Bob Lee tole Clabe to feed an' water the horses good an' let 'em blow 'bout an hour an' then drive back—slow. It was nearly sunup when he got home."

Cindy had enjoyed telling her tale and we all sat bug-eyed and silent for a few moments after she finished. Then Papa looked at Mama and drily remarked, "I believe last week's Sunday School Lesson was on casting your net where you are. The news you were looking for was right under your nose."

Mama grinned but she also pretended to shake her fist at him.

When Cindy returned to the dining room, she said, "Mister Hart, Floss holler at me just now that Mister Johnson's got worse. They've done sent for another doctor. may have to cut 'im open."

And that is exactly what did happen. Mr. Johnson had been ailing for several days and when Doctor Tinsley was finally called, he discovered he [*sic* the] visitor had appendicitis. A consultation was held with old doctor Figg and the patient was advised that surgery was necessary within the hour.

This all came on so quickly that the town couldn't take it in just then. In fact, it had not yet had time to chew its cud over the events of the last twelve hours. Many people were still trying to digest the facts about the runaway bride and bridegroom who had left the town holding the sack. Now, for the father of the missing bride to up and have acute appendicitis on the very afternoon of the wedding affair that had fizzled out—well, many thought the operation could have just waited.

But it couldn't wait—and didn't. In fact, before the final chapter of the Georgianna-Bob Lee story was in, Mr. Johnson's attack was the tail that wagged the dog.

Having made their decision, the harassed physicians hoisted Mr. Johnson on the makeshift operating table in Dr. Tinsley's office and between them, they plucked forth the offending appendix, but Mr. Johnson had waited too long. The appendix had ruptured.

Mrs. Johnson sent to Nashville for a nurse, and even with the best possible care, it was touch and go for a week as to whether Mr. Johnson would make it. The town walked on tiptoes and held its breath. Grandma Butler even killed her big Plymouth Rock rooster because she heard his lusty crowing every morning disturbed Mr. Johnson.

Georgianna was back at home right away, but her father was now so definitely in the limelight that nobody gave much thought to whether she wore a camisole or a French corset. Her honeymoon with Bob Lee in New Orleans had been cut in half—which meant they were there only two days instead of four—and their return home to set up housekeeping scarcely created a ripple. The town was hushed and spoke in whispers. Mothers fed their children absent-mindedly, scarcely aware of what they were doing. Merchants and lawyers and bankers attended to business half-heartedly.

Papa prepared what he considered one of his best sermons for the following Sunday, but it fell on fallow ground. His congregation's mind was on the events of the past week, and the fate of the sick man at the hotel.

Mr. Johnson meanwhile, used tantalizing tactics in pursuing his illness.

First off, Dr. Tinsley had put on a grim face and announced that the patient couldn't last more than a few days—no one ever did with a ruptured appendix[23]—but Mr. Johnson did. After eight or ten days he was sitting up and taking nourishment. Then suddenly his fever flared up and he had a sinking spell. This time his wife wired their Chicago doctor, who came South on the Panama Limited, took one look, shook his head and went back to Chicago. Mr. Johnson remained so low for the next week, that the town braced itself for the biggest funeral since the bull gored Mayor Storey.

The possibilities of where he would be buried furnished many man-hours of conversation.

Old Mrs. Charity Phillips made an extra batch of her famous salt-rising bread because she did not want to be caught short, and many a likely young rooster that might have otherwise escaped was penned up to fatten in anticipation of chicken salad that would be needed to feed the crowd when Mr. Johnson lay a corpse.

But Mr. Johnson would not be outdone and again he rallied. This time it seemed to be for keeps. He continued to mend right along and in a short time the nurse was rolling him in his wheelchair in front of the hotel.

That was when Mr. Johnson and I became friends.

Mrs. Johnson and Mama had exchanged calls. Now Mama wanted to do something to cheer the ailing husband. So she sent me to deliver a freshly baked cherry tart to tempt his taste.

I was in Sunday School frock, my curls freshly brushed, when I mounted the hotel stairs and delivered Mama's offering. I dare say I was awed by the nature of my errand, and for once I was more demure than assertive as I came into the friendly gaze of the affluent Chicagoan.

Mr. Johnson was quite chipper, considering what he had just been through. He thanked me warmly; then he entrusted me with additional effusive thanks, with expressions of gratitude and esteem, for my mother. I at once capitulated to his charms.

He bade me sit in a big chair where we both could look out the window. The nurse was busy, so we had a long chat. I told him I liked to skate on the cement walk near the church, and play hop-scotch, and read, and ride my uncle's pony.

When I finally remembered my manners and rose to leave, I said, "I hope you get well soon. I like you."

He smiled and winked at me. "I'm doing much better now, thank you," he said. "And please come to see me again."

I did. Every day for the next several days I ran by the hotel and chatted with my friend—about the funny wedding events, about my playmates, what my brothers were like and things like that.

He told me about Chicago and many other places he and Mrs. Johnson had visited. Once they had been on a long ocean voyage. I asked a lot of questions. My imagination was caught by his stories. We were pals.

Despite his rapid improvement, Mr. Johnson was unlucky enough to give one more fillip to his sensational illness.

The town had just caught up with its sleep, and a few citizens had slipped off to Reelfoot Lake on fishing expeditions to settle their nerves, when word came that the unpredictable Mr. Johnson had done it again! For his encore, he had eaten an over-ripe peach. It disagreed with him and brought about such violent abdominal contractions that he broke loose some stitches.

Without any further ado his wife and nurse hustled him onto the midnight Cannon Ball and headed him for home and a hospital in Chicago. It was just as well. The town could only take so much.

After a few more days, reassuring news came from Chicago, and the people sagged back into their porch rockers to recount over and over on long evenings the stimulating events of the last month.

There was scarcely a family that had not been touched in some way. Although there was grumbling about the new dresses and ribbons the women folks didn't get to wear, and about the whitewash wasted on many a paling fence . . . it didn't amount to much.

The walk and lawn in front of the Methodist Church had been mussed in several places when the marquee was put up. To this day, one can see where the holes in the walk were cemented over and the sight invariably prompts someone to recall the side-tracked wedding of Georgianna and Bob Lee.

Papa, of course, was a loser—no fee. For him, that was the big one that got away!

※

But these things were mere trifles compared with the woe of "Weepy" Wilson. Weepy was the town's enterprising undertaker, with a sideline of tombstones. He never missed an opportunity to be helpful, whether it was sitting up with the sick or assisting an old lady crossing the street. He always spoke in polite, subdued tones. And the town wag said the only time he ever really looked cheerful was during a 'grippe epidemic or the typhoid season,

Mama, who was rather frail, said the first time she met him she had the feeling he was "measuring her for size."

Weepy reportedly was in silent glee when he heard that Mr. Johnson was "lookin' to die." He immediately appraised his meager stock of caskets and realized that he had nothing suitable for a rich broker from Chicago. And he must "always be helpful and able to serve with the needs of anyone in sorrow"—so he told himself.

That very day he had the Memphis Wholesale Casket Company ship him a beautiful bronze coffin—gleaming and expensive—which he placed in the front of his showroom. He was ready. He had not let his enthusiasm carry him away entirely, however, He had exercised what he considered very shrewd judgment about it.

Mr. Johnson was a small man—not over five feet, six inches tall and weighing around 135 pounds. Because of this, Weepy ordered the small size of the high-priced casket, which he would sell to the prospective widow at the large-sized price. As he stood there in the shop, almost smiling over the fine profit he would make, Sam Dobson walked in.

"Hi, Weepy." After a pause, Sam walked over and peeped under the lid of the bronze casket.

"I thought maybe you were holding a dress rehearsal." This sally was followed by a loud guffaw. Then Sam took a serious tone,

"I'd roll that 'golden Calf' to the back of the room, if I were you. You may be a little previous. Old Doc Pigg just told me he was better."

The undertaker "had been took."

He carried the bronze casket item on his books for the next few years but he rarely had much hope. In fact, he soon realized that it probably would not be sold at any price. Most of the male citizens of that area were tall and hefty.

But wait—Weepy finally did get a chance.

The richest man in the county was Alonzo Cobb, a money lender, who lived on a farm a few miles out of town. He had been a frugal man all of his life, not-withstanding his substantial wealth; but when he died suddenly in the night, his widow unexpectedly took a fancy to Weepy's "Golden Calf." Weepy sold it to her, after a quick mark-up without batting an eye. The deceased, Mr. Cobb, was a tall man—well over six feet.

The tall Mr. Cobb was buried in the small-sized coffin. That's why the tales about the wedding of Georgianna and Bob Lee invariably end with the "So help me God" statement that when Weepy Wilson buried Alonzo Cobb he sawed several inches off the old man's legs to wedge him into his beautiful bronze casket.

At least that's the way the story goes.

❧

So much for the wedding that wasn't there. I had been drawn into the excitement, naturally, but I had been around and on the fringes of too many nuptial events to generate more than temporary interest. It was over. There were other things to occupy my thoughts.

I didn't forget the amiable Mr. Johnson though. As soon as we heard he was back home in Chicago, I asked Mama to let me write him a card. She helped me select one, and I wrote on it, wishing him a complete recovery, I signed it and added a line saying I hoped he would come back to see us. I also wrote: "I have just read a good book, "Penrod,"[24] by Booth Tarkington It's a boy's book, but I didn't mind."

In a week or so Mama and Papa unexpectedly called me into the living room from a romp outside. I thought they looked at me in an odd way.

"Sit down, honey," Mama said. "Papa has something to tell you. I think it's something you'll like."

My face, I'm sure, was a study in blank wonderment. Papa said: "We have a letter from your very good friend, Mr. Johnson. I think our ship may have come in at last."

Suddenly I was frozen. I couldn't think. I almost couldn't breathe.

Papa put on his glasses and took a letter from an envelope.

"Here's what he says:

"Tell my pal Hope that it's all right to read and enjoy boy's books, but I think she should have a girl's bicycle. Go to the Express Company; it should be there by the time you receive this letter!"

My heart flip-flopped.

"Papa, can we go now?" I shouted.

"Old Dick is already hitched," he said. "Come on."

It was waiting for me at the Express office. Papa quickly pried open the crate.

Wonder of wonders—it was a "Blue Bird" like the latest picture in the catalog!

And it was exactly right for me. It had a basket for my schoolbooks. It had a bell and a headlight with a battery and mud guard and a coaster brake—just as I had longed for. It had a springy seat and I rode it all the way home.

Then I ran in the house and cried.

After that I pedaled off on my "Blue Bird" in a flight of fanciful enchantment and rode . . . and rode . . . and rode!

Epilogue

MY STORY CLOSES.

I have told you of the weddings I saw and lived and knew as family legend.

A thousand weddings?

Perhaps there were more than a thousand—in reality, in my dreams, in the inevitable enlargement of things and events through the eyes of childhood.

I look back and I see Papa and Mama and a great passing throng of events, now ecstacy [*sic* ecstasy], now ineffable sadness, with a host of brides and bridegrooms, all in the dreamy accoutrements of Hymen,[1] marching in unending procession. I treasure the memories.

I hope the telling has entertained you,

And so . . . with love to all, goodbye.

NOTES

Introduction

1. "Prominent County Native Dies," *Dresden Enterprise* (hereafter *DE*), June 19, 1985, 3.
2. Hope Hart, "Among Kith and Kin," *DE*, February 9, 1973, 12.
3. Prenshaw, *Composing Selves: Southern Women and Autobiography* (Baton Rouge: Louisiana State University Press, 2011), 5, 26.
4. Prenshaw, *Composing*, 33.
5. Prenshaw, *Composing*, 37, 32–34.
6. Prenshaw, *Composing*, 27.
7. Cathryn Halverson, *Playing House in the American West: Western Women's Life Narratives, 1839–1987* (Tuscaloosa: University of Alabama Press, 2013), 1.
8. Judith (Judy) K. Lambert, Assignment of Rights to Unpublished Manuscript "A Thousand Weddings," Weakley County Historical and Genealogical Society, Martin, Tennessee, January 4, 2010. Notarized by Laura F. Phillips, Notary Public, Madison County, Tennessee.
9. Nelson Key Hart, "Sterling Reece Hart" and "Memoirs," Minutes of the Memphis Conference of the *Methodist Episcopal Church South Journal* (hereafter *MCJ*), 1957, 114.
10. Hart, "Kith," *DE*, February 9, 1973, 12. The survival food comes from the leaves of poke weeds; the berries are toxic, especially to children.
11. Hart, "Kith," *DE*, February 9, 1973, 12.
12. The territory stretched from Paducah, Kentucky, to the state of Mississippi's northern limit.
13. Due to abundant rainfall and soil type, early nineteenth-century land surveyor and speculator Memucan Hunt Howard wondered, however seriously, if the Chickasaws considered "the country leaked too much." Memucan Hunt Howard, "Recollections of Memucan Hunt Howard," *American History Magazine*, vii (January 1902), 64–65; Marvin Downing, "Old Christmasville: Its Lure and Lore," *Journal of the Jackson Purchase Historical Society* (hereafter *JJPHS*), July 1979, 34–44. (Such articles are also online at https:digitalcommons.murray

state.edu/jphs.) Indeed, there were several notable Purchase area rivers and numerous creeks making travel and occupational challenges. Sam McGowan, *West Tennessee: The Land Between the Rivers* (Lexington, KY: CreateSpace Independent Publishing Platform, 2018); Virginia C. Vaughan, *Weakley County* (Memphis: Memphis State University Press, 1983), 1–4. Retired Tennessee judge David Hayes claimed the Chickasaws called the area "the land of shakes" due to the frequent seismic activity. David G. Hayes, *The Historic Reelfoot Lake Region: An Early History of the People and Places of Western Obion and Present-Day Lake County* (Collierville, TN: InstantPublisher.com, Inc., 2017), 29.

14. Fred S. Rolater, "Treaties," *Tennessee Encyclopedia* (hereafter *TE*), Tennessee Historical Society; McGowan, *West Tennessee*, 69. Some sources differ about Chickasaw activity in the Jackson Purchase following the treaty ratification. Some American occupants last saw Chickasaw hunting temporarily on the Obion River in Weakley County during late 1820. Vaughan, *Weakley County*, 6, 9–10. The 1820 census showed some American squatters were already in the Jackson Purchase. E. Harrell Phillips, "Early Methodism in the Jackson Purchase: Before 1840," *Methodism in the Memphis Conference: 1840–1990*, ed. Kenneth Wilkerson (Memphis, TN: Memphis Conference Commission on Archives and History, 1990), 9.

15. Marvin Downing, "John Christmas McLemore," *TE*. More about McLemore and Christmasville's history in Carroll County, adjacent to Henry and Weakley Counties, is in Downing, "Old Christmasville," *JJPHS*, 34–44. The settlement likely began about the same time as Little Zion. Both flourished for a while but eventually waned into only people's memories. For more on McLemore's widespread land dealings, see Marvin Downing, "John Christmas McLemore: 19th Century Tennessee Land Speculator," *Tennessee Historical Quarterly* 42, no. 3 (1983): 254–65.

16. W. O. Inman, *Pen Sketches, Henry County, Tennessee* (Paris, TN: Henry County Historical Society, 1976), 26–27, 30, 67.

17. R. Scott Williams, *The Accidental Fame and Lack of Fortune of West Tennessee's David Crockett* (Union City, TN: TheRealDavidCrockett.com, 2021) 1, 4, 8, 15–18.

18. "Sampson Edward Kennedy," findagrave.com. His wife was "Nancy Killebrew Kennedy," findagrave.com. As early as 1823, there were Killebrews in the Cane Creek area of Palmersville. Vaughan, *Weakley County*, 11–12.

19. Hart, "Kith," *DE*, February 9, 1973, 12; Jesse King heirs et al., deed to Sampson Kennedy dated October 22, 1821, agreed January 6, 1831, Henry County. The transaction was in 1831, amounting to $262 for 121 acres of land in Weakley

County's 2nd range, 8th section 12th Surveyor's District. The document refers to an unrecorded warrant. *Weakley County Deed Book A–B*, Weakley County Courthouse, Dresden, Tennessee, 376.
20. Samuel Cole Williams, *Beginnings of West Tennessee in the Land of the Chickasaws, 1541–1841* (Nashville, Tennessee, Blue and Gray Press, 1971), 30.
21. Inman, *Pen Sketches*, 12, 15.
22. Vaughan, *Weakley County*, 38. Sometimes, as Crockett did, a man and a friend or two came temporarily just to choose a plot and make some preparatory improvements before fetching their family. Inman, *Pen Sketches*, 32, 34; Vaughan, *Weakley County*, 10–12.
23. Vaughan, *Weakley County*, 4.
24. "Nelson Kennedy," findagrave.com. There were also Killebrews in the Palmersville area. Vaughan, *Weakley County*, 12.
25. "Sterling Reece Hart," findagrave.com; Hope Hart, "Kith," *DE*, March 23, 1973, 6.
26. "Sterling Reece Hart," findagrave.com; Hart, "Kith," *DE*, March 9, 1973, 16.
27. Inman, *Pen Sketches*, 33. By 1850–1860, Tennessee possessed "an increasing population, expanding agriculture, developing industry, and rapidly growing towns." The greatest population concentration was in three Nashville Basin Counties and three southwestern cotton growing units near Memphis. Because agriculture was the main economic occupation, social and economic status identified with farming. Robert E. Corlew, *Tennessee: A Short History* (Knoxville: University of Tennessee Press, 2003), 220–28, 230.
28. Williams, *Beginnings*, 134.
29. Inman, *Pen Sketches*, 39–41.
30. Navigation of the shallow upper North Fork of the Obion River was challenging due to soft soil allowing dislodged trees to block passage. Otherwise, Vaughan speculated, settlers could have come into northwest Tennessee by watercraft. Vaughan, *Weakley County*, 38. However, a north-south link between Hickman, Fulton County, Kentucky and Union City, Obion County, Tennessee, both contiguous counties, happened after the Civil War began. Significantly, Hickman had immediate access to the Mississippi River. Weakley County got a Nashville connection during that conflict. Ron D. Bryant, "Fulton County," *The Kentucky Encyclopedia*, ed. John E. Kleber (Lexington: University Press of Kentucky, 1992), 360–36; Vaughan, *Weakley County*, 38, 41.
31. Donald L. Winters, "Agriculture," *TE*. For a general review of Southern agriculture around the mid-1800s, see Melissa Walker and James C. Cobb, eds. *Agriculture and Industry* (Chapel Hill: The University of North Carolina Press, 2008), 3–29.

32. Winters, "Agriculture," *TE*. Vaughan, *Weakley County*, 29, 43. By 1860, Henry and Weakley County farmers contributed to Tennessee being among the top five southern cotton-growing states and the leading corn growing southern state. Vaughan, *Weakley County*, 29, 43. Murray Miles, "Tobacco," *TE*; Wayne C. Moore, "Cotton," *TE*; Wayne C. Moore, "Corn," *TE*; and Inman, *Pen Sketches*, 50–52.
33. Vaughan, *Weakley County*, 43.
34. In Middle Tennessee, slaves comprised 29 percent of the population, primarily in three Nashville Basin counties. The East Tennessee slave population was the smallest at 9 percent. Corlew, *Tennessee*, 220, 224, and 227; Paul H. Bergeron, Jeannette Keith, and Stephen V. Ash, *Tennesseans and Their History* (Knoxville: University of Tennessee, 1999), 120 and 122.
35. Corlew, *Tennessee*, 210, 218. Tennessee—Slave Population—As Reported in the 1860 Census, Map. E. Hegesheimer, cartographer and Th. Leonhardt, engraver, *Map Showing the Distribution of the Slave Population of the United States-Compiled from the Census of 1860*, Census Office, Department of the Interior (Washington D.C., Sept. 9th, 1861). It is further identified as being "Sold for the Benefit of the Sick and Wounded Soldiers of the US Army." A copy in the Library of Congress in Washington, DC, was the source of this data. Charles A. Reeves, Jr., TN 1860 Slave Pop.Map.jpg https://teachtnhistory.org/file5.; Donald L. Winters, *Tennessee Farming, Tennessee Farmers: Antebellum Agriculture in the Upper South* (Knoxville: University of Tennessee Press, 1994), 135–36.
36. Bergeron, *Tennesseans*, 120, 122–24.
37. Corlew, *Tennessee*, 220, 224–25; Robert Tracy McKenzie, "Reconstruction," *TE*.
38. Historian David M. Kennedy believed issues about slavery in the western territories "the proximate cause of the Civil War." Richard White, *The Republic for Which It Stands: The United States during Reconstruction and the Gilded Age, 1865–1896* (New York: Oxford University Press, 2017), xvii. Historian David M. Potter saw that during the 1850s "slavery was indeed the overshadowing problem." David M. Potter, *The Impending Crisis, 1848–1861* (New York: Harper & Row, 1976), xiv. The highly respected scholar developed a well-established narrative of national events preceding the Civil War, covering from the Mexican Cession to the Fort Sumter attack of April 1861, including the Compromise of 1850, the Kansas-Nebraska Act, the Lincoln-Douglas debates, the 1860 Presidential election, and formation of the Confederate States of America.
39. In a referendum of June 8, 1861, 105,000 citizens preferred secession and 47,000 opposed withdrawal from the Union; by contrast, 33,000 East Tennesseans balloted to remain with the Union over 14,000 for withdrawal. Larry H. Whiteaker, "Civil War," *TE*.

40. Those wanting independence numbered 29,127 in contrast to the 6,117 residents who were against separation. "Table 4. Votes for and against Separaton of Tennessee from the Union," *Nashville Union and American*, June 16, 1861, cited in Corlew, *Tennessee*, 294.
41. For names of several Confederate and Union volunteers, see Vaughan, *Weakley County*, 49.
42. Webb, "Henry County," *TE*.
43. Vaughan, *Weakley County*, 49.
44. Whiteaker, "Civil War," *TE*. For a Weakley County clash of Federal and Confederate forces near the Obion River, see Dieter Ullrich, "They Met at Lockridge's Mills," West Tennessee Historical Society Papers (hereafter WTHSP) 51, 1997, 1–20; and Lonnie E. Maness, "Capt. Charles Cooper Nott and the Battle of Lockridge's Mills," *JJPHS*, June 1975, 12–20. In December 1863, USA general Thomas Kilby Smith camped at Dresden "and foraged heavily on the people in the area." Further, "guerrilla bands and bushwhackers infested the county during the war inflicting much damage." Those outlaws killed between 15 and 20 persons in the Dresden vicinity, one being a CSA Captain. Vaughan, *Weakley County*, 49.
45. In December 1862, Forrest's excursion seized much needed Union supplies while also capturing Humboldt and Trenton in Gibson County. Similarly, in 1864 his cavalry harassed Union posts, hindered rail capabilities, interdicted quartermaster, captured numerous prisoners. Whiteaker, "Civil War," *TE*; McGowan, *West Tennessee*, 158, 160; and Lonnie E. Maness, *An Untutored Genius: The Military Career of General Nathan Bedford Forrest* (Oxford, Mississippi: Guild Bindery Press, 1990), 106, 105.
46. Confederate troops were under the command of General Sterling Price. About March 8, 1862, That US victory strengthened the Union's hold in that area. William L. Shea and Earl J. Hess, *Pea Ridge: Civil War Campaign in the West* (Chapel Hill: University of North Carolina Press, 1992), 307–17.
47. Hart, "Weddings," chap. 8, "Grandma: 95 Pounds of Grit," 158; Hart, "Kith," *DE*, April 6, 1973, 5. An obituary claimed him as a Confederate officer. *MCJ* 1957, 114.
48. "Capt William Reuben 'Bill' McWherter," findagrave.com; "Capt. Thomas Leroy 'Roy' Killebrew," findagrave.com.
49. John Mark Hart was a Confederate 2nd Lt. in Company H of the Texas 15th Calvary Scouting Battalion. "John Mark Hart," findagrave.com; Hart, "Kith," *DE*, March 23, 1973, 6.
50. Hart, "Weddings," chap. 9, "The Mail-Order Bride," 175; "Calvin Simpson Moore," ancestry.com; Arthur Wyllie, *Tennessee Confederate Pensions* (New

York: Barnes and Noble, 2014), 370; "Pvt. James Franklin Killebrew," findagrave.com.
51. Silas's parents moved to Middle Tennessee where he was born in Davidson County. Hope Hart gave his death date as 1877, maybe a typo, whereas findagrave.com recorded it as 1897, the year after Silas Moore made his will. Hart, "Kith," *DE*, April 6, 1973, 5; "Silas Reuben Moore," findagrave.com.
52. She was the daughter of Nelson's son Isaac Kennedy (1817–1841) and Mary (Polly) Fields Kennedy (1817–1906). "Mary 'Polly' Fields Martin," findagrave.com; "Sarah Angeline Fields Kennedy," findagrave.com; Hart, "Kith," *DE*, February 9, 1973, 12. Angeline was a cousin of Martha "Mattie" Kennedy Hart, Hope Hart's mother. Nelson Kennedy was the father of Martha "Mattie" Howard Kennedy, Hope Hart's mother.
53. Their children were William Issac Moore (1862–1932), Emma Smith Moore Narron (1863–1941), Martha Emily Moore (1864–1961), and Mary Viola Moore (1866–1877). "William Issac Moore," findagrave.com; "Emma Smith Moore Narron," findagrave.com; "Martha Emily Moore," findagrave.com. Hope Hart did not list those children nor did she mention Calvin and Sarah Angeline Moore being in Illinois. There was an unusually brief time between the birth of Emma Smith Moore, August 8, 1863, and the arrival of Martha Emily Moore, February 2, 1864. "Mary Viola Moore," findagrave.com. However, Hope Hart only listed three children by Calvin Simpson Moore's first marriage. Hart, "Kith," *DE*, April 6, 1973, 5.
54. "Calvin Simpson Moore," findagrave.com.
55. "Life was hardest for southern farm women. They worked longer and harder than other members of the family and enjoyed the least recreation and social life." Gilbert C. Fite, *Cotton Fields No More: Southern Agriculture 1865–1980* (Lexington: The University Press of Kentucky, 1984), 1. "Washday in these homes must have made the strongest women shudder." Dorothy Schneider and Carl J. Schneider, *American Women in the Progressive Era, 1900–1920* (New York: Facts on File, Inc., 1993), 36. Like Paralee, most other country and small-towhousewives made clothes for their families. Schneider, *American Women*, 29. Small "Southern farmers lived little differently in 1900 than they had in 1880." How could they improve their lot? That was the basic but unanswered question in the late nineteenth and early twentieth centuries throughout the rural South." Schneider, *American Women*, 47.
56. Hart, "Weddings," chap. 7, "When Mama Laughed Again," 135.
57. Robert Tracy McKenzie, "Reconstruction," *TE*.
58. The total property loss of Tennessee farmers was about 200 million dollars, a figure 2.5 times more than yearly agricultural output around 1860. Winters, "Agriculture," *TE*; Winters, *Tennessee Farming*, 192–93.

59. Agricultural historian Gilbert C. Fite noted that after the war Southern "agriculture was in serious disarray." Nonetheless, the more independent and self-sufficient small white farmers generally more "quickly overcame most adverse economic effects of the fighting." Fite, *Cotton Fields*, 1.
60. Donald L. Winters concluded, "Tennessee never regained the national agricultural importance it held on the eve of the Civil War. At that time, no other state ranked as high in so many different products." Winters, "Agriculture," *TE;* Whiteaker, "Civil War," *TE*.
61. In 1880, Weakley was "the largest corn producing county in the state." Vaughan, *Weakley County*, 28.
62. Moore, "Cotton." Vaughan, *Weakley County*, 28. Those small and large farmers who married cotton were trapped economically. Fite, *Cotton Fields*, 6–7, 27; Moore, "*Cotton*," *TE*. Compounding rural woes, farm prices were low from the 1870s to 1900. Fite, *Cotton Fields*, 28. Some historians considered economic conditions a great depression between 1873 and 1896. Eric Foner, *Reconstruction: America's Unfinished Revolution, 1863–1877* (New York: Harper Perennial Modern Classics, 1988), 535; Eric Hobsbawn, *The Age of Empire, 1875–1914* (New York: Vintage Books, 1989), 35–36. Yet, in the 1865–1896 era, Richard White noted the general importance of farm products, especially cotton, extremely important to the economy and "critical to the development of capitalism." Richard White, *The Republic*), 886. More generally, White delved into the social, economic, and political events and forces of those years.
63. Winters, "Agriculture," *TE*.
64. Fite, *Cotton Fields*, 28, 22.
65. McGowan, *West Tennessee*, 310–11. Weakley County schools were likely representative of other rural counties with scattered populations. Vaughan, *Weakley County*, 23–24.
66. "Martha 'Mattie' Nelson Kennedy," findagrave.com.
67. Hart, "Memoirs," *MCJ* 1957, 114. Their mutual childhood attraction led to Reece, age 21, and Mattie, age 20, marrying in mid-December 1883. Hart, "Kith," *DE*, February 9, 1973, 12, March 16, 1973, 13.
68. Weakley County instructors taught 74 days a year and received $35.00 a month. Vaughan, *Weakley County*, 23–24. McGowan, *West Tennessee*, 311.
69. "Eva Elna Hart Harbert," findagrave.com.
70. "Ray Kennedy Hart," findagrave.com.
71. "Martha Reece Hart," findagrave.com.
72. "Ruth Lee Hart," findagrave.com.
73. "Hope Howard Hart," findagrave.com. Somewhat intriguing, in Hope Hart's family newspaper series, she did not mention Eva Elna, Martha Reece, and Ruth Lee. Hart, "Kith," *DE*, March 30, 1973, 16.

74. Hart, "Weddings," chap. 6, "Oh, Dem Golden Slippers," 111–12."
75. *MCJ* 1957, 114.
76. Phillips, "Early Methodism," 16; Louis B. Wright, *Culture on the Moving Frontier* (New York: Harper & Row, 1961), 175–76.
77. Phillips, "Early Methodism," 14; Elton Watlington, "Organization and Early Beginnings: 1840–1859," *Methodism in the Memphis Conference: 1840–1990*, ed. Kenneth Wilkerson (Memphis: Memphis Conference Commission on Archives and History, 1990), 25. The denomination routinely checked all minister's character. Phillips, *Early Methodism*, 9; John B. McFerrin, *Methodism in Tennessee* (Nashville: A. H. Redford, 1873), vol. 3, 182–83, 193–94.
78. Watlington, "Organization," 30.
79. Phillips, "Early Methodism," 10. Arminianism especially emphasized man's free will regarding grace in contrast to Calvinism that adhered to predestination. Phillips, "Early Methodism," 14; Watlington, "Organization," 25–26; Phillips, "Early Methodism," 14. Samuel Cole Williams believed that the camp meeting "was everywhere salutary." Williams, *Beginnings*, 196.
80. Phillips, "Early Methodism," 17; Watlington, "Organization," in *Methodism in the Memphis Conference: 1840–1990*, ed. Kenneth Wilkerson (Memphis: Memphis Conference Commission on Archives and History, 1990), 20–21.
81. Larry J. Daniel, "The Civil War and Reconstruction: 1860–1869," 40–43.
82. Daniel, "Civil War," 43–44, 48.
83. The Conference encouraged ordained and prospective ministers to study at one of eight two-year colleges scattered within the Purchase. Clarence E. Hare, Jr., "An Expanding Ministry: 1870–1899," *Methodism in the Memphis Conference: 1840–1990*, ed. Kenneth Wilkerson (Memphis: Memphis Conference Commission on Archives and History, 1990), 44, 48; Daniel, "Civil War," 45; Nancy K. Andersen, "Troubles and Triumphs, 1900–1939," *Methodism in the Memphis Conference: 1840–1990*, ed. Kenneth Wilkerson (Memphis, Tenn.: Memphis Conference Commission on Archives and History, 1990), 76. Included among those eight were Marvin College in Clinton, Kentucky; McTyeire Institute at McKenzie, Tennessee; and McFerrin College in Martin, Tennessee for both ministerial and laity training. Hare. "Expanding," 53–55, 57.
84. Hare, "Expanding," 57.
85. Andersen, "Troubles," 60–62, 64.
86. Some historians considered American agricultural distress of the 1870s–1890s worldwide. They termed the span as "the Long Depression" of the 1870s or "the Great Depression of 1873–1896." Hobsbawm, *The Age of Empire*, 535; Foner, *Reconstruction*, 535; Hobsbawn, *The Age of Empire*, 35–36.
87. Corlew, *Tennessee*, 501–2, 506. Donald L. Winters' assessment was a bit less rosy. Winters, "Agriculture," *TE*.

88. McGowan, *West Tennessee*, 305–6, 310; Fite, *Cotton Fields*, 30–32; ibid., 47, 90.
89. Begun in 1893, Sears, Roebuck and Company was a mail-order business that merchandised by catalog before morphing also into department stores. Some recipients called them wish books. Gordon L. Weil, *Sears, Roebuck, U.S.A.: The Great American Catalog Store and How it Grew* (Briarcliff Manor, N.Y., Stein and Day, 1977), 1–25.
90. McGowan, *West Tennessee*, 306; History.com Editors, "Model T," history.com. Yet, Fite considered the vast majority of small Southern farmers lived in 1900 much as in 1880 with little change by the 1930s. Fite, *Cotton Fields*, 47, 90. In 1900 and following, most American women, rural or urban, did housework without daily assistance. Schneider, *American Women*, 23, 26–27.
91. Hart, "Weddings," chap. 7, "Oh, Dem Golden Slippers," 117–18, 124; *MCJ* 1899, 31; and 1900, 29.
92. "Joe Reese Hart," findagrave.com.
93. "Nelson Key Hart," findagrave.com.
94. *MCJ* 1901, 9; 1902, 26; 1903, 23; and 1904, 21.
95. *MCJ* 1914, 60; 1915, 76; "Prominent," *DE*, June 19, 1985, 3.
96. *MCJ* 1927, 12, 48–49. The appointment times and locations appeared in *MCJ* 1899, 31; 1900, 29; 1901, 9; 1902, 26; 1903, 23; 1904, 21; 1905, 24; 1906, 27; 1907, 29; 1908,26; 1909, 35; 1910, 32; 1911, 41;1912, 39; 1913, 44; 1914, 60; 1915, 76; 1916, 54; 1917, 59; 1918, 59; 1919, 66; 1920, 57; 1921, 72; 1922, 85; 1923, 89; 1924, 79; 1925, 94; 1926, 59; and 1927, 49. The Memphis Conference admitted Sterling Hart to "Full Connection" in 1901 and ordained Deacon, too. In 1903, it ordained him an Elder. *MCJ* 1927, 12, 48–49; *MCJ* 1899, 25, 31. Superannuate meant retirement status due to infirmity, age, or formally stated regulations. The Memphis Conference Minutes dubbed him retired in 1939. *MCJ* 1939, 133–34. In 1957, Nelson Key Hart eulogized his father as having ministered 30 years. The son continued, "From Shiloh (Tennessee) he served charges at Pryorsburg, Sedalia, and Wingo, Kentucky; Obion, Ridgely, Finley, Gleason, Tennessee; Kirksey and Murray, Kentucky; Mason, Trenton, Covington, Curve, and Atwood, Tennessee." Nelson Key Hart, "Memoirs," *MCJ* 1957, 114.
97. "Nelson Kennedy," findagrave.com.
98. "Leroy Simpson Moore," findagrave.com. Hope Hart chose to give him some anonymity.
99. The bride was Weakley County native Ida May Brite Moore (1877–1966) whose parents were Lemuel Dewitt (1836–1913) and America Brite (1840–1891). Widowed Ida recovered to become a McWherter in 1902. "Ida May Brite McWherter," findagrave.com; Hart, "Kith," *DE*, April 6, 1973, 5.
100. Hart, "Weddings," chap. 8, "Grandma: 95 Pounds of Grit," 147–56.
101. *MCJ* 1901, 21–22.

102. "Perry Morton Harbert," findagrave.com.
103. Hope Hart, "Weddings," chap. 5, "Angel Music," 109–10.
104. "Laura Jane Simmons Kennedy," findagrave.com.
105. Providentially, the conference proposed $600 as the annual itinerant salary in 1908 and targeted $1,200 as the standard in 1918. Ministers also accrued some insurance benefits. Andersen, "Troubles," 67.
106. Hart, "Weddings," chap. 10, "A Gambol on the Mississippi," 179–80.
107. Ray Hart graduated from Cumberland College in Lebanon, Tennessee. "Weddings," chap. 4, "Go On with the Marryin' . . .," 85. Cumberland College, originally a Cumberland Presbyterian creation, developed a nationally recognized law department. Corlew, *Tennessee*, 240; "Ray Kennedy Hart," 1930 U.S. Public Census, ancestry.com.
108. "Prominent," *DE*, June 19, 1985, 3.
109. "Joe Reece Hart," *Ft. Myers Press*, Fort Myers, Florida, February 6, 1975.
110. "Nelson K. Hart," *Jackson Sun*, Jackson, Tennessee, May 30, 1998.
111. Hart, "Weddings," chap. 10, "Our Thanks to God," 206.
112. Hart, "Weddings," chap. 10, "A Gambol on the Mississippi," 178–79, chap. 11, "Our Thanks to God," 205–6,
113. Hart, "Weddings," chap. 11, "Our Thanks to God," 205–7.
114. Elaine Knight, synopsis, chap. 2, 1. For quick reference, Elaine Knight, a Weakley County Historical and Genealogical Society manuscript committee member in Martin, developed a typed five-page synopsis of each chapter.
115. Hart, "Weddings," chap. 2, "A Babe at Little Zion," 50.
116. Knight, synopsis, chap. 2, 1.
117. Knight, synopsis, chap. 2, 1.
118. Knight, synopsis, chap. 5 , 2.
119. Hart, "Weddings," chap. 5, "Angel Music," 96–97.
120. Hart, "Weddings," chap. 5, "Angel Music," 97–98; Knight, Synopsis, chap. 5, 2; Hart, "Weddings," chap. 5, "Angel Music," 100; Hart, "Weddings," chap. 5, "Angel Music," 100.
121. Hart, "Weddings," chap. 9, "The Mail-Order Bride," 195–96.
122. Hart, "Weddings," chap. 13, "The One That Got Away," 244–47, 250–51.
123. Knight, synopsis, chap. 12, 4.
124. Hart, "Weddings," chap. 12, "You Learned—or Else," 224–28.
125. Knight, synopsis, chap. 3, 1.
126. Knight, synopsis, chap. 4, 2.
127. Hart, "Weddings," chap. 4, "Go On with the Marryin' . . .," 75–80.
128. Edmund S. Morgan, *American Slavery, American Freedom: The Ordeal of Colonial Virginia* (New York, History Book Club, 2005), 119, 313–15, 325, 329, 338, 376, 380, 385–87, 385, 390–91; Alexander Saxton, *The Rise and Fall of the*

White Republic: Class Politics and Mass Culture in Nineteenth-Century America (New York, Verso, 2003), xiii–xviii, 1–3, 9–17. Saxton examined the origins and impacts of black minstrelsy. Blackface minstrelsy politically supported slavery and "faithfully reproduced the white slaveowners' viewpoint." Saxton, *Rise*, 176, 165–81.

129. Hart, "Weddings," chap. 4, "Go On with the Marryin' . . .," 85, 93.
130. Other lyrics included, "You've got to be taught to hate and fear / You've got to be taught from year to year."
131. He was born about 1835, presumably in Weakley County, Tennessee. No children were noted. "Dick Hutcherson," ancestry.com.
132. Hart, "Weddings," chap. 2, "A Babe at Little Zion," 50, 55–56, 59; and chap. 4, "Go On with the Marryin' . . .," 86.
133. Nelson Key Hart, "Memoirs," *MCJ* 1957, 14.
134. Knight, chap. 2, 1.
135. "Ray Kennedy Hart," findagrave.com; *DE*, May 11, 1962.
136. *Ft. Myers Press*, Fort Myers, Florida, February 6, 1975.
137. *Jackson Sun*, Jackson, TN, May 30, 1998.
138. "Prominent," *DE*, June 19, 2019, 2. The pallbearers were Richard Vaughan, Ned Ray McWherter (1930–2011), David Welles, Jim M. Perry, Tommy Thomas, and Robert Nanney. Hope and Nanney were cousins; his mother was a Hart who linked the surname back to the American Revolution. His unknown-numbered great-grandfather was Silas Moore, an early Palmersville settler. He claimed kin to "tons of others" in Weakley County. Somewhere along the way, Nanney and Ned Ray McWherter learned they were cousins. Robert Nanney to Marvin Downing, March 2, 2021, 11:03:01 a.m., 11:06:40 a.m. and 01:43 p.m., emails in Downing's possession. The most publicly known McWherter to emerge from the Little Zion-Palmersville local was McWherter, the prominent Weakley County businessman and Democratic politician. Successively, he served in the Tennessee House of Representatives 1969–1987, as House Speaker from 1973–1987, and as a popular Governor 1987–1995. Carroll Van West, "Ned Ray McWherter," *TE*. See also Billy Stair, *The Life and Career of Ned McWherter* (Nashville, Tennessee: State Public Affairs Office, 2011), 1–5; and "Ned Ray McWherter," findagrave.com.

Chapter 1

1. A parsonage is a pastor's residence usually provided by the denomination or the local church. For a broader view of West Tennessee families; see also Edward Walker Duck, "Memories of Family Life in West Tennessee from Around 1890 to 1910," WTHSP 25, 1971, 26–46.

2. According to the Methodist Memphis Conference appointments in late 1905, Reverend Sterling Reece Hart went to Obion, Obion County, Tennessee, immediately west of Weakley County and bordering southwest Kentucky. *Memphis Conference Minutes Journal* (hereafter *MCJ*) 1904, 21, 151; and *MCJ* 1905, 24, 227.
3. Papa was the local Methodist minister Reverend Sterling Reece Hart. His older family members called him Reece. Those seven family members were the father Sterling Reece Hart (1862–1956), mother Martha "Mattie" Nelson Kennedy Hart (1863–1945), sister Eva Elna Hart (Harbert) (1884–1907), brother Ray Kennedy Hart (1887–1967), Hope Howard Hart (1897–1985), brother "Joe" Reese Green Hart (1901–1998), and brother Nelson Key Hart (1901–1975). In the 1890s, the Hart's lost daughters Martha Reese Hart (1890–1892) and Ruth Lee Hart (1893–1896), "Sterling Reece Hart,"findagrave.com.
4. Hope Hart did not explain the background of the name Eleanor, and mostly referred to her just as Sister.
5. Whatever its origin, Joe was the commonly known name for this brother.
6. McGuffey Readers were general use textbooks for grades 1–6 in American schools from the mid-1800s into the 1900s. They contained a "strong emphasis on moral integrity and individualism." Consumers bought in excess of 150,000 volumes as late as 1983. Dolores P. Sullivan, *William Holmes McGuffey: Schoolmaster to the Nation* (Rutherford, N.J.: Fairleigh Dickinson University Press, 1994), 7, 9, 17, 191, 200, 204, 214.
7. Hope Hart possibly was eight years old at the time.
8. Sears, Roebuck and Company, incorporated by Richard Sears and Alvah Roebuck in 1893, was a mail-order business that merchandised by catalog before morphing also into department stores. Chris Isidore, "Sears' Extraordinary History: A Timeline," Cable News Network, https://www.cnn.com/interactive/2018/10/business/sears-timeline/index.html. Some catalog recipients also referred to them as wish books. Weil, *Sears*, 1–25.
9. Hope Hart generally used aliases, possibly because of legal issues. Consequently, the manuscript editor did not search for most persons.
10. "When his ships came in," a variation of "when my ship comes in," meant when a person was financially able or successful fortuitously.
11. Commonly in the American South, supper was the evening meal.
12. For decades before electrical service, many Southern households lighted their houses with kerosene lamps.
13. Eleanor would then be about twenty or twenty-one instead of nearing eighteen.
14. "Hearts and Flowers," subtitled "A New Flower Song," was published in the 1890s. Theodore M. Tobani and Mary D. Brine, "Hearts and Flowers," *DigitalCommons@UMaine*.

15. "Love is Fair," supposedly a song title of the early 1900s, was not found.
16. Joseph Eastburn Winner's "Little Brown Jug" was a novelty song from the days of American minstrel shows. Norm Cohen, *American Folk Songs: A Regional Encyclopedia* (Westport Conn: Greenwood Press, 2008), vol. 2, 652; and Theodore Raph, *The American Song Treasury* (Garden City, NY: Dover Publications, 1986), 171.
17. Alamo is the county seat of Crockett County in central West Tennessee around thirty miles east of the Mississippi River. The town and Crockett County names honored the famous David Crockett, aka Davy Crockett. Annie Laurie James, "Crockett County," TE. It took several efforts between 1845 and 1872, to create Crockett County, "a living memorial to Davy Crockett," 38. Ernest R. Pounds, compiler and editor, *An Early History of Gibson County and its Communities* (Clarksville, Tennessee: Jostens Printing and Publishing, 2011), 68.
18. The Methodist Discipline is a compilation of United Methodist Church General Conference policy decisions for more than two centuries. It contains the guidelines and processes of United Methodist governance. Brian K, Milford, editor, *The Book of Discipline of the United Methodist Church* (Nashville, TN: The United Methodist Publishing House, 2016), v.
19. The Obion River of upper northwest Tennessee consists of four major branches, being the North Fork, Middle Fork, South Fork, and Rutherford Fork. Once united into one stream it flows into the Mississippi River. Vaughan, *Weakley County*, 3–4.
20. Mainly formed around 1811, Reelfoot Lake is a shallow body in parts of Lake and Obion Counties in northwestern most northwest Tennessee just east of the Mississippi River. Hayes, *Reelfoot*, 1–2, 27–29.
21. The Ringling Brothers Circus began about 1884 and evolved thereafter. The last of the seven Ringling brothers, founders of their entertainment, died in 1936. John Cullhane, *The American Circus, An Illustrated History* (New York: Henry Holt and Company, 1991), 145–62, 403.
22. Diphtheria is a contagious bacterial throat infection that impairs breathing and sometimes becomes fatal. It was common in the United States prior to the 1920s when vaccines were developed. Centers for Disease Control. "Diphtheria," cdc.gov.
23. In 1904, the Louisiana Purchase Exposition at St. Louis, Missouri, commemorated the Louisiana Purchase and its exploration. The more common name was the St. Louis World's Fair. John Drabble, "A World on Display: The St. Louis World's Fair of 1904," American Historical Review 101 (Oct. 1996): 1168. In 1903–1904, Andrew B. Sterling and Kerry Mills, composers of "Meet Me in St. Louis, Louis," capitalized on the world's fair craze. Raph, The American Song, 295–99.

Chapter 2

1. Little Zion, likely begun early in the 1800s, was a small community with numerous Hope Hart relatives in northern Weakley County near Cane Creek and the North Fork of the Obion River. Hart, "Kith," *DE*, February 9, 1973, 12. Little Zion Church became a cultural feature in Weakley County. The primary coordinates for the Little Zion Church, marked now only by a cemetery, place it within the TN 38241 zip code delivery area. That location in northwest Tennessee is near the following communities: Cottage Grove, TN (4.3 miles E); Dresden, TN (10.1 miles WSW); Gleason, TN (11.3 miles SSW; Paris, TN (13.5 miles ESE); and Palmersville, TN (3.1 miles NW. Home-TownLocator, "Little Zion Church in Weakley County, TN (cultural)," tennessee.hometownlocator.com. Virginia Clark Vaughan, "Weakley County," *TE*. David W. Webb, "Henry County," *TE*.
2. Alice Ruth Moore Killebrew (1877–1962), Sterling Hart's youngest half-sister and Hope Hart's Aunt, was the fifth child of Calvin Simpson Moore (1837–1901) and Ruth Paralee McWherter Hart Moore. After both losing their first spouse earlier in the 1860s, Calvin and Paralee entered their second marriage in 1869; "Alice Ruth Moore Killebrew," findagrave.com.
3. Billy was William Thomas Killebrew (1869–1943) of Dresden, Weakley County, Tennessee, the Weakley County Circuit Clerk, 1898–1906. Vaughan, *Weakley County*, 129. "William Thomas Killebrew," findagrave.com.
4. Primitive Baptists, then and now, base their beliefs solely on the King James Version of the Bible of 1611. They do not support any religious practice if it is not in that Bible. They patterned their worship on early New Testament church custom, which is preaching, praying, and non-instrumental singing. In this case, the name Primitive means original. Howard Dorgan, "'Old Time' Baptists," *TE*.
5. Papa, often called Reece, was Sterling Reece Hart (1862–1956), the father of Hope Hart.
6. Grandpa was Calvin Simpson Moore. By his marriage to Paralee Hart, he became Sterling Reece Hart's stepfather and Hope Hart's step-grandfather. "Calvin Simpson Moore," findagrave.com.
7. The Baptist elder, the pastor of the Little Zion congregation, actually was George T. Mayo who was also the Weakley County Court Clerk. He was a longtime friend of the Moores and a Weakley County Courthouse colleague of William Killebrew, the prospective groom. W. T. Killebrew and Alice R. Moore, Marriage License No. 1209, State of Tennessee, Weakley County, Dresden, Tennessee, April 27, 1898. Weakley County Marriages, 1886–November 1898, Book C, 510. Later author Hart referred to him as Elder Maybank.

8. Uncle Pete, Sterling's Hart's half-brother, was Simon Peter Moore (1873–1938), the third child of the Calvin Simpson and Paralee Moore's. "Simon Peter 'SP' Moore," findagrave.com.
9. Ruth Paralee McWherter Hart Moore was the mother of Hope's father Sterling Reece Hart. She first married Palmersville native Thomas Greene Hart in 1857. He died July 30, 1863, in northwest Arkansas during the Civil War. "Ruth Paralee McWherter Moore," findagrave.com.
10. Aunt Susie Stone perhaps was Susan Emmaline Moore, the sister of Calvin Simpson Moore. "Calvin Simpson Moore," *TE*; Hart, "Kith," *DE*, April 6, 1973, 5. If not a blood relative, Aunt Susie might have been a Little Zion resident whom Hope Hart gave the Southern deference of Aunt.
11. A Punch and Judy show, as early as 1870, was a typical puppet show in which husband Punch was comically at odds with wife Judy. It existed as early as 1870.
12. In a typical Southern prejudiced perception, Aunt Susie Stone had in mind a minstrel show and its participants, especially blackface aspects. Whatever Dick Hutcherson's real age, possibly about 63, in her mind he was kind of a legacy of the end man in a minstrel band, the one always with bones and tambourine. Consequently, he represented the lowly "plantation 'nigger'" who excelled at bones, an instrument associated with that race. Alexander Saxton, *The Rise and Fall of the White Republic: Class Politics and Mass Culture in Nineteenth-Century America* (New York: Verso, 2003), 170, 165–82; and "Dick Hutcherson," ancestry.com. Hope Hart's use of the word "boys" may or may not have been in a pejorative sense. Whites, too, often refer to their mature progeny as boys rather than sons.
13. First Monday, a traditional trade day in many West Tennessee counties, happened on the first Monday of a month, weather permitting. Even more people gathered when the date coincided with court dates. Residents readily attended it as seen in a picture of a crowded courthouse street in Trenton, Gibson County, Tennessee during 1901. Frederick R. Culp and Mrs. Robert E. Ross, *Gibson County, Past and Present; The First General History of One of West Tennessee's Pivotal Counties* (Trenton, Tennessee: Gibson County Historical Society, 1961), xvi–1; and Marvin Downing, "'First Monday': A Trade Day and Social Institution in Trenton, Tennessee," WTHSP 46 (1992), 73–83. Richard E. Davis often mentioned Trenton's First Monday in his personal front-page column begun in 1942. Marvin Downing, "Richard E. Davis and the Trenton Herald-Register: An Editor's Return Home, 1941–1942," *JJPHS*, 1992, 29. For more specific information about a regular participant at First Monday, see Marvin Downing, "Jack of All Trades: Early 20th Century Master Mule Trader Walter Bonaparte 'Bone' Phelan of Trenton, Tennessee," *JJPHS* 16 (1988): 27–34.

14. "O Promise Me" was a traditional love song of 1889 often sung at weddings. Raph, *The American Song*, 222.
15. Hope Hart, meant her sister was an instrumental soloist and a vocal accompanist.
16. Uncle Jim, Sterling Reece Hart's half brother, was James Silas Moore (1871–1949), the second son of Calvin and Paralee Moore. "James Silas Moore," findagrave.com.
17. Ellum Tree and the "marryin' squire" refer to S. M. Futrell of Fulton, Kentucky, who became "known as the 'Marrying Squire.'" He was also a Justice of the Peace in Obion County, Tennessee. His fame stemmed from his performing ceremonies for 600 couples along the Kentucky and Tennessee state lines. "The Marrying Squire Catches the Fever Himself and Claims a Kentucky Bride," *The Commercial* (Union City, TN), November 29, 1907, 6. He might have lived on or near Elm Creek in northern Weakley County. Perhaps Hope Hart became a bit creative here with Elm Creek. Many people then, and some people now, pronounced Elm as Ellum.
18. Weakley County Historian Virginia "Jenny" Vaughan made no mention of the Palmersville Academy in her county history.
19. William "Uncle Billy" Killebrew was the Weakley County Circuit Clerk between at least 1898 and 1906. Vaughan, *Weakley County*, 129.
20. Grandma's first marriage was to fellow Palmersville native Thomas Green Hart (1836–1863) on November 11, 1857, four years before the Civil War began in 1861. Her second marriage was to Calvin Simpson Moore. "Ruth Paralee McWherter Moore," findagrave.com, and Thomas Reynolds, "Grave site: Thomas Green Hart," genealogy.com.
21. Though slavery had officially ended in the 1860s, Hope Hart presented Grandpa Moore and Uncle Israel more in a demeaning master-slave relationship than as an employer and employee. Since Uncle Israel was elderly, Hope's use of the term "boys" was pejorative. A reader can only imagine the intimidating words Grandpa Moore said to the alleged underling Israel about the barbeque being ready and tasty.
22. The North Fork of the Obion River begins in northern Weakley County and eventually merges with the Middle Fork, the South Fork, and the Rutherford Fork of the Obion River near Dyersburg, Tennessee. The Obion then flows into the Mississippi River. HomeTownLocator, "North Fork of the Obion," tennessee.hometownlocator.com.
23. Pigeon wing was a folk dance back to at least the 1800s in the United States. It was little more than shaking a leg in the air. According to tradition, in the early 1820s, newly arriving settlers at Christmasville, near McLemoresville, in Carroll County, Tennessee, celebrated with that dance shortly after the

Jackson Purchase opened. Marvin Downing, "Old Christmasville," *JJPHS* 7, 1979, 33–34.
24. "Old Dan Tucker" or "Dan Tucker," a minstrel song by Daniel Emmett, was also a dance tune and a fiddle instrumental. Olin Downes and Elie Siegmeister, *A Treasury of American Song* (New York: Alfred A. Knopf, 1943), 139–41. Surely, Uncle Clabe was a competent fiddler even if Hope Hart chose the descriptive word "scraped."
25. Aunt Annie, Sterling Reece Hart's half-sister and Aunt Alice's older sister, was Sarah Annie Moore Hodges (1877–1962), the fourth child of the second Calvin Moores. "Sarah Annie Moore Hodges," findagrave.com.
26. Morgan's Raiders were famous Confederate cavalrymen led by Tennessean General John Hunt Morgan (1825–1864). Like Nathan Bedford Forrest, Morgan was among the leading Southern cavalrymen and raiders. William P. Morelli, "John Hunt Morgan," *TE*. Maness, *Untutored*, 71, 77, 86. James A. Ramage, "General John Hunt Morgan and His Great Raids into Kentucky," in *The Civil War in Kentucky: Battle for the Bluegrass State*, ed. Kent Masterson Brown (Mason City, Iowa: Savas Publishing Company, 2000), 243–70. Charles P. Roland, *Albert Sidney Johnston: Soldier of Three Republics* (Austin: University of Texas Press, 1984), 335–39, 326–51.
27. Acting the fool meant to be playful or comical.
28. Squire Killebrew was Thomas Leroy Killebrew (1839–1907), the father of William Thomas Killebrew. "William Thomas Killebrew," findagrave.com.
29. Aunt Sammy, Squire Killebrew's wife and William Thomas Killebrew's mother, was Martha Ann Kennedy Killebrew (1841–1928). For an unknown reason, Hope Hart called her "Sammy." "Sarah Angeline Kennedy Moore," findagrave.com. She was also the sister of Sarah Angeline Kennedy (1837–1868), Calvin Simpson Moore's first wife.
30. Henry County, which originated during 1821 in honor of Patrick Henry (1736–1799), lies easterly adjacent to Weakley County, Tennessee. Its western boundary was only a few miles from Little Zion. David W. Webb, "Henry County," *TE*.
31. Shiloh in Hardin County was the site of one of the bloodiest battles of the American Civil War. The clash of April 6–7, 1862, happened in the southeast corner of West Tennessee near the Mississippi and Alabama state lines. James L. McDonough, "Battle of Shiloh," *TE*; and Maness, *Untutored*, 60–66.

Chapter 3

1. Starched meant adding starch, a laundry compound, to textile to stiffen it.
2. About 1900, a stereoscope was originally an apparatus enabling a viewer to see

in three dimension a picture or design. Sometimes the gadget also had a clip to hold special cards for viewing.
3. Venice by Moonlight consisted of lighted images of the famous Italian city of Venice.
4. The post-Cleveland era began after President Grover Cleveland completed his second term, 1893–1897. Hope Hart was born in the latter year.
5. Harness was the equipment put onto horses that connected or hitched one or more of them to whatever they were to pull.
6. Hitching, or hitched, was an idiom or informal name for marrying.
7. Squire in this instance was a Justice of the Peace or a judge.
8. Reverend Hart's saying was a variation of the proverb "Two can live as cheaply as one."
9. Hope was four in September 1901 when the Harts resided at Pryorsburg, Kentucky, in Graves County of south-central West Kentucky or at Sedalia, Kentucky, near Murray, Calloway County, Kentucky close to Henry County, Tennessee. Lon Carter Barton, "Graves County," in *The Kentucky Encyclopedia*, ed. John E. Kleber (Lexington: University Press of Kentucky, 1992), 384–85. Ron D. Bryant, "Calloway County," in *The Kentucky Encyclopedia*, ed. John E. Kleber (Lexington: University Press of Kentucky, 1992), 152–53. *Memphis Conference Minutes Journal* (hereafter *MCJ*) 1900, 29; and *MCJ* 1901, 9.
10. Union suit was a one-piece undergarment combining a shirt and drawers.
11. Children's Day is a special day observed by some Protestant churches with special events for children.
12. Ambrosia was a dessert with coconut and oranges.
13. Adding water to granulated gelatin produces an edible jelly or gel, also called gelatin.
14. Mayfield is the county seat of Graves County, Kentucky, in south central West Kentucky on the Kentucky-Tennessee line. Barton, "Graves County," 384.
15. Aunt Nannie was Sarah Annie Moore Hodges (1877–1962), a sibling of Hope Hart's father Sterling Reece Hart by the Hart-Moore marriage. "Sarah Annie Moore Hodges," findagrave.com.
16. Belshazzar's feast is in the Bible book of Daniel chapter 5. Surely, the wedding Hope Hart described had a better result than King Belshazzar's feast; Belshazzar literally saw handwriting on the wall and died that night. Daniel, 5. NKJV.
17. Hope Hart referred to the wedding in Cana of Galilee at which Jesus turned water into wine. Christianity regards this as Jesus' first miracle. John 2:1–11. NKJV.
18. Uncle Jimmy was James Silas Moore (1871–1949), a sibling of Hope Hart's father Sterling Reece Hart from the Hart-Moore marriage. James was the

second son of the Paralee Hart-Calvin Moore union. "James Silas Moore," findagrave.com.

19. Hope Hart's grandmother and grandfather were Laura Jane Simmons (1823–1908), and Nelson Kennedy (1817–1900). They were parents of Martha "Mattie" Nelson Kennedy Hart, Hope Hart's mother. "Laura Jane Simmons Kennedy," findagrave.com; "Nelson Kennedy," findagrave.com. Hope Hart only referred to her grandfather once as Nelson Kennedy II to distinguish him from an uncle also named Nelson Kennedy. Hart, "Kith," *DE*, February 9, 1973, 12.

20. "Oh Promise Me" was a popular wedding song first published in the 1880s. Raph, *The American Song*, 222.

Chapter 4

1. Papa was Methodist Reverend Sterling Reece Hart (1862–1956), commonly called Reece by older kin.
2. The Methodist Discipline is a compilation of United Methodist Church General Conference policy decisions for than two centuries. It contains the guidelines and processes of United Methodist governance. Brian K, Milford, editor, *The Book of Discipline of the United Methodist Church 2016* (Nashville, TN: The United Methodist Publishing House, 2016), v.
3. "Throw Out the Life Line," composed by a late 19th century Maine-Massachusetts Baptist minister, was well known in several denominations; Hope Hart would naturally be familiar with it in Methodist circles.
4. Supernumerary meant either unnecessary or old.
5. Key, born in 1904, would have been in high school around 1918, meaning the Harts acquired a car around World War I or its end.
6. Sterling Reece Hart and other Methodist ministers were assigned to a circuit within a district. Though appointed to a particular location, traveling preachers also had responsibility to minister to other points in the circuit. The Sterling Hart family had stints in Graves County, Kentucky between 1901 and 1905 at the towns of Pryorsburg, Sedelia, and Wingo and between 1913 and 1915 in Murray, Calloway County, Kentucky. Ron D. Bryant, "Calloway County," in *The Kentucky Encyclopedia*, ed. John E. Kleber (Lexington: University Press of Kentucky, 1992), 152–53. Barton, "Graves County," 384. During the second span, Hope Hart graduated from Murray High School. *MCJ* 1900, 29; *MCJ* 1901, 9; *MCJ* 1902, 26; *MCJ* 1903, 23; *MCJ* 1904, 21; *MCJ* 1912, 39; *MCJ* 1913, 44; and *MCJ* 1914, 60.
7. Hope Hart, born in 1897, would have started school around 1903 about age six in either Sedelia or Wingo, Kentucky. *MCJ* 1902, 26; or *MCJ* 1903, 23.

8. A charge was another name for a circuit or circuit appointment.
9. Upon Reverend Hart's appointment in late 1905, the Harts moved from Wingo, Graves County, in central West Kentucky to Obion County, Tennessee, which borders the southern West Kentucky line. *MCJ* 1904, 21, 151; *MCJ* 1905, 24, 227.
10. The thriving little town was likely Obion, Obion County, Tennessee, which is about 15 miles south of Union City, the Obion County seat. *MCJ* 1904, 21, 151; *MCJ* 1905, 24, 227.
11. Nelson Key Hart (1904–1975), born in Wingo, Kentucky, was the youngest child of the Sterling Reece Hart family.
12. Cumberland University began in 1842 by Cumberland Presbyterians in Lebanon, Tennessee. In 1847, it opened a law school that was Tennessee's first and the first in the trans-Appalachian west. Corlew, *Tennessee*, 240, 242, 535.
13. Fulton, Hickman County, Kentucky, is a West Kentucky town in the Jackson Purchase on the Kentucky-Tennessee line. Fulton is adjacent to South Fulton, Tennessee, and near Union City, Tennessee, and Hickman, Kentucky. Ron D. Bryant, "Hickman," in *The Kentucky Encyclopedia, ed. John E. Kleber (Lexington: University Press of Kentucky, 1992)*, 427. In the late 1800s and early 1900s, it was a significant rail link between New Orleans and Chicago, especially in tending and transmitting bananas. Each September in recent years, Fulton has celebrated that role with its unique one-ton banana pudding. Christine J. Batts, "The Golden Banana and the Banana Festival Story," *JJPHS* 7, no. 1 (June 1979): 44–48. Virginia Honchell Jewell, "Hickman County," in *The Kentucky Encyclopedia*, ed. John E. Kleber (Lexington: University Press of Kentucky, 1992), 42–28. Fulton County, Kentucky, is contiguous with Hickman County and only a short distance from the city of Fulton. Ron D. Bryant, "Fulton County," in *The Kentucky Encyclopedia*, ed. John E. Kleber (Lexington: University Press of Kentucky, 1992), 360–61.

Chapter 5

1. Hope Hart was in school at Obion, Obion County, Tennessee, about 15 miles south of Union City, the county seat of Obion County along the southern West Kentucky line. *MCJ* 1904, 21, 151; *MCJ* 1905, 24, 227; *MCJ* 1906, 27; and *MCJ* 1907, 25.
2. *Pilgrim's Progress* by Englishman John Bunyan, published in 1667, is an allegory generalized about the life of Christians and different stages through which they pass. John Bunyan, *Pilgrim's Progress* (New York: Frederick A. Stokes Company, 1939).

3. *Twenty Thousand Leagues Under the Seas: Tour of the Underwater World* was an early science fiction novel by Frenchman Jules Verne (1828–1905) which appeared in print during 1870. Jules Verne, *Twenty Thousand Leagues Under the Sea* (Charlottesville, Va.: University of Virginia Library, Generic NL Freebook Publisher, 1995).
4. "Thanatopsis" is a poem written about 1813 by the famous American poet William Cullen Bryant (1794–1878). The word means "a consideration of death." Emory Elliott, General Editor, *Columbia Literary History of the United States* (New York: Columbia University, 1988), 281.
5. A Google search did not show a periodical with that title.
6. *The Three Bears, or The Story of the Three Bears* was a children's fairytale story about young Goldlocks and her encounter with a family of friendly bears consisting of a mother, father, and baby bear. James Marshall, *Goldilocks and the Three Bears* (New York: Dial Books for Young Readers, 1988).
7. *The Little Tin Soldier* by the Danish author Hans Christian Andersen (1805–1875) is an 1838 children's story about a little boy, his little tin soldier toy, and the tin soldier's love for a ballerina. H. C. Andersen, *The Brave Tin Soldier* (Champaign, Ill.: Project Gutenberg, 1998).
8. Br'er Fox and Br'er Rabbit were main characters in the Uncle Remus stories of folklorist and author Joel Chandler Harris (1848–1908) of Atlanta, Georgia. His accounts of those and other characters were in dialect of 19th century African-Americans in the South. Emory Elliott, General Editor, *Columbia Literary History of the United States* (New York: Columbia University, 1988), 513–15.
9. "Little Boy Blue" is a traditional children's nursery rhyme dating back to the 1740s. Wiltshire Marlborough, *Little Boy Blue* (New York: Adam Matthew Digital, McLoughlin Bros., 2020).
10. The two quite different creatures set out on a voyage. Edward Lear, *The Owl and the Pussycat* (New York: Lothrop, Lee & Shepard Books, 1991).
11. *Gulliver's Travels* by Englishman Jonathan Swift is a literary satire of his country's life in the 18th century. Jonathan Swift, *Gulliver's Travels* (New York: Knopf, 1991).
12. *Treasure Island* by Robert Louis Stevenson (1850–1894) is a sea adventure about pirates. Robert Louis Stevenson, *Treasure Island* (New York: Scholastic, 19880).
13. "Hero Tales of All Nations" was not found.
14. James Fenimore Cooper (1789–1851) was a prolific writer of novels about the early American frontier and Native Americans. His most famous book was *The Last of the Mohicans*, featuring the hero Natty Bumpo. Emory Elliott, gen. ed., *Columbia Literary History of the United States* (New York: Columbia University, 1988), 241–43.

15. In the late nineteenth century, George Alfred Henty, a prolific English novelist wrote popular historical adventure stories. G. A. Henty, *St. George for England* (Unknown: CreateSpace Independent Publishing Platform, 2013).
16. Horatio Alger (1832–1899) was a prolific American author of inexpensive fiction emphasizing "rags-to-riches successes of young males. Gary Scharnhorst, Horatio Alger, Jr. (Boston: Twayne Publisher, 1980). Emory Elliott, General Editor, *Columbia Literary History of the United States* (New York: Columbia University, 1988), 556–58.
17. *Little Women*, a classic girls' story authored by American novelist Louisa May Alcott (1832–1888), followed the lives of the young daughters of the fictional March family. Louisa May Alcott, *Little Women* (Garden City, N.Y.: Literary Guild of America, 1950). Emory Elliott, General Editor, *Columbia Literary History of the United States* (New York: Columbia University, 1988), 301–4.
18. "Clarion" was supposedly a local weekly newspaper of Obion or Obion County.
19. About 1900 a stereoscope was an apparatus enabling a viewer to see in three dimension a picture or design. The gadget also had a clip to hold special cards for viewing.
20. In 1888, George Eastman formed the Eastman Kodak Company, maker of the first convenient consumer camera. "George Eastman" in Howard Bromberg, editor, *Great Lives from History: The Incredibly Wealthy* (Hackensack, N.J.: Salem Press, Inc., 2011), 300–303. Eastman Kodak Company, "The Birth of Eastman," eastman.com.
21. Due to President Theodore Roosevelt sparing a small Mississippi bear during a 1902 hunting trip there, such stuffed toy bears popularly became called "Teddy Bears." Aida D. Donald, *Lion in the White House, A Life of Theodore Roosevelt* (New York: Basic Books, 2007), 172–73.
22. Velocipede was an early type of bicycle with movement provided by foot pedals on the front axle, some resembled tricycles. Pryor Dodge, *The Bicycle* (New York: Flammarion, 1996), 30–32, 70–71.
23. Hope Hart possibly was possibly referring to the financial Panic of 1907, one of several sporadic economic downturns in United States history. Jon R. Moen and Ellis W. Tallman, "Panic of 1907," *Federal Reserve History*, https://www.federalreservehistory.org/essays/panic-of-1907.
24. Nainsook is a white lightweight muslin, both fine and lightweight.
25. A bolt of cloth is on a roll of specific width and length.
26. Paducah in McCracken County, Kentucky along the Ohio River is the northern most part of the Jackson Purchase and the United Methodist Church Memphis Conference. John E. L. Robertson, "Paducah," in *The Kentucky Encyclopedia*, ed. John E. Kleber (Lexington: University Press of Kentucky, 1992), 705–6.
27. Organdy is a light cotton fabric.

28. The Little Zion community in northeastern Weakley County of extreme northwest Tennessee was the home area of Sterling Reece Hart (1862–1956).
29. Grandma, Hope Hart's paternal grandmother, was Ruth Paralee McWherter Hart Moore, Sterling Hart's mother.
30. Buster Brown clothes were a popular line of children's apparel begun in 1878 by George Warren Brown, originally a shoe manufacturer before venturing into clothing. Buster Brown was a comic character with a Dutch boy hairstyle created for the St. Louis World Fair of 1904.
31. Parcel Post, begun in 1913, was the United States government move to generate competition in product delivery.
32. Trencherman was a hearty eater or otherwise a person who sponged off others.
33. Conference was the Methodist name for both a specific geographic area of ministry and for a usual quarterly or traditional fall ministerial gathering to conduct denominational business. Sterling Hart ministered in the Memphis Conference.
34. Big Sandy is a small West Tennessee town in Benton County along the Tennessee River. Johnathan K. T. Smith, "Benton County," *TE*.
35. The Gibson Girl was the embodiment of an ideal attractive young woman as the 1800s ended and the 1900s began. The original image was the creative drawing generated by artist Charles Dana Gibson.
36. Cousin Lou was possibly Louisa "Lucy B" Killebrew Rawls (1875–1936) and possibly Cousin Irene was her daughter Thomas Irene Rawls Pentecost (1901–1998). Louisa was the daughter of Martha Ann Kennedy Killebrew (1841–1928), who was the sister of Sarah Angeline Kennedy (1837–1868). Sarah was the first wife of Grandpa Calvin Simpson Moore. Louisa "Lucy B" Killebrew Rawls, findagrave.com. It was less likely that Cousin Lou was Louisa Jane Kennedy Pentecost (1839–1928), the sister of Grandpa Calvin Simpson Moore. That Lou would have been an aunt. Hart, "Kith," *DE*, February 9, 1973, 12.
37. Aunt Sally was possibly Sarah Ann Kennedy Bondurant (1841–1919) who married Churchill Edwin Bondurant (1841–1928) in 1869. Hope Hart's mother Martha Nelson Kennedy Hart was a sister of Sarah Ann Kennedy Bondurant. "Sarah Ann Kennedy Bondurant," findagrave.com.
38. The bridegroom was Perry Morton Harbert (1878–1959) of Savannah, Tennessee who married Sister, aka Eva Elna "Eleanor" Hart, on August 23, 1907, at Obion, Obion County, Tennessee. "Perry Morton Harbert," findagrave.com.
39. Savannah, Hardin County, Tennessee is along the Tennessee River near Shiloh, the site of the first ministerial appointment of Sterling Reece Hart. James B. Phillips, "Hardin County," *TE*.
40. The Jamestown Exposition of 1907 was the three hundredth anniversary of the settlement of Jamestown and Virginia. Brian de Ruiter, "Jamestown

Ter-Centennial Exposition of 1907," *Encyclopedia Virginia*, https://www.encyclopediavirginia.org/Jamestown_Ter-Centennial_Exposition_of_1907.

Chapter 6

1. Sister, a.k.a. Eva Elna "Eleanor" Hart (1884–1907), was Hope Hart's oldest sibling who had passed away unexpectedly during late 1907.
2. Mama, Hope Hart's mother, was still grieving the loss of her daughter.
3. The Memphis Conference encompassed the Jackson Purchase area of Western Tennessee and West Kentucky. *MCJ* 1899, 31.
4. The Shiloh appointment was "a testing ground" in part because Methodist ministerial prospects were "On Trial" status for a minimum of two years before receiving full status as a Methodist minister.
5. Shiloh, Hardin County is in extreme southeastern Tennessee along the Tennessee River near the Mississippi and Alabama state lines. The Harts actually resided at Hurley, Tennessee about 1.7 miles from Shiloh and received their mail there. *MCJ* 1899, 31.
6. Shiloh was the site of the major bloody Civil War battle on April 6–7, 1862. Union sources note this as the battle of Pittsburg Landing. James L. McDonough, *Shiloh: In Hell before Night* (Knoxville: University of Tennessee Press, 1977), 152–53. See also Larry J. Daniel, *Shiloh: The Battle That Changed the Civil War* (New York: Simon & Schuster, 1997).
7. Cottage Grove of northwest Henry County, Tennessee in uppermost northwest Tennessee was just under 60 miles from Shiloh, less than the 100 miles Hope Hart gave.
8. Sister (1884–1907) was fifteen in 1899 and sixteen in 1900. Ray (1887–1967), Hope's oldest brother, was twelve in 1899 and thirteen in 1900.
9. Grandmother was Laura Jane Simmons Kennedy (1823–1908), wife of Nelson Kennedy (1817–1900) of Palmersville, Weakley County, Tennessee near the southern border of West Kentucky. Hart, "Kith," *DE*, February 9, 1973, 3.
10. Union suits were a somewhat loose undergarment combining the shirt and the drawers worn by women and men as early as the 1800s.
11. The term "Campbellite" is a somewhat offensive term to Church of Christ adherents in that they profess following only Christ in the New Testament and not the teachings of Alexander Campbell, a prominent spokesman in the Disciples of Christ.
12. "Oh, Dem Golden Slippers" was a popular minstrel song from 1879 with perhaps a seemingly biblical reference, certainly a religious fervor. Richard Jackson, *Popular Songs of Nineteenth-Century America* (New York: Dover Publications, Inc., 1976), 144–47, 276–77.

13. "When the Roll is Called up Yonder" was composed by musician and Methodist Sunday School teacher James Milton Black. His concern about a poor little girl's absence one Sunday inspired him to write the song and tune. Kenneth W. Osbeck, *Amazing Grace, 366 Inspiring Hymn Stories for Daily Devotions* (Grand Rapids, Michigan, Kregel Publications, 1990), 99.
14. A congregant had provided a young butchered hog.
15. Seth Thomas clock was a line produced by Seth Thomas (1785–1859) in the Seth Thomas Seth Thomas Clock Company. His family continued their ownership into the 1930s.
16. "Onward Christian Soldiers" was originally an English children's school festival day as they walked along to a meeting. Sabine Baring-Gould (1834–1924) wrote it in 1865 for such an occasion. Sir Arthur S. Sullivan (1842–1900) of comic opera fame composed the stirring tune. Osbeck, *Amazing Grace*, 308.
17. The U.S. government created Shiloh National Military Park when President Grover Cleveland signed the Congressional bill on December 27, 1894. "The desire to honor and preserve was formed in their (preservationists) mind when they established the isolated and less-visited battle field of Shiloh," the earlier parks being near big cities. The first thought of a park at Shiloh was in 1893, beginning locally and the thought built gradually upwardly. Workers soon after appointed. Surveying started in May 1895. 127. Shiloh National Military Park preceded the National Cemetery there. Timothy B. Smith, *The Golden Age of Battlefield Preservation: The Decade of the 1890s and the Establishment of America's First Five Military Parks* (Knoxville: University of Tennessee Press, 2008), 115, 123, 127.
18. Minnie ball was a conical shaped bullet for muzzle loading firearms.
19. Nathan Bedford Forrest (1821–1877) entered the Civil War as a private and became a Lieutenant General in Confederate cavalry forces. As a superb cavalry officer, he was at the famous battles of Shiloh, Chickamauga, and Franklin, Tennessee and numerous raids and skirmishes in West Tennessee and northern Mississippi. Maness, *Untutored*, 60–66. Brian Steel Wills, *A Battle from the Start: The Life of Nathan Bedford Forrest* (New York: Harper Collins, 1993), 66–69. Brian S. Wills, "Nathan Bedford Forrest," *TE*.
20. Albert Sidney Johnston (1803–1862), previously a U.S. Army officer, became a Confederate general in 1861. While commanding at Shiloh, Tennessee, on April 6, 1862, he was hit by a bullet that severed a femoral artery leading to his death. McDonough, *Shiloh*, 152–153; Maness, *Untutored*, 61–62; Charles P. Roland, *Albert Sidney Johnston: Soldier of Three Republics* (Austin: University of Texas Press, 1984), 335–39.
21. During each calendar quarter, Methodist ministers met at different locations within the Memphis Conference to discuss ministerial matters.

22. Selmer, the county seat of McNairy County, Tennessee is located in lower West Tennessee. Bill Wagoner, "McNair County," *TE*.
23. Grandfather Kennedy was Nelson Kennedy (1817–1900), the father of Martha Nelson "Mattie" Kennedy Hart and Hope Hart's maternal grandfather. His wife was Laura Jane Simmons (1823–1908), Mattie's mother and Hope Hart's maternal grandmother. Hart, "Kith," *DE*, February 13, 1973, 3–4. "Nelson Kennedy," findagrave.com. Nelson had an older uncle Nelson Kennedy who was the older brother of Sampson Kennedy, Hope Hart's great-grandfather.
24. Jackson in central West Tennessee is the county seat of Madison County. Williams, *Beginnings*, 135–36. Emma Inman Williams, *Historic Madison; The Story of Jackson and Madison County, Tennessee* (Jackson, Tenn.: Madison County Historical Society, 1972), 37–39. Harbert Alexander, "Madison County," *TE*.
25. Dresden, Weakley County, Tennessee is the county seat in upper West Tennessee near West Kentucky's southern border. Vaughan, Weakley County, 14.
26. Uncle Potter was Lemuel Potter Moore (1879–1958) who was the last-born child of Calvin Simpson Moore (1837–1901) and Ruth Paralee McWherter Hart Moore (1841–1916) and sibling half-brother of Sterling Reece Hart (1862–1956). "Calvin Simpson Moore," findagrave.com.
27. Little Zion, the home of the Nelson Kennedy family, is in northeastern upper Weakley County, Tennessee, near the southwest West Kentucky line.
28. There was a total solar eclipse on May 28, 1900, that covered much of the southeastern United States. Portions of the continental United States saw fifteen total eclipses between 1867 and 2017. Christopher Burt, "Historical Perspective on Total Solar Eclipses in the U.S." *Underground*, July 28, 2017, 12:43 EDT, https://www.wunderground.com/cat6/historical-perspective-total-solar-eclipses-us. In this instance, Hope Hart grouped her narrative by location whereas chronologically the eclipse occurred in the spring of 1900 and her grandfather died in October that year.
29. Hope Hart was correct that her father Sterling Reece Hart was an itinerant or traveling preacher. However, in Methodist terms, he remained "on trial" until the annual Memphis Conference of 1901. Perhaps in lay thinking he was fully a Methodist minister from his 1899 appointment. In November 1901 he received "full connection" and also ordained deacon. *MCJ* 1899, 31; *MCJ* 1900, 29; and *MCJ* 1901, 9.

Chapter 7

1. Sister was Eva Elna "Eleanor" Hart (1884–1907), Hope Hart's oldest sibling. She died in late 1907 from an unspecified cause. Interestingly, her grave marker

neither specifies the month and day of her birth nor her death. "Eva Elna Hart Harbert," findagrave.com.
2. Reelfoot Lake is a famous hunting and lodging site in Lake and Obion County in upper northwestern most West Tennessee. Hayes, *Reelfoot*, 1–2.
3. Grandmother Laura Jane Simmons Kennedy (1823–1908) was eighty-four by then. The mother of Mattie Hart became a widow in early October 1900 at Little Zion, Weakley County, Tennessee. Hart, "Kith," *DE*, February 9, 1973, 12. Grandmother Kennedy died January 17, 1908. "Laura Jane Simmons Kennedy," findagrave.com.
4. Grandfather was Nelson Kennedy (1817–1900), Mattie Hart's father who died in early October 1900 at Little Zion, Weakley County, Tennessee. Hart, "Kith," *DE*, February 9, 1973, 12. "Nelson Kennedy," findagrave.com.
5. Grandmother and Grandfather Kennedy were married in 1838.
6. It is unclear what relative Hope Hart had in mind. All of the sisters of Mattie Kennedy Hart, Hope Hart's mother, were married or were deceased. One of the sisters had married in the 1860s and died that decade. "Martha Nelson "Mattie" Kennedy Hart," findagrave.com.
7. "Joe" Reece Green Hart (1901–1975), was a younger brother of Hope Hart. If the Hart family trip was in late 1907 or early 1908, Joe was six years old.
8. Hollow Rock in northwest Tennessee is a small community in Carroll County some forty-three miles northeast of Jackson, Tennessee. It is about thirty-seven miles southeast of Dresden, Weakley County, Tennessee. Joe David McClure, "Carroll County," TE.
9. Weakley County, Tennessee is in upper northwest Tennessee on the southern border of Kentucky.
10. Neither the distant cousin nor the couple living with Grandmother Kennedy were otherwise identified.
11. Uncle John was John Calvin Kennedy (1861–1940), the son of Nelson Kennedy (1817–1900) and Laura Jane Simmons Kennedy (1823–1908). Hart, "Kith," *DE*, February 9, 1973, 12.
12. Uncle Harris was Green Harris Kennedy (1858–1925), the son of Nelson Kennedy (1817–1900) and Laura Jane Simmons Kennedy (1823–1908). Hart, "Kith," *DE*, February 9, 1973, 12. "Nelson Kennedy," findagrave.com.
13. Hart, "Kith," *DE*, February 9, 1973, 12.
14. Grandfather Nelson Kennedy and Grandmother Laura Jane Simmons Kennedy, Hope Hart's maternal grandparents, married September 18, 1838. Hart, "Kith," *DE*, February 9, 1973, 2.
15. Nelson Kennedy's father was Sampson Edward Kennedy (1787–1845). "Sampson Edward Kennedy," findagrave.com. Hart, "Kith," *DE*, February 9, 1973, 12.

16. A section of land was six hundred and forty acres, measuring a mile on each side if rectangular.
17. A patent was a document or an instrument conveying public lands or the land itself. "Patent." In this instance, the original conveying governmental authority was North Carolina or the University of North Carolina.
18. According to the U. S. Census of 1840, the somewhat newlywed Kennedys had no slaves. "Nelson Edward Kennedy [Canedy]," ancestry.com.
19. Dog trot is a roofed breezeway connecting two cabins.
20. An ell of a building is an addition at a right angle to the original structure. In some respects, the configuration resembles a human elbow.
21. A churn is a mechanism or container for making butter from cream.
22. Sterling Reece Hart's mother was Ruth Paralee McWherter Hart Moore (1841–1916). For a few years, she was Hope Hart's Grandmother Hart. When she married Calvin Simpson Moore (1837–1901) in 1869, she became Grandma. She became widowed again in 1901 when Grandpa Moore died.
23. Uncle Potter, Sterling Hart's youngest half-brother, was Lemuel Potter Moore (1879–1958) who married in 1913 and 1919. "Lemuel Potter Moore," findagrave.com.
24. The War of 1812 subdued and fragmented Indians along the Wilderness Road. By treaty those Indians did move westward.
25. From Virginia and North Carolina, the Wilderness Trail ran through Cumberland Gap in the Appalachian Mountains into bluegrass Kentucky and limestone Tennessee. Harriette Simpson Arnow, *Seedtime on the Cumberland* (Lexington: The University of Kentucky Press, 1983), 6–7, 18, 20, 64–65, 242. "Historically, the best-known segment of the road ran from the Long Island of the Holston to the Bluegrass area of north-central Kentucky by way of Cumberland Gap." Rebecca A. Vial, "Wilderness Road," *TE*.
26. The Obion and Forked Deer country meant the northern West Tennessee watershed and flow of the four forks of the Obion River and the central West Tennessee watershed and flow of the three forks of the Forked Deer River.
27. Side meat is salt pork generally from a hog's sides.
28. Old Scratch was a nickname for the Devil.
29. Varmints usually meant an animal pest.
30. A press was a storage area, a cabinet or closet for household items, often linens.
31. Grandfather Nelson Kennedy's parents were Sampson Edward Kennedy (1787–1845) and Nancy Killebrew Kennedy (1787–1867), Hope Hart's great-grandfather and great-grandmother. Hart, "Kith," *DE*, February 9, 1973, 12.
32. Effie May's great-grandfather was otherwise unidentified. In the newspaper genealogical series, Hope Hart was vague about the Piggs though she did connect them with some McWherters. Hart, "Kith," *DE*, March 2, 1973, 13.

33. Effie May was otherwise unidentified other than as the granddaughter of Cousin Pigg. Hope Hart also gave little identity to Cousin Pigg.
34. Lydia Killebrew Kennedy was Nelson Kennedy's aunt. She was the wife of Nelson Kennedy, the older brother of Sampson Edward Kennedy (1787–1845). Lydia died in 1823 on the Wilderness Road. She was also the sister of Nancy Killebrew Kennedy, Sampson Edward Kennedy's wife. Hart, "Kith," *DE*, February 9, 1973, 12.
35. Milk glass is a type of milk-colored glass for decorative items.
36. French Chalk is a kind of talc for marking cloth lines and cleaning an item.
37. A sleeper is usually a horizontal timber on a solid base to support upper structure, such as floor joists.

Chapter 8

1. Grandmother, during early 1908 living in the Little Zion community of northeastern Weakley County of northwest Tennessee on the Kentucky border, was Laura Jane Simmons Kennedy (1823–1908). She was the widow of Nelson Kennedy (1817–1900) and mother of Martha "Mattie" Kennedy Hart. The Sterling Hart family visit to Grandmother Kennedy's in early 1908 happened shortly before Mrs. Kennedy's death though Hope Hart did not discuss that.
2. In early 1908, the Sterling Hart family was ministering at Obion in Obion County, a county in upper northwest Tennessee along the West Kentucky line. *MCJ* 1907, 29.
3. The Obion River is a four-branched stream in northwest Tennessee; in this instance, it was the North Fork.
4. In mumblety-peg a player from various positions attempts to flip a knife so that the blade sticks in the ground.
5. Ray, Hope Hart's oldest brother then about twenty years old, studied law at Cumberland College in Lebanon, Tennessee.
6. Uncle Charlie, the oldest son of Calvin Simpson and Paralee Moore, was Leroy Simpson Moore (1870–1901). He was the oldest Hart-Moore sibling of Sterling Reece Hart. Records did not show whether he was really nicknamed Charlie or whether Hope Hart just authored him an alias. "Leroy Simpson Moore," findagrave.com.
7. Grandma Moore was first Grandmother Ruth Paralee McWherter Hart, the wife of Thomas Green Hart (1836–1863). She and fellow Palmersville native Thomas Hart married in 1857. The sons of Ruth and Thomas were Thomas Loesco Hart (1860–1955), born in Weakley County, and Sterling Reece Hart (1862–1956), born at Dardanelle, Yell County, Arkansas.
8. Hope Hart's real grandfather was Thomas Green Hart (1836–1863).

9. Actually, Paralee Hart's first son was three when his father Thomas Green Hart died in western Arkansas during July 1863 and the second son Sterling Reece was a year old.
10. According to genealogical records, in the 1860s, Grandpa Calvin Simpson Moore, then the husband of Sarah Angeline Kennedy Moore (1837–1868) whom he married in 1861, had three or four children, William Issac Moore (1862–1932), Emma Smith Moore (Narron) (1863–1941), Martha Emily Moore (1864–1961), and Mary Viola Moore (1866–1877). Interestingly, William was born in Weakley County, Emma was born August 8, 1863, in Quincy, Illinois, and Martha was born in Weakley County on February 2, 1864. Perhaps curiously, only six months separates the birth of Emma and Martha. Mary Viola was born in Weakley County.
11. Uncle Charlie (1870–1901) became thirty-one on May 31, 1901.
12. Little Zion was the home and church location of the Calvin Simpson Moores who lived in upper Weakley County, Tennessee near Cane Creek.
13. Dr. Busby was an otherwise unidentified Elm Grove physician. Elm Grove possibly was at Elm Springs or Elm Creek that was on some early maps. Otherwise, Elm Grove was unidentified.
14. Instead of limiting herself to the local Obion River tributaries, perhaps Hope Hart mentioned the southerly Forked Deer River in central West Tennessee to emphasize Uncle Charlie's far ranged appeal. Otherwise, she meant the Obion River rather than the southerly Forked Deer River in central West Tennessee.
15. Ore's Spring, also Ore Springs, was the small unincorporated community on the Paris-Dresden route seven miles east of Dresden, Weakley County and fourteen miles west of Paris. Vaughan, *Weakley County*, 115–16.
16. Squire Grimes could have been a storekeeper and cattle buyer, but he was primarily a farmer. He was actually Lemuel Dewitt Brite, a Weakley County father of three sons and nine daughters. "Lemuel Dewitt Brite," findagrave.com.
17. Carrie Griggs was an alias author Hope Hart created. Caroline "Carrie" Griggs was actually Ida May Brite (1877–1966) of Weakley County, Tennessee, the daughter of farmer Lemuel Dewitt Brite (1836–1913) of Weakley County, Tennessee. She was his ninth child and seventh daughter. "Ida May Brite McWherter," findagrave.com. "Lemual Brice [Brite]," 1900 United States Federal Census, ancestry.com. "Lemuel D. Bright [Brice]," 1880 United States Federal Census, ancestry.com.
18. Carrie, a.k.a. Ida May, was 24 years old in 1901.
19. Squire Grimes, a.k.a. Lemuel Dewitt Brite, was widowed by 1891. One genealogical site showed he married Emma Lee Cloys Page, but did not specify what year. Ida May was 15 years younger than her oldest surviving sister.
20. Carrie had several sisters between her and her oldest surviving sister.

21. The marriage license date was October 11, 1901, and Uncle Charlie died eight days later. There was no death certificate. In an email, Greg Roach to Marvin Downing, 10:23 a.m., February 23, 2021, Roach indicated Carrie, a.k.a. Ida Mae Bright, "married Oct. 11, 1901, to Leroy Moore. He died 8 days later no death certificate. Remarried Dec. 30, 1902 to Andrew McWherter." Email in Downing's possession.
22. Weakley County Clerk George Mayo issued the marriage certificate and added Baptist beside his name. Seemingly, he united Charlie and Carrie. L. S. [Leroy] Moore to Ida Brite. Marriage certificate to Moore Ancestry.com–Tennessee, U.S., Marriage Records, 1780–2002, October 11, 1901. Similarly, Mayo issued the 1898 marriage certificate and presided at the wedding of Aunt Alice and Uncle Billy Killebrew. Hart, "Weddings," chap. 1, "A Babe at Zion," i.
23. Widow's weeds were black dresses and veils worn by proper widows in the late 1800s and early 1900s in the United States, generally for a year.
24. A bureau and linen press were wooden clothing containers.
25. Hart family tradition had Thomas Greene Hart (1836–1863) both a Confederate and an officer. Hart, "Memoirs," *MCJ* 1957, 114. So far, the only military record located showed that he enlisted as a Private, Tenth Infantry, unit unknown, December 12, 1862, at Frenandina, location unknown. U.S., Confederate Soldiers Compiled Service Records, 1861–1865. "Thomas Greene Hart," ancestry.com. David Coffey, a published Civil War and military history professor of the University of Tennessee at Martin, claimed Confederate military records sometimes to be sketchy at best. David Coffey to Marvin Downing, email, Sunday March 14, 2021, 8:36 p.m. in Downing's possession. His older brother John Mark Hart (1832–1911), however, was a Confederate Lieutenant. "John Mark Hart," findagrave.com. Perhaps Hart relatives confused the ranks of the two brothers.
26. Ruth Paralee McWherter Hart became a widow at age twenty-two with a three-year old son and a one-year-old son.
27. The Battle of Pea Ridge, known to Union forces as the Battle of Elkhorn, occurred on March 7–8, 1862, in northwestern Arkansas near the Missouri state border. Though the Confederates were under the overall command of CSA General Sterling Price (1809–1867), in the theater, they were more immediately under CSA Major General Earl Van Dorn who ultimately had to withdraw partially due to a lack of supplies. The disastrous CSA defeat left Missouri in the Union. William L. Shea and Earl J. Hess, *Pea Ridge: Civil War Campaign in the West* (Chapel Hill: The University of North Carolina Press, 1992), 307–17. Albert E. Castel, *General Sterling Price and the Civil War in the West* (Baton Rouge: Louisiana State University Press, 1968), 66–83. Arthur B. Carter, *The Tarnished Cavalier: Major General Earl Van Dorn, C.S.A.* (Knoxville: University

of Tennessee Press, 1999), 42–67. Robert G. Hartje, *Van Dorn: The Life and Times of a Confederate General* (Nashville, Tennessee: Vanderbilt University Press, 1967), 137–61.

28. Thomas Loesco Hart (1860–1955) was the first son of the Thomas Green Hart, born in Tennessee, presumably in the Palmersville area of Weakley County. "Thomas Loesco Hart." findagrave.com.
29. Dardanelle, Arkansas is a town in Yell County on the Arkansas River in northwest Arkansas.
30. Papa was Sterling Reece Price (1862–1955), Hope Hart's father. The battle at Pea Ridge was March 6–8, 1862, approximately two and a half months before Sterling Reece Hart's birthday on May 11, 1862, at Dardanelle, Yell County, Arkansas. The precise sequence of Hart family events in 1862 was a bit difficult to sort out.
31. In late July 1863, Thomas Greene Hart died of a typhus fever, a bacterial disease carried by vermin, such as fleas, lice, and chiggers, and transmitted to human. Centers for Disease Control and Prevention, "Typhus," cdc.gov.
32. Hope Hart's ages for Thomas L. Hart and Sterling R. Hart were a bit off. By late July 1863, Thomas Loesco Hart, born March 29, 1860, was three years and four months old and Sterling, born May 11, 1862, was about fourteen and a half months old.
33. Federal forces attempted to control Confederate traffic on the Arkansas and Mississippi Rivers.
34. A roustabout is a boat deckhand.
35. The Arkansas and White Rivers merge in southeastern Arkansas.
36. Sawyer's Landing was an otherwise unidentified location.
37. Leoso (*sic* Loesco) and Papa were Paralee's two sons.
38. Bush-whackers ranged from irregular Union and Confederate forces to common criminals and even individuals seeking revenge for major or minor personal reasons. Robert R. Mackey, *The Uncivil War: Irregular Warfare in the Upper South, 1861–1865* (Norman, Okla.: University of Oklahoma Press, 2004), 5–11, 19–27, 195–204. Sometimes Unionists were called bushwhackers and Southerners termed them guerrillas. McGowan, *West Tennessee*, 171. Bergeron, *Tennesseans*, 152–53.
39. Thomas Green Hart was not a recorded member of the Masonic Lodge at Palmersville though his older brother John Mark Hart (28 Jan 1832–24 Feb 1911) definitely was.
40. Hickman, Kentucky on the Mississippi River is the county seat of Fulton County along the extreme southwest Western Kentucky line. It is about forty-three miles from Palmersville-Little Zion, Tennessee. Fulton County is on the northern line of Weakley County, Tennessee. Ron D. Bryant, "Hick-

man," in *The Kentucky Encyclopedia*, ed. John E. Kleber (Lexington: University Press of Kentucky, 1992), 427. Virginia Honchell Jewell, "Hickman County," in *The Kentucky Encyclopedia*, ed. John E. Kleber (Lexington: University Press of Kentucky, 1992), 427–28.

41. Dresden is the county seat of Weakley County, Tennessee on the Kentucky-Tennessee line. Paralee Hart was still some eleven miles from home, Little Zion and Palmersville. Vaughan, *Weakley County*, 14, 55.
42. In this instance, Hope Hart did not specify the name of Paralee McWherter Hart's brother. Her brothers were William Reuben, Leroy W. George Rufus, James Monroe, Almus Clayton, and Thomas Benton. Hart, "Kith," *DE*, March 9, 1973, 16.
43. Captain William Reuben, CSA, died at the battle of Chickamauga. Upon William's death, Thomas Killebrew, a Palmersville cousin, assumed that command. Other CSA relatives were Almus McWherter, F. l. Mcwherter and Robert McWherter. "Captain William Reuben 'Bill' McWherter," findagrave.com.

Chapter 9

1. The Sterling Reece Hart family was in Obion about 1908. *MCJ* 1906, 27; *MCJ* 1907, 29, Union City District, Obion, TN Circuit, 3.
2. Pokey refers to something slow moving or small.
3. Chicago's "Daily Blade" was a weekly from 1887 by the Chicago Blade Publishing Company until at least June 21, 1913, and distributed in Cook County, Illinois. Chronicling America, "About The Saturday Blade. [volume] (Chicago, Ill.) 1887–19??." Library of Congress, https://chroniclingamerica.loc.gov/lccn/sn84024076/.
4. Gibbs Junction might have been a railroad stop or designation in or near Union City, Tennessee or a Hope Hart created name. General George Washington Gibbs, a lawyer, likely wanted to create a town where two railroads met and planned to name it Junction City. Instead, he named it Union City, the county seat of Obion County, Tennessee on the southern Kentucky border after learning there was already a Junction City, Tennessee. Historical Marker Project, "Union City Junction (HM204R)," *Union City, TN 38261 Obion County*, https://historicalmarkerproject.com/markers/HM204R_union-city-junction_Union-City-TN.html.
5. Bon Ami, meaning "Good Friend," was a special powdered formula household cleaner begun in 1886. The container famously showed a freshly hatched baby chick and claimed, "Hasn't Scratched Yet."
6. The first state militia contingent arrived at Union City. A bit later, the Forrest Rifles from Memphis detrained at Obion. The troops did have communication

connection via the Illinois Central railroad station at Obion, Tennessee. Paul J. Vanderwood, *Night Riders of Reelfoot Lake* (Tuscaloosa: University of Alabama Press, 2003), 62, 56; R. C. Forrester and Betty Burdick Wood, *Night Riders of Reelfoot Lake: The Untold Story* (Union City, TN: Forrester Wood Publication, 2001), 72.

7. Malcolm Patterson (1861–1935) was Tennessee's governor for two terms 1907–1911. By 1909, he enjoyed considerable acclaim for putting down the vigilante night riders of 1908 at Reelfoot Lake in the extreme upper northwestern part of the state. Timothy P. Ezzell, "Malcom R. Patterson," *TE*.

8. During 1908 in Lake and Obion County in upper northwest Tennessee, vigilante subsistence farmers, fishermen, and hunters disputed the West Tennessee Land Company's title to land around the natural Reelfoot Lake. They wanted continued access to and use of the water and adjacent land. They questioned the alleged ownership of the company and protested its planned partial lake drainage for cotton production. Their differences resulted in weeks of violence and culminated the night of October 19, 1908, when some especially aggressive masked vigilantes kidnapped company executives R. Z. Taylor and Quinton Rankin, murdered Taylor, and would have killed Rankin but for his successful escape.

At that point, Governor Malcom Patterson ordered Tennessee National Guard troops to restore order. Within days, the Guard rounded up over seventy-five suspects into a temporary stockade. Six were convicted for murder and received death sentences. In 1909, the Tennessee Supreme Court ruled against their convictions. Perhaps as a result of public opinion heavily favoring the Reelfoot Lake residents, in 1914 the state of Tennessee took ownership of the lake. Bill Threlkeld, "Night Riders of Reelfoot Lake." *TE*. Hayes, *Reelfoot*, 303, 313–14, 320–23.

9. Reelfoot Lake primarily in Lake and Obion County in upper northwest Tennessee was formed in part due to the New Madrid earthquakes of 1811–1812 along the Mississippi River near Missouri, Kentucky, Arkansas, and Tennessee. Those Mississippi Valley shakes were felt eastward to at least Washington, D.C. Emma Walker, "The Fascinating Story Behind Reelfoot Lake," National Forest Foundation Roots Rated, https://rootsrated.com/stories/the-fascinating-story-behind-reelfoot-lake. Hayes, *Reelfoot*, 1–2.

10. Joe Green Hart (1901–1975) and Key Nelson Hart (1904–1998) were the youngest brothers of Hope Hart (1897–1985) and the Sterling Reece Hart family.

11. The otherwise unidentified sheriff was possibly Obion County Sheriff T. J. Easterwood in 1908 and 1909. Obion County, TNGenWeb, "Court Clerks, Sheriffs, etc," tngenweb.org.

12. Since the town of Obion was not a county seat. It did not have a traditional town square.
13. Shiloh, Tennessee was the site of the bloody major Civil War battle of April 7–8, 1862 in extreme southeastern West Tennessee. James L. McDonough, "Battle of Shiloh," *TE*.
14. Grandpa Moore was Hope Hart's step-grandfather Calvin Simpson Moore (1837–1901). He was the second husband of Grandma Ruth Paralee McWherter Hart Moore (1840–1916). "Calvin Simpson Moore." findagrave.com.
15. While Calvin Simpson Moore might have fought at Shiloh, he received an elbow wound at Tishimingo Springs, Mississippi in 1863. C.S.A. military records showed it as a slight elbow injury. Shortly after the Civil War, his petition for a disability pension was denied though his widow Ruth Paralee Moore received one. Arthur Wyllie, *Tennessee Confederate Pensions* (New York: Barnes and Noble, 2014), 370.
16. Palings are often narrow pointed wooden pieces of a fence.
17. Paducah, McCracken County, Kentucky along the Ohio River is the northern most part of Western Kentucky, the Jackson Purchase, and the United Methodist Church Memphis Conference.
18. Stem-winder is an energetic and focused person of action. The term likely originated when pocket and wristwatches had stems to wind the internal spring to keep time.
19. Radiators were metal devices along a wall to transfer steam heat into a room.
20. Linoleum is a thin laying of material for covering a floor.
21. Lye soap refers to a common homemade soap in this instance.
22. The Woman's Christian Temperance Union began during 1874 in Ohio and spread throughout the United States. It particularly focused on prohibition in the late 1800s and early 1900s. Ruth Birgitta Anderson Bordin, *Francis Willard: A Biography*. Chapel Hill: University of North Carolina, 1986. History.com Editors, "Woman's Christian Temperance Union," history.com.
23. "Damn Yankee" is a Southern term disparaging a person from north of the Mason-Dixon Line.

Chapter 10

1. A gambol is an outing or play occasion.
2. A Methodist Conference was the governing body for a designated geographical area. Conferences were held quarterly and annually. At the fall session of the Memphis Conference in November, the presiding Bishop announced ministerial assignments
3. The presiding Methodist bishop headed each Methodist conference in religious

policy and ministerial appointments. A national bishop is the leading ministerial officer of the United Methodist Church.
4. John Clark Ridpath (1840–1900), Editor in chief, revisions and additions by William Montgomery Clark (1860–1931), *The Ridpath Library of Universal Literature; A Biographical and Bibliographical Summary of the World's Most Eminent Authors, Including the Choicest Selections and Masterpieces from Their Writings* (New York: The Fifth Avenue Library Society, 1899–1912).
5. Perhaps Hope Hart had in mind Evelyn Abbott, ed., The Heroes of the Nations (New York: G. P. Putnam's Sons, 1890). It consisted of biographies of famous persons who greatly impacted their nations and others.
6. Dr. Charles W. Eliot, then the Harvard University President, compiled fifty-one volumes into a five foot shelf about literary and historical documents; it aimed to provide a liberal education. Charles W. Eliot, compiler, *The Harvard Classics* (New York: P. F. Collier and Son, 1909).
7. "David Cooperfield" was a major novel of the mid-1800s by Englishman Charles Dickens about a poor youngster becoming a successful novelist. Charles Dickens, Edited with an Introduction by George H. Ford, *David Cooperfield* (Boston: Houghton Mifflin, 1958).
8. "Oliver Twist" was the second novel of Englishman Charles Dickens before the 1850s about a young London orphan unwittingly drawn into the criminal underworld. Charles Dickens, edited by Kathleen Tillotson, *Oliver Twist* (Oxford: Clarendon Press, 1974).
9. *The Adventures of Tom Sawyer* is a major Mark Twain novel about the mid-1850s adventures or misadventures of a young mischief along the Mississippi River. Emory Elliott, ed., *Columbia Literary History of the United States* (New York: Columbia University Press, 1988), 628–30, 638–39.
10. *The Adventures of Huckleberry Finn* is a famous Mark Twain novel about Huck Finn, sometimes pal of Tom Sawyer but more so friend of fugitive slave Jim. Elliott, *Columbia Literary History*, 134, 308–9.
11. *The Last of the Mohicans* is a James Fenimore Cooper novel during the French and Indian War of the mid-eighteenth century northern New York frontier. Natty Bumppo, a.k.a. Hawkeye, and his Indian friends Chingachgook and Uncas are major characters. Elliott, *Columbia Literary History*, 241–43, 256–58.
12. *Mrs. Wiggs of the Cabbage Patch* is the early 1900s novel of Alice Caldwell Hegan Rice about a poor but optimistic southern woman's skillfully rearing her five children. Alice Caldwell Hegan Rice, *Mrs. Wiggs of the Cabbage Patch* (Lexington: University Press of Kentucky, 2015).
13. "David Harum" in *David Harum: A Story of American Life*, a novel about 1900, was a New York area country banker noted for his skillful "horse trading."

Edward Noyes Westcott, *David Harum: A Story of American Life* (New York: Appleton, 1898).

14. *Ben Hur: A Tale of the Christ* by General Lew Wallace, a novel of 1880, concerned a young Jewish noble's devotion to Christ. It was quite popular with youngsters. Elliott, *Columbia Literary History*, 336.
15. *The Old Curiosity Shop* was an 1840–1841 work of Charles Dickens about Londoner Nell Trent who lived with her grandfather in *The Old Curiosity Shop*. Charles Dickens, *The Old Curiosity Shop* (New York: Oxford University Press, 1951).
16. E. P. Roe, Edward Payson Roe (1838–1888) was a prolific New York fiction author and minister who lectured and wrote romantic novels.
17. E. P. Roe wrote popular religious fiction after 1850. This book dealt with a young fellow's attempts to relate personally to his employer's reluctant daughter. E. P. Roe, *Barriers Burned Away* (New York, New York: Dodd MeadAMS, 1898).
18. *In His Steps*, an 1897 novel by Congregationalist minister Charles W. Sheldon (1857–1946) challenged Christian character based on the standard "What would Jesus do?" Elliott, *Columbia Literary History*, 529.
19. A search did not locate that book. Hope Hart might have meant Sue F. Dromgoole Mooney's *My Moving Tent*, the memoirs of a traveling Methodist parson's wife during the Civil War in Tennessee and Alabama. Sue F. Dromgoole Mooney, *My Moving Tent* (Nashville: Publishing House Methodist Episcopal Church South, Bigham & Smith Agents, 1903).
20. "St. Elmo," by Augusta Jane Evans Wilson of Georgia was a late 1800s novel about Southern life involving a devout heroine Edna Earl and a cynical male St. Elmo. Augusta Jane Evans, *St. Elmo: Or, Saved at Last* (Tuscaloosa: The University of Alabama Press, 2015).
21. *At the Mercy of Tiberius* by Augusta Jane Evans Wilson of Georgia is a novel concerning Tiberius prosecuting heroine Beryl for allegedly murdering her grandfather over their differences. Augusta Jane Evans Wilson, *At the Mercy of Tiberius* (N.P: G. W. Dillingham, Company, 1887).
22. *Les Miserables* by French novelist Victor Hugo (1802–1885) was a highly popular classic about a paroled convict who broke his parole but became a respectable citizen while being pursued by a jailer. Victor Hugo, Translated by Charles E. Wilbour, *Les Miserables* (New York: Modern Library, 1992).
23. Fantine was a downtrodden female worker befriended by the main character of Les Miserables.
24. Jack London, a.k.a. John Griffith Chaney (1876–1916), was noted especially for his adventure novels. Elliott, *Columbia Literary History*, 540–41.
25. *The Call of the Wild* chronicled the development of the Yukon sled dog Buck and his master. Elliott, *Columbia Literary History*, 540–41.

26. Jack London's *The Sea-Wolf* depicted a sea captain's dominance. Elliott, *Columbia Literary History*, 541.
27. *Vanity Fair* by William Makepeace Thackery (1811–1863) portrayed the lives of Becky Sharp and her friend Amelia Sedley, two women of different morals and disposition in a very-male world. William Makepeace Thackery (1811–1863), *Vanity Fair* (Champaign, Ill.: 1996).
28. *The Scarlet Letter* by American novelist Nathaniel Hawthorne (1804–1864) concerns Hester Prynne's sin of adultery with her child's father, local minister Arthur Dimmesdale whose sin was unknown to their community. Elliott, *Columbia Literary History*, 39, 421.
29. "Treasure Island" by Robert Louis Stevenson (1850–1894) created a fictional world about pirates and their adventures. Robert Louis Stevenson, *Treasure Island* (New York: Scholastic, 1988).
30. Mary Ann Evans, better known as George Eliot (1819–1880), authored seven novels with *Adam Bede*, *The Mill on the Floss*, and *Silas Marner* among them. Elizabeth Deeds Ermarth, George Eliot (Boston: Twayne, 1985).
31. *Ivanhoe* by Scotchman Sir Walter Scott (1771–1832) depicted a chivalrous English knight in his adventures. Walter Scott, *Ivanhoe* (Mt. View, Calif.: Generick NL Freebook Publisher, 1993).
32. *Tess of the D'Urbervilles* by Englishman Thomas Hardy (1840–1928) was a novel about a poor girl torn between deceitful access to wealth or genuine love with a promising young suitor. Thomas Hardy, *Tess of the D'Urbervilles* (Evanston, Ill.: McDougal Littell, 1998).
33. *The Light that Failed*, a novel by Englishman Rudyard Kipling (1865–1936), pictured a war correspondent going blind who had to decide whether to stay with his sweetheart or return to soldiers who supported him in war. Rudyard Kipling, *The Light that Failed* (Garden City, N.Y.: Doubleday, 1915).
34. Tom Brown's *Schooldays* by English lawyer Thomas Hughes (1822–1896) told of an early 1800s English boy's activities at an elite school. Thomas Hughes, *Tom Brown's Schooldays* (New York: Crowell, [n.d.]).
35. *The Vicar of Wakefield* by Oliver Goldsmith (1730–1774) chronicled the blessings and woes of an 1800s vicar's family in a comical way. Oliver Goldsmith, *The Vicar of Wakefield* (London: Oxford University Press, 1967).
36. *The Little Shepherd of Kingdom Come* by Kentuckian John Fox Jr. (1862–1919) painted the fictional life of an orphaned Kentucky mountain boy seeking his identity before and during the Civil War. John Fox, Jr., *The Little Shepherd of Kingdom Come* (New York: Charles Scribner's Son, 1910).
37. In *The Last of the Mohicans* by James Fenimore Cooper (1789–1851), Chingachgook and Uncas were Indian allies and friends of the American frontiersman Natty Bumppo. Elliott, *Columbia Literary History*, 241–43, 256–58.

38. *The House of Seven Gables* by Nathaniel Hawthorne (1804–1864) dealt with the guilt of more than one generation in a large New England dwelling. Elliott, *Columbia Literary History*, 225, 417, 424, 427–28.
39. *The Count of Monte Cristo* by Alexandre Dumas (1802–1870) traced a wrongfully convicted early 1800s sailor who escaped incarceration and sought Monte Cristo's treasure to gain revenge against his wrongdoers. Alexandre Dumas, *The Count of Monte Cristo* (New York: Modern Library, 1996).
40. Sherlock Holmes was the fictional master detective created by Scottish author Arthur Conan Doyle (1859–1930).
41. Arthur Conan Doyle (1859–1930) was the Scottish author, a.k.a. Sir Arthur Conan Doyle, whose most famous characters are Sherlock Holmes and Dr. Watson. Russell Miller, *The Adventures of Arthur Conan Doyle: A Biography* (New York: Thomas Dunne Books, 2008).
42. *The Hound of the Baskervilles* by Arthur Conan Doyle concerned attempted murder related to a legend about an unusual dog and the Baskerville estate. Sir Arthur Conan Doyle, *The Hound of the Baskervilles* (Cutchogue, N.Y.: Buccaneer Books, 1986).
43. *The Sign of the Four* by Arthur Conan Doyle was the second novel focusing on Sherlock homes. Sir Arthur Conan Doyle, *The Sign of the Four* (New York: Oxford University Press, 1993).
44. John Trotwood Moore (1858–1929) was an Alabama and Tennessee author. Sandra G. Hancock, "John Trotwood Moore," Encyclopediaofalabama.org, http://www.encyclopediaofalabama.org/article/h-2437.
45. *The Bishop of Cottonwood* concerned child labor in southern cotton mills. John Trotwood Moore, *The Bishop of Cottonwood: A Story of the Southern Cotton Mills* (Philadelphia: The J. C. Winston Company, 1906).
46. A hayseed is a bumpkin, yokel, simpleton, or unsophisticated person.
47. By parsonage standards meant that the family income was limited.
48. No information was found about a multivolume series of "Cozy Journeys to Faraway Lands."
49. A circuit was a local Methodist ministerial appointment site located within a larger district inside a geographical conference.
50. Promotion was an unofficial term because officially or commonly all Methodist appointments are of an equal status. However, in effect, there were really promotions.
51. A spur-line railroad was a short line of or off the main railroad line, sometimes only a short distance into an industrial or commercial area.
52. Rubber-tired buggy was an improvement over the traditional metal wheel.
53. Kid gloves were soft gloves made from the skin of a young goat.
54. A ginner referred to an owner of a cotton gin or sometimes a worker at a gin.

55. Baptized in Methodist practice is generally sprinkling though a baptismal candidate may opt for immersion.
56. Mr. Jim Frampton was an otherwise unidentified heavy drinker or alcoholic Methodist church member of the Reverend Sterling Hart's Methodist congregation.
57. Variety store was a business selling notions and other small items.
58. Queer in this instance meant odd or different without a sexual reference.
59. John Barleycorn was hard liquor.
60. Calaboose was another name for a jail.
61. Reece was the name Mattie Kennedy called her husband Sterling Reece Hart. Other relatives often called him Reece.
62. Holy Ghost is another name for the Holy Spirit, the third person of the Christian Trinity.
63. Mormon missionaries travel in pairs in their evangelizing efforts as required by their practices.
64. Hoboes were unemployed or homeless poor individuals.
65. The word "scriptures" is often capitalized in Christian circles.
66. "Love's Old Sweet Song," originally a poem by G. Clifton Bingham about 1884, set to music, retaining the name. Poetry Nook, "Love's Old Sweet Song." Poetrynook.com, https://www.poetrynook.com/poem/loves-old-sweet-song.
67. Calomel was a white tasteless laxative.
68. Sister Hart was Martha "Mattie" Kennedy Hart, the wife of Sterling Reece Hart. In some church circles, it is often customary to acknowledge fellow Christians by the words brother or sister.
69. Cottonwood Landing was in the Dyersburg area, according to Dr. Bill Austin, a retired University of Tennessee Math Professor from that area and member of the Weakley County Historical and Genealogical Society. He introduced Downing to Hope Hart's "Thousand Weddings." Marvin Downing and Bill Austin, a brief and unrecorded conversation in Martin, Tennessee, April 11, 2021. Home Town Locator, "Cottonwood Point Ferry (historical)." Home Town Locator, Tennessee, https://tennessee.hometownlocator.com/maps/feature-map,ftc,3,fid,1309785,n,cottonwood%20point%20ferry.cfm.
70. Showboats were large steam crafts with actors performing at places located on or beside a river.
71. Calliope was an instrument somewhat similar to an organ with whistles produced by steam or pressured air.
72. Usually devout Methodists and Baptists, especially ministers and family, avoided such entertainment as immoral or unrespectable. Hare, Jr., "Expanding," 51; McGowan, *West Tennessee*, 309.
73. Old Scratch was a nickname for the Devil.

74. Beale Street originally was a commercial avenue in Memphis that became an entertainment section through decades.
75. A bluenose is a prude.
76. Cairo, a small southernmost Illinois settlement, is at the junction of the Mississippi and Ohio Rivers.
77. A search found no Mississippi River showboat by that name. Perhaps it was a small local enterprise.
78. "The Shepherd of the Hills," Harold Bell Wright's 1907 novel, depicted life in the Ozark Mountains around 1900. Harold Bell Wright, *Their Yesterdays* (Chicago, Ill.: Book Supply Co., 1912). Andrew R. L. Cayton ed., *The American Midwest: An Interpretative Encyclopedia* (Bloomington: Indiana University Press, 2007), 117.
79. Hope Hart rather jumbled her writing and her father's concern about the propriety of mixing a performance and a ceremony.
80. "Turkey in the Straw," is a quite famous American folk song, particularly a fiddle tune, possibly originating about the 1820s. Downes, *"Treasury,"* 144–45.
81. Pigeon wing was a folk-dance movement with a leg out like a pigeon's wing. The dance was mentioned in relation to the settlement at Christmasville, near McLemoresville, in Carroll County, Tennessee shortly after the Jackson Purchase opened. Downing, "Old Christmasville," *JJPHS*, 34–35.
82. "Dixie" is a shortened popular name for Daniel Decatur Emmett's 1859 minstrel song "(I Wish I Was in) Dixie's Land." Daniel Decatur Emmett, "Dixie's Land," genius.com.

Chapter 11

1. Key, Hope Hart's youngest brother Nelson Key Hart (1904–1975), would have entered school about 1910 if he began at age six. He was the youngest child of Reverend Sterling Reece Hart (1862–1956) and Martha "Mattie" Nelson Kennedy Hart (1863–1945). At that time the Sterling Hart family was living in the Methodist Memphis Conference of the Dyersburg Circuit in the Dyersburg District. *MCJ* 1909, 35.
2. Joe was Reece Green "Joe" Hart (1901–1998), Hope Hart's second brother; he would have been about nine in 1910.
3. Hope Hart Howard (1897–1985), the manuscript author, was about thirteen around 1910.
4. Hope Hart's claim of living all her life along streams flowing into the Mississippi River was not entirely accurate. During Sterling Hart's first ministerial appointment, her family was at Shiloh, Hardin County, Tennessee quite near the Tennessee River. After Shiloh, her family was in pastoral assignments at

Pryorsburg, Sedalia, and Wingo, all Graves County, Kentucky communities away from the Mississippi River. *MCJ* 1899, 31; *MCJ* 1900, 29; *MCJ* 1901, 9; *MCJ* 1902, 26; *MCJ* 1903, 23; and *MCJ* 1904, 21. Between 1912 and 1915, the Sterling Hart Family was in Calloway County, Kentucky, closer to the Tennessee River. *MCJ* 1912, 39; *MCJ* 1913, 44; and *MCJ* 1914, 60.

5. During 1908, 1912, and 1913 the Mississippi River flooded notably. National Weather Service, "Mississippi River Flood History 1543-Present," National Oceanic and Atmospheric Administration, https://www.weather.gov/lix/ms_flood_history.

6. "Laid by." After cotton was planted and was well established it could be largely left alone till harvest time except for some chopping down weeds or grass. Once a crop or field was laid by during the early 1900s the cultivators had a less pressing schedule and might even go for a visit of several days. The term also applied to some other plants. Van Hawkins, "Cotton Industry." *Encyclopedia of Arkansas*, https://encyclopediaofarkansas.net/entries/Cotton-Industry-2092. The progression of corn production was the spring planting as early as possible, "cultivated through May and June, 'laid by' in July and August, then picked by hand in early autumn." Moore, "Corn," *TE*.

7. "A season of revivals," meaning especially evangelistic meetings to revive any slacking members and to win converts, would be during the late spring and summer in several evangelistic denominations.

8. A Bishop or the Bishop was the presiding officer of the Memphis Conference of the Methodist Church.

9. Malaria is "a mosquito-borne disease caused by a parasite" often accompanied by high fever and chills. The disease may be mild to fatal. Centers for Disease Control and Prevention, "Malaria." cdc.gov.

10. The Cottonwood Ferry was discontinued after the bridge over the Mississippi River connecting Tennessee and Missouri was completed, according to Bill Austin, a Dyer County native and Weakley County Genealogical and Historical Society member. Informal conversation between Austin and Downing, April 21, 2021, Martin, Tennessee. "Cottonwood Point Ferry (historical) is a cultural feature (crossing) in Dyer County. The primary coordinates for Cottonwood Point Ferry (historical) places it within the TN 38030 zip code delivery area." HomeTownLocator, "Cottonwood Point Ferry (historical)," Tennessee *Gazetteer*, https://tennessee.hometownlocator.com/maps/feature-map,ftc,3,fid,1309785,n,cottonwood%20point%20ferry.cfm.

11. The ell is a building portion at a right angle to the main structure. It is shaped like the letter L or a human elbow, often due to a larger addition.

12. Lye soap meant a common homemade soap, especially in rural areas, containing lye, fat drippings, and ashes.

13. A wood burning stove was common at that time in large part due to readily available wood and remoteness from other fuel sources.
14. "Dressed up" meant the residents were wearing their best clothes, not every day wear.
15. Gingham was a white cotton fabric with colored squares.
16. Calico was inexpensive cotton cloth with patterns.
17. A sacque was a woman's loose jacket or covering.
18. Mother Hubbards were women's loose clothing without a special form. The term sometimes referred to maternity clothes.
19. "Pass Me Not O Gentle Savior" by Fanny J. Crosby was a Christian hymn written after the blind author had visited a prison about 1870. It was often used as an altar call to repentance. Michael Hawn, "History of Hymns: 'Pass Me Not, O Gentle Savior,'" United Methodist Church Discipleship Ministries, https://www.umcdiscipleship.org/resources/history-of-hymns-pass-me-not-o-gentle-savior.
20. Funny paper was a newspaper section with comics and humorous items.
21. Game leg was a hurt or injured leg, hampering but not incapacitating a person.
22. Galluses are a type of suspenders generally attached to men's trousers, sometimes in lieu of a waist belt.
23. Buttermilk is the semi-sour milk or liquid byproduct of making butter usually from cream. It may also be a beverage and cooking product.

Chapter 12

1. It is unclear whether the family of Methodist Reverend Sterling Reece Hart (1862–1956) was possibly still at their 1910 Dyersburg, Tennessee, location or if Hope Hart was mentioning events that more nearly fit their 1906–1907 assignment at Obion, Tennessee. Though Gleason, Weakley County, Tennessee, would have approximately sixty miles from the Mississippi River. *MCJ* 1906, 27; *MCJ* 1907, 29; *MCJ* 1909, 35; *MCJ* 1910, 32, 207, 227; *MCJ* 1906, 27; *MCJ* 1907, 29, 3; *MCJ* 1909, 35, 1; *MCJ* 1910, 32, 2.
2. Bellows were blacksmith devices for intake and expulsion of air to provide oxygen for stoking a metal heating fire.
3. Reece Green "Joe" Hart (1901–1998) and Nelson Key Hart (1904–1975), Hope Hart's younger brothers.
4. Bean ball was a variety of kid's games, all using a bean bag in the manner agreed on.
5. Jump the rope was an assortment of games with a person at each end of the rope moving it and a third person jumping over it as it was moved in various ways.

6. Red light, sometimes called red light-green light, freeze, or statues, was a game in which one player, sometimes known as "it," alternately says green light allowing distant players lined side by side to advance until "it" says red light. Players had to stop instantly or be out of the game. The first player to reach "it" became it or the caller of commands.
7. Wolf-over-the-river was an otherwise unidentified schoolyard game.
8. Run sheep run was a game of players hiding until their leader thinks they can safely run home while eluding an imaginary wolf or other predator.
9. A free-for-all meant an activity open to anyone with few, or even no, rules.
10. Normal School was a teacher training institution.
11. "Yre'rlin's" was Hart's particular spelling meaning fractious youngsters or otherwise creatures a year old.
12. Hardscrabble is characterized by poverty or barely scratching out a living on poor soil.
13. A postmaster was in charge of a postal office.
14. Domineck or Dominecker was a common black and white chicken breed.
15. Jonathan Rigdon, *Rigdon's English Grammar for the Common School* (New York: Hinds, Noble & Eldredge, 1896).
16. "Head marks" meant special recognition or rewards for exceptional achievement.
17. "Turned down" meant to outcompete someone in a contest particularly in a school or academic competition.
18. Teddy or Teddy Roosevelt, a term of affection for the popular man, was Theodore Roosevelt (1858–1919), the former New York governor who was the twenty-sixth President of the United States between 1901 and 1909. Nathan Miller, *Theodore Roosevelt: A Life* (New York: Morrow, 1992), 333–495, 520–31.
19. Even after the passage of the Civil Service Act, a postmaster's position was traditionally a political plum or reward given to a faithful party member by the political party holding the Presidency.
20. President Cleveland, a Democrat, was Grover Cleveland, the twenty-second and twenty-fourth President of the United States.
21. Republican Vice President Theodore "Teddy" Roosevelt became the United States President in 1901 upon the assassination of President William McKinley. He continued in the Presidency after the 1904 election and served until March 4, 1909.
22. By the name "The Commercial Appeal," the Memphis newspaper began in 1894 and has continued to the present. Bernard Fisher, ed., "The Commercial Appeal," HMdb.org, the Historical Marker Database, https://www.hmdb.org/m.asp?m=55377.

23. Former President Roosevelt was on a 1912 political campaign to become the U.S. president.
24. Pall meant to find less enjoyable or less interesting.
25. Mid-Victorian meant something associated with or characteristic of the middle years of British Queen Victoria's reign, 1837–1901.
26. Gayoso Hotel or Gayoso House Hotel, built during 1842, was a famous downtown business in Memphis, Tennessee. Blythe Semmer, "Gayoso Hotel," *TE*.
27. In 1912, four years removed from the Presidency, Progressive Party or Bull Moose Party candidate Roosevelt was the only Presidential candidate to campaign in Tennessee. During late September 1912, he spoke at fairs in both Jackson and Memphis. Corlew, *Tennessee*, 438, Phillip Langsdon, *Tennessee: A Political History* (Franklin, TN: Hillsboro Press, 2000), 279. That year, Hope Hart, then 15, was at Gleason, Weakley County, Tennessee, a community on a less major train line. *MCJ* 1912, 390.
28. Bishop Thomas Frank Gailor (1856–1929) was the Episcopal Bishop of the diocese of Tennessee. Donald S. Armentrout, "Gailor, Thomas Frank," *TE*.
29. Hope Hart was indicating a particular way of speaking.
30. In 1898 during the Spanish-American War Theodore "Teddy" Roosevelt was first a Lieutenant Colonel in the Rough Riders of the First Volunteer Cavalry under Colonel Leonard Wood. When Wood became a Brigadier General, Roosevelt was also promoted to full Colonel. In the 1890s, the popular song "A Hot Time in the Old Town Tonight" was popular and in 1898 became publicly associated with the Rough Riders and subsequently Roosevelt commonly used it in his political campaigns. Rick Marschall, *Bully: The Life and Times of Theodore Roosevelt* (Washington, D.C.: Regency Publishing, Inc., 2011), 116–28. H. Paul Jeffers, *Colonel Roosevelt: Theodore Roosevelt Goes to War, 1897–1898* (New York: J. Wiley and Sons, 1996), 226–28, 243.
31. General Nathan Bedford Forrest was one of the most famous and controversial Confederate cavalrymen of the U.S. Civil War, known for his swift and daring raids. Forrest's raid on Memphis formed in the pre-dawn hours of Sunday, August 21, 1864. Maness, *Untutored*, 288–90.
32. The phrase "time to light" meant the riders did not necessarily dismount and tie their horses quickly. At least Captain William H. Forrest, General Forrest's brother, did ride his horse into the hotel. The Confederates were instantly into the structure and futilely seeking Federal general Stephen A. Hurlbut who was overnighting at a fellow officer's house. Maness claimed the riders went mounted into the Gayoso House. Maness, *Untutored*, 289. Other historians claimed that only Captain William Forrest, the general's brother, went mounted in. Jack Hurst, *Nathan Bedford Forrest: A Biography* (New York: A.A.

Knopf, 1993), 212–16; and Eddy W. Davis and Daniel Foxx, *Nathan Bedford Forrest: In Search of the Enigma* (Gretna, New York: Pelican Pub. Co., 2007), 311.

33. At his headquarters away from the Gayoso Hotel, Federal general Cadwallader C. Washburn received a warning of the raid and departed, albeit in a nightshirt. The general successfully eluded Colonel Jesse Forrest, another of General Forrest's brothers. Maness, *Untutored*, 289.
34. Bacchanal was a huge feast or orgy.
35. Queen Victoria (1819–1901) ascended to the British throne at eighteen and reigned over sixty-three years, a time of unprecedented growth industrially, scientifically, and imperially. Julia Baird, *Victoria, The Queen: An Intimate Biography of the Woman Who Ruled an Empire*s (New York: Random House, 2016), 462–83.
36. Queen Isabella (1451–1504) and King Ferdinand (1452–1516) of Spain ruled over a united kingdom and their influence reached well beyond its borders. John Edwards, *The Spain of the Catholic Monarchs, 1474–1520* (Malden, Mass.: Blackwell Publishers, 2000), viii–ix, 38–67, 282–83.
37. Charlotte Corday (1768–1793) was a French Revolutionary individual who was guillotined for the murder of Jean-Paul Marat (1743–1793), another contemporary who helped cause more radicalism during that revolution. Ian Davidson, *The French Revolution: From Enlightenment to Tyranny* (New York: Pegasus Books, 2016), 113, 117, 168.
38. More properly, Corday and Marat were contemporary revolutionists. If friends, a definitely strained relationship.
39. Hope Hart just used an adjective to describe a somewhat ogre, a dreaded person.
40. Parcel Post in the United States did not actually begin until 1913. Hope Hart was using the term generally applying it to packages shipped from a business to a customer that at first would be by rail or private carriers. Implementation of the idea resulted in booming business for catalog companies like Montgomery Ward and Sears, Roebuck and Company. The convenience of ordering for home delivery notably bettered the quality of rural residents. "Parcel Post: Delivery of Dreams, Introduction." Smithsonian Libraries and Archives, https://www.sil.si.edu/ondisplay/parcelpost/intro.htm.
41. "THE NATIONAL CLOAK & SUIT COMPANY," formed during 1888 in New York City, and "BELLAS-HESS," as Hope Hart typed the names, emerged during 1927 as the National Belles Hess Company in Kansas City, Missouri. The mail-order company, emphasizing quality women's apparel, was among the top five mail order houses that included Sears and Montgomery Wards. James Worthy, *Shaping An Institution: Robert E. Wood and Sears, Roebuck* (Urbana: University of Illinois, 1984), 16. Cecil C. Hoge, Sr., *The First Hundred Years Are The Toughest: What We Can Learn from the Century of Com-*

petition between Sears and Wards (Berkley, California: Ten Speed Press, 1988), 82–83, 99. Boris Emmet and John E. Jeuck, *Catalogues and Counters: A History of Sears, Roebuck and Company* (Chicago: University of Chicago Press, 1950), 22, 171, 204. Hope Hart did not explain her reason for putting the names of the two companies in all uppercase letters.

Chapter 13

1. There was not enough internal evidence to pinpoint a location or year of the events in this chapter.
2. Grenada consists of three islands as a West Indies Caribbean nation northeast of Venezuela.
3. Futures are financial agreements obligating the signers to sell a commodity at a preset future time and price irrespective of the current market price at the end of the contract.
4. *Entre Nous* in French means between us as in confidence. Hope Hart probably coined a term for a social group or club that might meet to play cards, more specifically the game Rook.
5. Chine in the fashion world is a garment with a high neck and large sleeves made of a soft silky fabric.
6. Teddies are short one-piece female undergarments.
7. Camisoles are short sleeveless undergarment cover for women.
8. Spirella was a brand name for a corset, a tight-laced fitted garment around a woman's midsection.
9. Uncle Billy and Aunt Alice were William Thomas Killebrew (1869–1943) and Alice Moore Killebrew (1877–1962). "William Thomas Killebrew," findagrave.com. Alice was the youngest child of Calvin Simpson Moore (1837–1901) and Ruth Paralee McWherter Hart Moore (1840–1916) of Little Zion near Palmersville in northeastern Weakley County. "Alice Ruth Moore Killebrew," findagrave.com.
10. Mule is a footwear with no heel back usually for but not limited to household wear.
11. Northerner was a general term for relative newcomers not from the American south, often said in somewhat pejorative tone.
12. "Ja'nders" was a local use of the word jaundice that means yellow or yellowish. It referred to discolored skin and whites of the eye.
13. Woodmen's Hall was a building where the Woodmen's Club met.
14. Dancing was either prohibited by Baptist, Church of Christ, and Methodists churches or frowned on by them. However, McGowan stated that Methodists and Presbyterians permitted dancing. McGowan, *West Tennessee*, 309.

15. Reelfoot Lake was a natural lake formed partially by the New Madrid earthquakes of 1811–1812 in upper northwest Tennessee mainly in Lake and Obion Counties, Tennessee. Hayes, *Reelfoot*, 1–2, 25–29.
16. Prince Albert was a long double-breasted formal outer coat featuring a fitted upper body. The man himself was the Prince Consort of Queen Victoria.
17. "Jump the broomstick" meant to get married or the formalizing of vows.
18. "Howlin' on the church steps" was likely some obscure local superstition or supposed omen.
19. Fulton was Fulton, Fulton County, Kentucky, a town adjacent to South Fulton, Obion County, Tennessee.
20. "How-de-do" is an indication of an unexpected result.
21. "Queer" meant different or out of the ordinary in the early twentieth century.
22. Since the late 1890s in Memphis, Tennessee, "The Commercial Appeal" has been a daily newspaper.
23. Could it be the diagnosis was wrong or was the outcome a miracle?
24. Penrod, an aspiring male adventure writer, disliked having to act in a school play and rather drastically turned a serious production on its head. Booth Tarkington, *Penrod* (New York: Grosset & Dunlap, 1946).

Epilogue

1. Hymen was the Greek god of marriage. "Hymen." Merriam-Webster Online, https://www.merriam-webster.com/dictionary/hymen.

BIBLIOGRAPHY

Abbott, Evelyn, ed. *The Heroes of the Nations*. New York: G. P. Putnam's Sons, 1890.
Alcott, Louisa May. *Little Women*. Literary Guild of America, 1950.
Alexander, Harbert. "Madison County." *Tennessee Encyclopedia*. Tennessee Historical Society. https://tennesseeencyclopedia.net/entries/madison-county/.
Andersen, H. C. *The Brave Tin Soldier*. Project Gutenberg, 1998.
Andersen, Nancy K. "Troubles and Triumphs, 1900–1939." In *Methodism in the Memphis Conference: 1840–1990*, edited by Kenneth Wilkerson, 59–82. Memphis Conference Commission on Archives and History, 1990.
Armentrout, Donald S. "Gailor, Thomas Frank." *Tennessee Encyclopedia*. Tennessee Historical Society. https://tennesseeencyclopedia.net/entries/thomas-frank-gailor/.
Arnow, Harriette Simpson. *Seedtime on the Cumberland*. University of Kentucky Press, 1983.
Baird, Julia. *Victoria, The Queen: An Intimate Biography of the Woman Who Ruled an Empire*. Random House, 2016.
Barton, Lon Carter. "Graves County." In *The Kentucky Encyclopedia*, edited by John E. Kleber, 384–85. University Press of Kentucky, 1992.
Batts, Christine J. "The Golden Banana and the Banana Festival Story." *Journal of the Jackson Purchase Historical Society* 7, no. 1 (June 1979).
Bergeron, Paul H., Stephen V. Ash, Jeanette Keith. *Tennesseans and Their History*. University of Tennessee Press, 1999.
Black, Roy W., Sr. "The Genesis of County Organization in the Western District of North Carolina and in the State of Tennessee." Vol. 2 of West Tennessee Historical Society *Papers*, 95–118. 1948.
"Bondurant, Sarah Ann Kennedy." Find a Grave. https://www.findagrave.com/memorial/66514017/sarah-ann-bondurant.
Bordin, Ruth Birgitta Anderson. *Francis Willard: A Biography*. University of North Carolina, 1986.
Boylston, James R., and Allen J. Wiener. *David Crockett in Congress: The Rise and Fall of the Poor Man's Friend: With Collected Correspondence, Selected Speeches and Circulars*. Bright Sky Press, 2009.

"Brice [Brite], Lemual [Lemuel]." 1900 United States Federal Census. Ancestry.com. https://www.ancestry.com/discoveryui-content/view/61423515:7602.

"Bright [Brite], Lemuel D." 1880 United States Federal Census. Ancestry.com. https://www.ancestry.com/discoveryui-content/view/16993350:6742

"Brite, Ida May Vanola." Ancestry.com. https://www.ancestry.com/genealogy/records/ida-may-vanola-brite-24-1b1s70.

"Brite, Lemuel Dewitt." Find a Grave. https://www.findagrave.com/memorial/74011377/lemuel-dewitt-brite.

Bromberg, Howard, ed. "George Eastman." In *Great Lives from History: The Incredibly Wealthy*. Salem Press, Inc., 2011.

Bryant, Ron D. "Calloway County." In *The Kentucky Encyclopedia*, edited by John E. Kleber, 152–53. University Press of Kentucky, 1992.

———. "Fulton County." In *The Kentucky Encyclopedia*, edited by John E. Kleber, 360–61. University Press of Kentucky, 1992.

———. "Hickman." In *The Kentucky Encyclopedia*, edited by John E. Kleber, 427. University Press of Kentucky, 1992.

Bunyan, John. *Pilgrim's Progress*. Frederick A. Stokes Company, 1939.

Burt, Christopher. "Historical Perspective on Total Solar Eclipses in the U.S." Weather Underground. https://www.wunderground.com/cat6/historical-perspective-total-solar-eclipses-us.

"Canedy, Nelson [Nelson Kennedy]." 1840 United States Federal Census. Ancestry.com. https://www.ancestry.com/search/collections/8057/.

Carter, Arthur B. *The Tarnished Cavalier: Major General Earl Van Dorn, C.S.A.* University of Tennessee Press, 1999.

Cashman, Sean Dennis. *America in the Gilded Age: From the Death of Lincoln to the Rise of Theodore Roosevelt*. New York University Press, 1994.

Castel, Albert E. *General Sterling Price and the Civil War in the West*. Louisiana State University Press, 1968.

Cayton, Andrew R. L., ed. *The American Midwest: An Interpretative Encyclopedia*. Indiana University Press, 2007.

Centers for Disease Control and Prevention. "Diphtheria." https://www.cdc.gov/diphtheria/index.html.

———. "Malaria." https://www.cdc.gov/parasites/malaria.

———. "Typhus." https://www.cdc.gov/typhus/index.html.

Chester, William Wayne. "The Skirmish at Lockridge Mill in Weakley County, Tennessee—May 6, 1862." Vol. 15 of *Journal of the Jackson Purchase Historical Society*, 51–54. June 1987.

Chronicling America, "About The Saturday Blade. [volume] (Chicago, Ill.) 1887–19??." Library of Congress. https://chroniclingamerica.loc.gov/lccn/sn84024076/.

Civil War Centennial Commission of Tennessee. *Tennesseans in the Civil War: A Military History of Confederate and Union Units with Available Rosters of Personnel.* Civil War Centennial Commission of Tennessee, 1964.

Cohen, Norm. *American Folk Songs: A Regional Encyclopedia.* Vol. 2. Greenwood Press, 2008.

Corlew, Robert E. *Tennessee, A Short History.* University of Tennessee Press, 1990.

Cullhane, John. *The American Circus, An Illustrated History.* Henry Holt and Company, 1991.

Culp, Frederick R., and Mrs. Robert E. Ross. *Gibson County, Past and Present; The First General History of One of West Tennessee's Pivotal Counties.* Gibson County Historical Society, 1961.

Daniel, Larry J. *Shiloh: The Battle That Changed the Civil War.* Simon & Schuster, 1997.

———. "The Civil War and Reconstruction: 1860–1869." In *Methodism in the Memphis Conference: 1840–1990*, edited by Kenneth Wilkerson, 38–47. Memphis Conference Commission on Archives and History, 1990.

Davidson, Ian. *The French Revolution: From Enlightenment to Tyranny.* Pegasus Books, 2016.

Davis, Eddy W., and Daniel Foxx. *Nathan Bedford Forrest: In Search of the Enigma.* Pelican Pub. Co., 2007.

De Ruiter, Brian. "Jamestown Ter-Centennial Exposition of 1907." Encyclopedia Virginia. https://www.encyclopediavirginia.org/Jamestown_Ter-Centennial_Exposition_of_1907.

Dickens, Charles. *David Copperfield.* Edited with an Introduction by George H. Ford. Houghton Mifflin, 1958.

———. *Oliver Twist.* Edited by Kathleen Tillotson. Clarendon Press, 1974.

———. *The Old Curiosity Shop.* Oxford University Press, 1951.

Dodge, Pryor. *The Bicycle.* Flammarion, 1996.

Donald, Aida D. *Lion in the White House: A Life of Theodore Roosevelt.* Basic Books, 2007.

Dorgan, Howard. "'Old Time' Baptists." *Tennessee Encyclopedia.* Tennessee Historical Society. https://tennesseeencyclopedia.net/entries/old-time-baptists/.

Downes, Olin, and Elie Siegmeister. *A Treasury of American Song.* Knopf, 1943.

Downing, Marvin. "An Admiring Nephew-in-Law: John Christmas McLemore and His Relationship to 'Uncle' Andrew Jackson." West Tennessee Historical Society Papers 44 (1990): 38–44.

Downing, Marvin. "'First Monday': A Trade Day and Social Institution in Trenton, Tennessee." West Tennessee Historical Society Papers 46 (1992): 73–83.

———. "Jack of All Trades: Early 20th Century Master Mule Trader Walter Bonaparte "Bone" Phelan of Trenton, Tennessee." *Journal of the Jackson Purchase Historical Society* 16 (June 1988): 27–34.

———. "John Christmas McLemore." *Tennessee Encyclopedia.* Tennessee Historical Society. http://tennesseeencyclopedia.net/entries/john-christmas-mclemore/.

———. "John Christmas McLemore: 19th Century Tennessee Land Speculator." *Tennessee Historical Quarterly* 42, no. 3 (1983): 254–65. http://www.jstor.org/stable/42626381.

———. "Old Christmasville: Its Lure and Lore." *Journal of the Jackson Purchase Historical Society* 7 (June 1979): 34–43.

———. "Richard E. Davis and The Trenton Herald-Register: An Editor's Return Home, 1941–1942." *Journal of the Jackson Purchase Historical Society* 20: (June 1993), 25–31.

Doyle, Arthur Conan, Sir. *The Hound of the Baskervilles.* Buccaneer Books, 1986.

———. *The Sign of the Four.* Edited by Christopher Roden. Oxford University Press, 1993.

Drabble, John. "A World on Display: The St. Louis World's Fair of 1904." *American Historical Review* 101 (Oct. 1996).

Duck, Edward Walker. "Memories of Family Life in West Tennessee from Around 1890 to 1910." West Tennessee Historical Society Papers 25 (1971): 26–46.

Dumas, Alexandre. *The Count of Monte Cristo.* Modern Library, 1996.

Eastman Kodak Company. "The Birth of Eastman." https://www.eastman.com/company/about_eastman/history/stories/pages/birth-of-eastman.aspx.

Edwards, John. *The Spain of the Catholic Monarchs, 1474–1520.* Blackwell Publishers, 2000.

Eliot, Charles W., compiler. *The Harvard Classics.* P. F. Collier and Son, 1909.

Elliott, Emory, gen. ed. *Columbia Literary History of the United States.* Columbia University, 1988.

Emmet, Boris, and John E. Jeuck. *Catalogues and Counters: A History of Sears, Roebuck and Company.* University of Chicago Press, 1950.

Emmett, Daniel Decatur. "Dixie's Land." Genius. https://genius.com/Daniel-decatur-emmett-i-wish-i-was-in-dixies-land-lyrics.

Ermarth, Elizabeth Deeds. *George Eliot.* Twayne, 1985.

Evans, Augusta Jane. *At the Mercy of Tiberius.* G. W. Dillingham Company, 1887.

———. *St. Elmo: Or, Saved at Last.* University of Alabama Press, 2015.

Ezzell, Timothy P. "Malcom R. Patterson." *Tennessee Encyclopedia.* Tennessee Historical Society. http://tennesseeencyclopedia.net/entries/malcolm-r-patterson/.

Fisher, Bernard, ed. *"The Commercial Appeal."* Historical Marker Database. https://www.hmdb.org/m.asp?m=55377.

Fite, Gilbert C. *Cotton Fields No More: Southern Agriculture, 1865–1980.* University Press of Kentucky, 1984.

Fleming, Cynthia Griggs. "Elementary and Secondary Education." *Tennessee*

Encyclopedia. Tennessee Historical Society. http://tennesseeencyclopedia.net/entries/elementary-and-secondary-education/.

Folmsbee, Stanley. "David Crockett and West Tennessee." West Tennessee Historical Society Papers 28 (1974): 5–24.

Foner, Eric. *Reconstruction: America's Unfinished Revolution, 1863–1877*. HarperCollins, 2002.

Forrester, R. C., and Betty Burdick Wood. *Night Riders of Reelfoot Lake: The Untold Story*. Forrester Wood Publication, 2001.

Fox, John, Jr. *The Little Shepherd of Kingdom Come*. Charles Scribner's Sons, 1910.

Freeberg, Ernest. *The Age of Edison: Electric Light and the Invention of Modern America*. Penguin, 2013.

Goldsmith, Oliver. *The Vicar of Wakefield*. Oxford University Press, 1967.

Gundersen, Lawrence G., Jr. "West Tennessee and the Cotton Frontier." West Tennessee Historical Society Papers 52 (1998): 25–43.

Hancock, Sandra G. "Moore, John Trotwood." Encyclopedia of Alabama. http://www.encyclopediaofalabama.org/article/h-2437.

"Harbert, Eva Elna Hart." Find a Grave. https://www.findagrave.com/memorial/74462633/eva-elna-harbert.

"Harbert, Perry Morton." Find a Grave. https://www.findagrave.com/memorial/138445528/perry-morton-harbert.

Hardy, Thomas. *Tess of the D'Urbervilles*. McDougal Littell, 1998.

Hare, Jr., Clarence E. "An Expanding Ministry: 1870–1899." In *Methodism in the Memphis Conference: 1840–1990*, edited by Kenneth Wilkerson, 48–58. Memphis Conference Commission on Archives and History, 1990.

"Hart, Benjamin, Lt." Daughters of the American Revolution. https://www.geni.com/people/Lt-Benjamin-Hart/6000000003199457750.

"Hart, Benjamin Umpstead." Ancestry.com. https://www.ancestry.com/genealogy/records/benjamin-umpstead-hart-24-18lp1c.

Hart, Hope. "Among My Kith and Kin." *Dresden Enterprise*, February 9, 1973–April 6, 1973.

"Hart, Hope Howard." Find a Grave. https://www.findagrave.com/memorial/74195751/hope-howard-hart.

"Hart, Joe Reese." Find a Grave. https://www.findagrave.com/memorial/67918633/joe-reese-hart.

Hart, "Joe Reece." *Ft. Myers* (Florida) *Press*. February 6, 1975.

"Hart, John Mark." Find a Grave. https://www.findagrave.com/memorial/46072690/john-mark-hart.

"Hart, Martha Nelson 'Mattie' Kennedy." Find a Grave. https://www.findagrave.com/memorial/74196032/martha-nelson-hart.

"Hart, Martha Reece." Find a Grave. https://www.findagrave.com/memorial/139980840/martha-reese-hart.

"Hart, Nelson K." *Jackson* (Tennessee) *Sun*, May 30, 1998.

Hart, Nelson Key. "Memoirs." Memphis Conference Minutes Journal (1957): 114.

"Hart, Ray Kennedy." Find a Grave. https://www.findagrave.com/memorial/74462586/ray-kennedy-hart.

"Hart, Ray Kennedy." 1930 U.S. Public Census. Ancestry.com. https://www.ancestry.com/search/collections/6224/.

"Hart, Ruth Lee." Find a Grave. https://www.findagrave.com/memorial/139980791/ruth-lee-hart.

"Hart, Sterling Reece." Find a Grave. https://www.findagrave.com/memorial/74195995/sterling-reece-hart.

"Hart, Thomas." U.S. Confederate Soldiers Compiled Service Records, 1861–1865. Ancestry.com. https://www.ancestry.com/search/collections/2322/.

"Hart, Thomas Greene." Ancestry.com. https://www.ancestry.com/genealogy/records/thomas-green-hart-24-18lpdr.

Hartje, Robert G. *Van Dorn: The Life and Times of a Confederate General*. Vanderbilt University Press, 1967.

Hawkins, Van. "Cotton Industry." Encyclopedia of Arkansas. https://encyclopediaofarkansas.net/entries/Cotton-Industry-2092.

Hawn, Michael. "History of Hymns: 'Pass Me Not, O Gentle Savior.'" United Methodist Church Discipleship Ministries. https://www.umcdiscipleship.org/resources/history-of-hymns-pass-me-not-o-gentle-savior.

Hayes, David G. *The Historic Reelfoot Lake Region: An Early History of the People and Places of Western Obion and Present-Day Lake County*. Collierville, TN: InstantPublisher.com, Inc., 2017.

Henty, G. A. (George Alfred). *St. George for England*. CreateSpace Independent Publishing Platform, 2013.-

Historical Marker Project. "Union City Junction (HM204R)." Union City, TN 38261 Obion County. https://historicalmarkerproject.com/markers/HM204R_union-city-junction_Union-City-TN.html.

Hobsbawm, Eric. *The Age of Empire, 1875–1914*. Vintage Books, 1989.

"Hodges, Sarah Annie Moore." Find a Grave. https://www.findagrave.com/memorial/96910216/sarah-annie-hodges.

Hoge, Cecil C., Sr. *The First Hundred Years Are the Toughest: What We Can Learn from the Century of Competition Between Sears and Wards*. Ten Speed Press, 1988.

HomeTownLocator. "Cottonwood Point Ferry." *Tennessee Gazetteer*. https://tennessee.hometownlocator.com/maps/feature-map,ftc,3,fid,1309785,n,cottonwood%20point%20ferry.cfm.

———. "Little Zion Church, Weakley County, Tennessee." *Tennessee Gazetteer.* https://tennessee.hometownlocator.com/maps/feature-map,ftc,2,fid,1291716,n,little%20zion%20church.cfm.

———. "North Fork of the Obion." *Tennessee Gazetteer.* https://tennessee.hometownlocator.com/maps/feature-map,ftc,1,fid,1295906,n,north%20fork%20obion%20river.cfm.

Hughes, Thomas. *Tom Brown's Schooldays.* Crowell, [n.d.].

Humphreys, Cecil C. "The Formation of Reelfoot Lake and Consequent Land and Social Problems." West Tennessee Historical Society Papers 14 (1960): 32–73.

Hurst, Jack. *Nathan Bedford Forrest: A Biography.* A. A. Knopf, 1993.

Isidore, Chris. "Sears' Extraordinary History: A Timeline." Cable News Network. https://www.cnn.com/interactive/2018/10/business/sears-timeline/index.html.

Jackson, Richard. *Popular Songs of Nineteenth-Century America.* Dover Publications, 1976.

James, Annie Laurie. "Crockett County." *Tennessee Encyclopedia.* Tennessee Historical Society. http://tennesseeencyclopedia.net/entries/crockett-county/.

"Jamestown Exposition of 1907." Encyclopedia Virginia. https://www.encyclopediavirginia.org/Jamestown_Ter-Centennial_Exposition_of_1907.

Jeffers, H. Paul. *Colonel Roosevelt: Theodore Roosevelt Goes to War, 1897–1898.* J. Wiley and Sons, 1996.

Jewell, Virginia Honchell. "Hickman County." In *The Kentucky Encyclopedia*, edited by John E. Kleber, 427–28. University Press of Kentucky, 1992.

Joiner, Harry M. *Tennessee Then and Now.* Southern Textbook Publishers, 1983.

Kennedy, David M. *Over Here: The First World War and American Society.* Oxford University Press, 1980.

"Kennedy, Laura Jane Simmons." Find a Grave. https://www.findagrave.com/memorial/110633161/laura-jane-kennedy.

"Kennedy, Martha 'Mattie' Nelson." Find a Grave. https://www.findagrave.com/memorial/74196032/martha-nelson-hart.

"Kennedy, Nancy Killebrew." Find a Grave. https://www.findagrave.com/memorial/140108781/nancy-kennedy.

"Kennedy, Nelson." Find a Grave. https://www.findagrave.com/memorial/110632762/nelson-kennedy.

"Kennedy, Sampson Edward." Find a Grave. https://www.findagrave.com/memorial/140108731/sampson-edward-kennedy.

"Kennedy, Sarah Angeline Fields." Find A Grave. https://www.findagrave.com/memorial/23797568/sarah-angeline-moore.

"Killebrew, Alice Ruth Moore." Find a Grave. https://www.findagrave.com/memorial/139600949/alice-ruth-killebrew.

"Killebrew, Capt. Thomas Leroy 'Roy.'" Find a Grave. https://www.findagrave.com/memorial/66720495/thomas-leroy-killebrew.

"Killebrew, Thomas Leroy." *Dresden Enterprise* and *Sharon Tribune*, April 12, 1907.

Killebrew, W. T., and Alice R. Moore. Marriage License No. 1209, State of Tennessee, Weakley County, Dresden, Tennessee, April 27, 1898. Weakley County Marriages, 1886–November 1898, Book C, 510.

"Killebrew, William Thomas." Find a Grave. https://www.findagrave.com/memorial/139600822/william-thomas-killebrew.

King, Jesse, et al., heirs. Deed to Sampson Kennedy, October 22, 1821—Original recording in Henry County. April term 1831. Agreed upon January 6, 1831. Weakley County Deed Book A-B, Weakley County Courthouse, Dresden, Tennessee, 376.

Kipling, Rudyard. *The Light that Failed*. Doubleday, 1915.

Langsdon, Phillip. *Tennessee: A Political History*. Hillsboro Press, 2000.

Laughter, Verne. "An Ordinary Family's Changing Lifestyle, 1902–1982." West Tennessee Historical Society Papers 64 (2010): 90–118.

Lear, Edward. *The Owl and the Pussycat*. Lothrop, Lee & Shepard Books, 1991.

Lears, Jackson. *Rebirth of a Nation: The Making of Modern America, 1877–1920*. Harper, 2001.

Lofaro, Michael A., and Joe Cummings, Eds. *Crockett at Two Hundred: New Perspectives on the Man and the Myth*. University of Tennessee Press, 1989.

Mackey, Robert R. *The Uncivil War: Irregular Warfare in the Upper South, 1861–1865*. University of Oklahoma Press, 2004.

Maness, Lonnie E. *An Untutored Genius: The Military Career of General Nathan Bedford Forrest*. Guild Bindery Press, 1990.

———. "Capt. Charles Cooper Nott and the Battle of Lockridge's Mills." *Journal of the Jackson Purchase Historical Society* 3 (June 1975): 12–20.

Marlborough, Wiltshire. *Little Boy Blue*. Adam Matthew Digital, McLoughlin Bros., 2020.

Marschall, Rick. *Bully: The Life and Times of Theodore Roosevelt*. Regency Publishing, 2011.

Marshall, James. *Goldilocks and the Three Bears*. Dial Books for Young Readers, 1988.

"Martin, Mary 'Polly' Fields." Find a Grave. https://www.findagrave.com/memorial/160941825/mary-martin.

McClure, Joe David. "Carroll County," *Tennessee Encyclopedia*. Tennessee Historical Society. http://tennesseeencyclopedia.net/entries/carroll-county/.

McCormac, Eugene Irving. *James K. Polk: A Political Biography*. Russell & Russell, 1965.

McDonough, James L. "Battle of Shiloh." *Tennessee Encyclopedia*. Tennessee Historical Society. http://tennesseeencyclopedia.net/entries/battle-of-shiloh/.

McDonough, James Lee. *Shiloh—In Hell before Night*. University of Tennessee Press, 1977.

McFerrin, John B. *Methodism in Tennessee*. Vol. 3. A. H. Redford, 1873.

McGowan, Sam. *West Tennessee: The Land Between the Rivers*. CreateSpace Independent Publishing Platform, 2018.

McPherson, James M. *Battle Cry of Freedom: The Civil War Era*. Oxford University Press, 1988.

"McWherter, Capt. William Reuben 'Bill.'" Find a Grave. https://www.findagrave.com/memorial/76063385/william-reuben-mcwherter.

"McWherter, Ida May Brite." Find a Grave. https://www.findagrave.com/memorial/103529139/ida-may-mcwherter.

Memphis Conference, United Methodist Church, Journals 1862 to Present, https://www.memphis-umc.net/journals1862topresent.

Miles, Murray. "Tobacco." *Tennessee Encyclopedia*. Tennessee Historical Society. http://tennesseeencyclopedia.net/entries/tobacco/.

Milford, Brian K., ed. *The Book of Discipline of the United Methodist Church 2016*. United Methodist Publishing House, 2016.

Miller, Nathan. *Theodore Roosevelt: A Life*. Morrow, 1992.

Miller, Russell. *The Adventures of Arthur Conan Doyle: A Biography*. Thomas Dunne Books, 2008.

Moen, Jon R., and Ellis W. Tallman. "Panic of 1907." Federal Reserve History. https://www.federalreservehistory.org/essays/panic-of-1907.

Mooney, Sue F. Dromgoole. *My Moving Tent*. Publishing House Methodist Episcopal Church South, Bigham & Smith Agents, 1903.

"Moore, Calvin Simpson." Ancestry.com. https://www.ancestry.com/discoveryui-content/view/114630015:60525.

"Moore, Calvin Simpson." Find a Grave. https://www.findagrave.com/memorial/139599310/calvin-simpson-moore.

"Moore, J. S. [Leroy Moore]." Tennessee, U.S., Marriage Records, 1780–2002. Ancestry.com. https://www.ancestry.com/search/collections/1169.

"Moore, James Silas." Find a Grave. https://www.findagrave.com/memorial/36713447/james-silas-moore.

Moore, John Trotwood. *The Bishop of Cottonwood: A Story of the Southern Cotton Mills*. J. C. Winston Company, 1906.

"Moore, Lemuel Potter." Find a Grave. https://www.findagrave.com/memorial/136933600/lemuel-potter-moore.

"Moore, Leroy Simpson." Ancestry.com. https://www.ancestry.com/genealogy/records/leroy-simpson-moore-24-1bmqrc.

"Moore, Leroy Simpson." Find a Grave. https://www.findagrave.com/memorial/103530661/leroy-simpson-moore.

"Moore, Martha Emily." Find a Grave. https://www.findagrave.com/memorial/210061676/martha-emily-moore.

"Moore, Mary Viola." Find a Grave. https://www.findagrave.com/memorial/23797497/mary-viola-moore.

"Moore, Ruth Paralee McWherter." Find a Grave. https://www.findagrave.com/memorial/81398874/ruth-paralee-moore.

"Moore, Sarah Angeline Kennedy" Find a Grave. https://www.findagrave.com/memorial/23797568/sarah-angeline-moore.

"Moore, Silas Reuben." Find a Grave. https://www.findagrave.com/memorial/139631206/silas-reuben-moore.

"Moore, Simon Peter 'SP'." Find a Grave. https://www.findagrave.com/memorial/91464523/simon-peter-moore.

Moore, Wayne C. "Corn." *Tennessee Encyclopedia*. Tennessee Historical Society. http://tennesseeencyclopedia.net/entries/corn/.

———. "Cotton." *Tennessee Encyclopedia*. Tennessee Historical Society. http://tennesseeencyclopedia.net/entries/cotton/.

"Moore, William Issac." Find a Grave. https://www.findagrave.com/memorial/210060267/william-issac-moore.

Morelli, William P. "John Hunt Morgan." *Tennessee Encyclopedia*. Tennessee Historical Society. http://tennesseeencyclopedia.net/entries/john-hunt-morgan/.

N. A. "The Marrying Squire Catches the Fever Himself and Claims a Kentucky Bride." *The Commercial* (Union City, TN), November 29, 1907, 6.

National Park Service. "Shiloh Battlefield—Site of Shiloh Church." Shiloh National Military Park. https://www.nps.gov/places/shiloh-battlefield-site-of-shiloh-church.htm

National Weather Service. "Mississippi River Flood History 1543-Present." National Oceanic and Atmospheric Administration. https://www.weather.gov/lix/ms_flood_history.

Obion County, Tennessee, Genealogy and History. "Court Clerks, Sheriffs, etc." https://tngenweb.org/obion/court-clerks-sheriffs-etc/.

Osbeck, Kenneth W. *Amazing Grace: 366 Inspiring Hymn Stories for Daily Devotions*. Kregel Publications, 1990.

Ouzts, Clay. "Nancy Hart." New Georgia Encyclopedia. https://www.georgiaencyclopedia.org/articles/history-archaeology/nancy-hart-ca-1735-1830/.

"Parcel Post: Delivery of Dreams, Introduction." Smithsonian Libraries and Archives. https://www.sil.si.edu/ondisplay/parcelpost/intro.htm.

Phillips, E. Harrell. "Early Methodism in The Jackson Purchase: Before 1840." In *Methodism in the Memphis Conference: 1840–1990*, edited by Kenneth Wilkerson, 7–19. Memphis Conference Commission on Archives and History, 1990.

Phillips, James B. "Hardin County." *Tennessee Encyclopedia*. Tennessee Historical Society. http://tennesseeencyclopedia.net/entries/hardin-county/.

Poetry Nook. "Love's Old Sweet Song." https://www.poetrynook.com/poem/loves-old-sweet-song.

Potter, David M. *The Impending Crisis, 1848–1861*. Harper & Row, 1976.

Pounds, Ernest R., comp., ed. *An Early History of Gibson County and Its Communities*. Jostens Printing and Publishing, 2011.

Pruitt, Sarah. "When the Sears Catalog Sold Everything from Houses to Hubcaps." History.com. https://history.com/news/sears-catalog-houses-hubcaps.

Ramage, James A. "General John Hunt Morgan and His Great Raids into Kentucky." In *The Civil War in Kentucky: Battle for the Bluegrass State*, edited by Kent Masterson Brown. Savas Publishing Company, 2000.

Randall, James G., and David Donald. *The Civil War and Reconstruction*. Little, Brown and Company, 1969.

Raph, Theodore. *The American Song Treasury: 100 Favorites*. Dover Publications, 1986.

Rasmussen, Frederick N. "Pullman porters, once the backbone of passenger rail service laid the groundwork for what became the civil rights movement." *Baltimore Sun*, March 25, 2021. https://www.baltimoresun.com/features/retro-baltimore/bs-fe-retro-pullman-porters-20210325-ennht430pbchjmkfbhjysynja4-story.html.

"Rawls, Louisa 'Lucy B' Killebrew." Find a Grave. https://www.findagrave.com/memorial/24717227/louisa-rawls.

Reeves, Charles A. Jr. "Slave Population of the United States Map." Teach History. https:///teachtnhistory.org/file/5. tn 1860 Slave Pop.Map./jpg.

Reynolds, Thomas. "Grave site: Thomas Green Hart." *Genealogy.com*. February 26, 2012.

Rice, Alice Caldwell Hegan. *Mrs. Wiggs of the Cabbage Patch*. University Press of Kentucky, 2015.

Ridpath, John Clark, ed. *The Ridpath Library of Universal Literature; A Biographical and Bibliographical Summary of the World's Most Eminent Authors, Including the Choicest Selections and Masterpieces from Their Writings*. Revisions and additions by William Montgomery Clark. New York: The Fifth Avenue Library Society, 1899–1912.

Rigdon, Jonathan. *Rigdon's English Grammar for the Common School*. New York: Hinds, Noble & Eldredge, 1896.

Robertson, John E. L. "Paducah." In *The Kentucky Encyclopedia*, edited by John E. Kleber, 705–6. University Press of Kentucky, 1992.

Roe, E. P. *Barriers Burned Away*. N.p.: Dodd Mead AMS, 1898.

Roland, Charles P. *Albert Sidney Johnston: Soldier of Three Republics*. University of Texas Press, 1984.

Rothrock, Mary U., ed. "Home Life in Madison and Carroll Counties, Tennessee, 1864–1867." *West Tennessee Historical Society Papers* 23 (1969): 110–28.

———. "Home Life in Madison and Carroll Counties, Tennessee, 1868." *West Tennessee Historical Society Papers* 24 (1970): 106–28.

Scharnhorst, Gary. *Horatio Alger, Jr.* Twayne Publisher, 1980.

Schneider, Dorothy, and Carl J. Schneider. *American Women in the Progressive Era, 1900–1920.* Facts on File, 1993.

Seigenthaler, John. *James K. Polk.* Times Books, 2004.

Semmer, Blythe. "Gayoso Hotel." *Tennessee Encyclopedia.* Tennessee Historical Society. https://tennesseeencyclopedia.net/entries/gayoso-hotel/.

Shackford, James Atkins. *David Crockett: The Man and the Legend.* University of North Carolina Press, 1956.

Shea, William L., and Earl J. Hess. *Pea Ridge: Civil War Campaign in the West.* University of North Carolina Press, 1992.

Smith, Johnathan K. T. "Benton County." *Tennessee Encyclopedia.* Tennessee Historical Society. http://tennesseeencyclopedia.net/entries/benton-county/.

Smith, Timothy B. *The Golden Age of Battlefield Preservation: The Decade of the 1890s and the Establishment of America's First Five Military Parks.* University of Tennessee Press, 2008.

Stevenson, Robert Louis. *Treasure Island.* Scholastic, 1988.

Sullivan, Dolores P. *William Holmes McGuffey: Schoolmaster to the Nation.* Fairleigh Dickinson University Press, 1994.

Tarkington, Booth. *Penrod.* Grosset & Dunlap, 1946.

Thackery, William Makepeace. *Vanity Fair.* London, 1867. https://archive.org/details/vanityfairnovelwo1thac_0.

Threlkeld, Bill. "Night Riders of Reelfoot Lake." *Tennessee Encyclopedia.* Tennessee Historical Society, http://tennesseeencyclopedia.net/entries/night-riders-of-reelfoot-lake/.

Tobani, Theodore M., and Mary D. Brine. "Hearts and Flowers." DigitalCommons@UMaine. https://digitalcommons.library.umaine.edu/cgi/viewcontent.cgi?article=1440&context=mmb-vp.

Trefousse, Hans. *Andrew Johnson: A Biography.* Norton, 1989.

Uffelman, Minoa D., Ellen Kanervo, Phyllis Smith, and Eleanor Williams, eds. *The Diary of Nannie Haskins Williams: A Southern Woman's Story of Rebellion and Reconstruction, 1863–1890.* University of Tennessee Press, 2014.

———. *The Diary of Serepta Jordan: A Southern Woman's Struggle with War and Family, 1857–1864.* University of Tennessee Press, 2020.

Ullrich, Dieter. "They Met at Lockridge's Mills." *West Tennessee Historical Society Papers* 51 (1997): 1–20.

Vanderwood, Paul J. *Night Riders of Reelfoot Lake*. University of Alabama Press, 2003.
Vaughan, Virginia C. *Weakley County*. Memphis State University Press, 1983.
Vaughan, Virginia Clark. "Weakley County." *Tennessee Encyclopedia*. Tennessee Historical Society. http://tennesseeencyclopedia.net/entries/weakley-county/.
Verne, Jules. *Twenty Thousand Leagues Under the Sea*. University of Virginia Library. Generic NL Freebook Publisher, 1995.
Vial, Rebecca A. "Wilderness Road." *Tennessee Encyclopedia*. Tennessee Historical Society. http://tennesseeencyclopedia.net/entries/wilderness-road/.
Wagoner, Bill. "McNairy County." *Tennessee Encyclopedia*. Tennessee Historical Society. http://tennesseeencyclopedia.net/entries/mcnairy-county/.
Walker, Emma. "The Fascinating Story Behind Reelfoot Lake." National Forest Foundation Roots Rated. https://rootsrated.com/stories/the-fascinating-story-behind-reelfoot-lake.
Walker, Melissa, and James C. Cobb, eds. *Agriculture and Industry*. University of North Carolina Press, 2008.
Watlington, Elton. "Organization and Early Beginnings: 1840–1859." In *Methodism in the Memphis Conference: 1840–1990*, edited by Kenneth Wilkerson, 20–37. Memphis Conference Commission on Archives and History, 1990.
Webb, David W. "Henry County." *Tennessee Encyclopedia*. Tennessee Historical Society. http://tennesseeencyclopedia.net/entries/henry-county/.
Weil, Gordon L. *Sears, Roebuck, U.S.A.: The Great American Catalog Store and How It Grew*. Stein and Day, 1977.
Westcott, Edward Noyes. *David Harum: A Story of American Life*. New York: Appleton, 1898.
White, Richard. *The Republic for Which It Stands: The United States During Reconstruction and the Gilded Age, 1865–1896*. Oxford University Press, 2017.
Whiteaker, Larry H. "Civil War." *Tennessee Encyclopedia*. Tennessee Historical Society. http://tennesseeencyclopedia.net/entries/civil-war/.
Wiebe, Robert H. *The Search for Order, 1877–1920*. Hill and Wang, 1967.
Wilkerson, Kenneth, ed. *Methodism in the Memphis Conference: 1840–1990*. Memphis Conference Commission on Archives and History, 1990.
Williams, Emma Inman. *Historic Madison: The Story of Jackson and Madison County, Tennessee*. Madison County Historical Society, 1972.
Williams, Joseph S. *Old Times in West Tennessee: Reminiscences, Semi-Historic, of Pioneer Life and the Early Emigrant Settlers in the Big Hatchie Country*. W. G. Cheeney, 1873.
Williams, Samuel Cole. *Beginnings of West Tennessee in the Land of the Chickasaws, 1541–1841*. Blue and Gray Press, 1971.

Wills, Brian S. "Nathan Bedford Forrest." *Tennessee Encyclopedia*. Tennessee Historical Society. http://tennesseeencyclopedia.net/entries/nathan-bedford-forrest/.

Wills, Brian Steel. *A Battle from the Start: The Life of Nathan Bedford Forrest*. Harper Collins, 1993.

Winters, Donald L. "Agriculture." *Tennessee Encyclopedia*. Tennessee Historical Society. http://tennesseeencyclopedia.net/entries/agriculture/.

———. *Tennessee Farming, Tennessee Farmers: Antebellum Agriculture in the Upper South*. University of Tennessee Press, 1994.

"Woman's Christian Temperance Union." History.com. https://www.history.com/topics/womens-history/womans-christian-temperance-union

Worthy, James. *Shaping An Institution: Robert E. Wood and Sears, Roebuck*. University of Illinois, 1984.

Wright, Harold Bell. *Their Yesterdays*. Chicago: Book Supply Co., 1912.

Wright, Louis B. *Culture on the Moving Frontier*. Harper & Row, 1961.

Wyllie, Arthur. *Tennessee Confederate Pensions*. Barnes & Noble, 2014.

INDEX

Angela, Miss, 174
Annie Sue, 173
Arkansas River, 119
Atwood, Tennessee, 22, 197n96
Aunt Alice, (Alice Ruth Moore Killebrew), 16, 36, 202n2, 205n25, 235n9
Aunt Callie, 178
Aunt Liddy, 127, 131
Aunt Lisa, 75, 90
"Aunt" Liza, 61–65
Aunt Nannie (Sarah Annie Moore Hodges), 48–49, 206n15
Aunt Sally (Sarah Ann Kennedy Bondurant), 76, 211n37
Aunt Sammy (Martha Ann Kennedy Killebrew), 43, 206n29
Aunt Susie (Susan Emmaline Moore), 38, 203nn10–11
Austin, Bill, x, 3, 228n69, 230n10, 231n28
Aydlotte, Mrs., 174

Baker, Pansy, ix, 3
Barleycorn, John, 141, 228n59
Baxter, Mary Ann, ix, 3
Bellas-Hess, 168
Belle of Memphis, 147–50
Big Deal soap, 83
Big Preach, Little Preach, Preachie and Baby Preach, 60–62
Blakemore, Mr., 159
Bon Ami, 126, 221n5

Brite, America, 197n99
Brite, Ida May, 19, 198n99, 218n17
Brite, Lemuel D., 19, 218n17
Brite, Lemuel Dewitt, 197n99, 218n16, 218n19
Britton, Mr., 24–32, 126
Britton, Carrie, 25, 28–30
Britton, Essie, 28–33
Buckner, "Mudcat" Captain, 121–22
Busby, Dr., 112, 115, 218n13
Buster Brown, 72, 211n30

Ca'line, 118
Calloway County, Kentucky, 13, 22, 206n9, 207n6, 230n4
Carter, Bob Lee, 172, 180
Carter, Old Mr., 180
Chicago "Saturday Blade," 125, 221n3
Chickasaw Indians, 3, 189n13, 190nn13–14
Christmasville, Tennessee, 5, 189n13
Cindy, 175, 177–81
Civil War, 7, 9, 11–13, 40, 79, 136–37, 191n30, 193n44
Clarion, 68
Cleveland, Grover, 46, 162, 206n4, 213n17, 232n20
Cobb, Alonzo, 185
Cooper, Jere Prentice, 1
Corey, Bob Brother, 116
Corinth, Mississippi, 8

Cottage Grove, Tennessee, 3, 5, 8, 10, 22, 79, 202n1, 212n7
Cottonwood Landing, Tennessee, 145–46, 228n69
Cousin Elroy, 111
Cousin Irene, 75, 211n36
Cousin Lou, 75, 211n36
Cousin Pigg, 18, 99–101, 217n33
Covington, Tennessee, 22, 197n96
Crandall, Miss, 25, 32
Crandall, Mr., 70
Crider, Janice, ix, 3
Crockett, David, 5, 201n17
Crockett County, 22, 29, 191n22, 201n17
Curve, Tennessee, 22, 197n96

Daisy, 52
Dardanelle, Arkansas, 8, 119, 217n7, 220nn29–30
Daughters of the American Revolution, 1
"Dixie," 130, 229n82
Donie, 173
Downing, Sandra Kay "Sandy" Mitchell, ix
Dresden, Tennessee, 1, 13, 22, 204n22, 228n69, 229n1, 231n1
Dresden Enterprise, 20, 102
Dyersburg, Tennessee, 1, 13, 22, 204n22, 228n69, 229n1, 231n1

Elder Maybank, 19, 39–40, 202n7
Elizabeth, 126
Elmore, Karen, ix
Everett, Robert A. "Fats," 1

Figg, Dr., 181
"Fighting Parson, The," 57
Finley, Tennessee, 198n96
Floss and Clabe, 180–81

Ford, Henry, 12
Forked Deer River, 96, 113, 216n26, 218n14
Forrest, Bill, 164
Forrest, Jesse, 234n33
Forrest, Nathan Bedford, 8, 39, 86, 162, 164, 205n26, 213n19, 233nn31–32, 234n33
Fort Donelson, Tennessee, 8
Fort Henry, Tennessee, 8
Fort Scott, Kansas, 20
Frampton, Jim, 140–42, 228n56
Fulton, Kentucky, 19, 22, 64, 178, 180–81, 204n17, 208n13, 236n19
Fulton County, 192n30, 208n13, 220n40, 236n19
Futrell, Eloise, 114
Futrell, S. M., 264n17

Gailor, Bishop, 163, 233n28
Galloway, Judge, 111
Gaye, Eva, 148–50
Gayoso Hotel, 163–65, 233n26, 233n32, 234n33
George Washington's 1785 treaty, 5
Gibbs, George Washington, 221n4
Gibbs Junction, Tennessee, 125, 221n4
Gleason, Tennessee, 22, 197n96, 202n1, 231n1, 233n27
Grandfather Kennedy, 86, 214n23, 215n5
Grandma (Mrs. Calvin Simpson Moore, Ruth Paralee), 33, 37–41, 71–72, 95–96, 110–14, 116–24, 193n47, 197n100, 204n20, 211n29, 216n22, 218n7, 223n14
Grandma Butler, 181
Grandmother Kennedy, 18, 86, 215n10, 215n12, 217n1
Graves, Gladys, 162–63
Graves, Mr., 162–65

Graves County, Kentucky, 12, 22, 206n9, 207n6, 208n9, 230n4
Grenada, 171, 235n2
Griggs, Caroline "Carrie" (Ida May Brite), 113–17, 218n17; Mrs. Leroy Simpson "Uncle Charlie" Moore, 117–19, 124
Griggs, Squire, 19, 113–18, 218n17

Harbert, Perry Morton, 14, 198n102, 211n38
Hardin County, Tennessee, 12, 22, 211n39, 212n5, 229n4
Hard Shells, 37–38, 40
Hart, Benjamin Umpstead, 6
Hart, Bill R., 20
Hart, Mrs. Edith S., 21
Hart, Eva Elna "Eleanor", 211n38, 212n1, 214n1; Eleanor, 10, 12, 14–17, 23–24, 27, 30, 33–34, 59,74, 102, 200n4, 201n13, 211n38, 212n1, 214n1; Sister, 27, 30, 32–34, 37–40, 48–49, 51, 59, 68, 70–72, 74–77, 80–83, 85, 88–89, 91–93, 102
Hart, Hope Howard, ix-x, 1–21, 50, 102, 186, 194nn51–53, 195n73, 197n98, 199n138, 200nn3–4, 200n7, 200n9, 202nn1–2, 202nn5–6, 203nn9–10, 203n12, 204n15, 204n17, 204n21, 205n24, 205n29, 206n4, 206n9, 206nn15–19, 207n3, 207nn6–7, 208n1, 210n23, 211n29, 211n37, 212n1, 212n2, 212nn7–8, 214n23, 214nn28–29, 214n1, 215nn6–7, 215n14, 216n22, 216nn31–33, 217n1, 217nn5–6, 217n8, 218n14, 218n17, 220n30, 221n32, 221nn41–42, 222n10, 223n14, 224n5, 225n19, 228n69, 229n47, 229nn1–4, 231n1, 231n3, 233n27, 233n29, 234nn39–41, 235n4

Hart, "Joe" Reece Green, 12, 15, 20, 23, 26, 55, 59, 61, 67, 69, 71–72, 79, 90, 96–98, 109–10, 128, 130, 134, 139, 153–54, 159, 200n3, 200n5, 215n7, 220n10, 229n2, 231n3
Hart, John Mark, 8, 193n9, 219n25, 220n39
Hart, Larry M., 20
Hart, Leoso (Leosco), 121, 220n37
Hart, Martha Nelson "Mattie" Kennedy, 215n6, 214n23; Mama, 4, 23–28, 30, 32–34, 37–42, 44–46, 48–52, 54–55, 57–101, 109–11, 117, 126–27, 129–30, 132, 134–39, 141–45, 147–48, 150, 154, 156, 163, 172, 174–85, 187, 212n2; Mattie, 4, 6, 10, 13–15, 25, 64–65, 69, 72, 142, 147, 175, 179–80, 194n52, 195n67, 200n3, 207n19, 214n23, 215nn3–4, 215n6, 217n1, 228n61, 228n68, 229n1; Sister Hart, 25, 73, 145, 147, 228n68
Hart, Martha Reece, 10, 195n73
Hart, Nelson Key, 10, 13–16, 21, 23, 26, 55–56, 59, 67, 72, 79, 95–96, 109, 129, 134, 137, 139–40, 146, 153–54, 159, 189n9, 197n96, 200n3, 207n5, 208n11, 223n10, 229n1
Hart, Ray Kennedy, 10, 12, 15, 20, 23, 27–31, 33, 51, 53–54, 59, 73, 75–76, 80–81, 83, 85, 110, 198n107, 212n8, 217n5
Hart, Ruth Lee, 10, 200n3
Hart, Sterling Reece, 2–3, 8, 10, 12, 22, 29, 189n9, 200n2, 200n3, 202n5, 202n6, 203n9, 204n16, 205n23, 206n15, 206n18, 207n1 206n6, 208n11, 211n28, 211n39, 214n26, 214n29, 216n22, 217n6, 220n30, 221n1, 222n10, 228n6 228n68, 229n1, 231n11; Papa, 23, 25–34, 36, 41–42, 44, 46–63, 68–74, 76–77, 79–84, 86–90, 93, 95–97, 100–101, 109–11, 117, 119, 121,

Hart, Sterling Reece (*cont.*)
125–30, 132, 134–35, 137–38, 163,
175–77, 179–82, 184–87, 200n3, 202n5,
207n1, 220n30, 220n17; Reece, 26,
117, 141–42, 147, 179; Reverend Hart,
2, 4, 14, 18, 20, 29, 148, 200nn2–3,
206n8, 207n1, 208n9, 228n56, 229n1,
231n1; Brother Hart, 29, 33, 46–47,
73, 141, 145–47
Hart, Sterling Reese, 21
Hart, Thomas Green, 6, 8, 203n9,
204n20, 217n7, 227n8, 218n9, 219n25,
220n28, 220n31, 220n39; Grandfather
Hart, 6, 111, 119, 122, 217n8
Hart, Ray K., II, 20
Hayes, David Judge, 190
"Hearts and Flowers," 27, 30, 200n14
Henry County, Tennessee, 3, 5, 8–10, 13,
43, 205n30, 206n9, 212n7
Hickman, Kentucky, 123, 208n13,
220n40
Hickory Grove, Tennessee, 113
Hollow Rock, Tennessee, 90–91, 215n8
Hollow Rock Junction, Tennessee,
90–92
Holy Ghost, 32, 52, 141–42, 228n62
Howard, Memucan Hunt, 189n138
Hudson, Squire, 181
Humberfield, Mr. John, 125–31
Humberfield, Mrs., 131–32
Humboldt, Tennessee, 193
Hutcherson, Dick, 19, 38, 203n12
Hurley, Tennessee, 12–13, 212n5
Hymen, 187

Infare, 16, 41

Jack, Captain Bill, 148
Jackson, Andrew, 5
Jackson Purchase, 2, 4–5, 11–12, 16, 20,
190n14, 205n23, 208n13, 210n26,
212n3, 223n17, 229n81
Jamestown Exposition, 76, 211n40
Jeff and Dovie, 179
Jim Crow, 18
Johnson, Georgianna, 171–78, 180–82,
184–85
Johnson, Mr. and Mrs., 175–77, 179–86
Johnston, Albert Sidney, 86, 213n20
Junie, 179

Kennada, Ann, 19
Kennedy, Isaac, 194n52
Kennedy, Laura Jane Simmons, 18, 50,
194n32, 215n14; Grandmother Kennedy, 80, 90, 93–101, 109, 207n19,
212n9, 214n23, 215n3, 215n5, 215n10,
215n14, 217n1, 217n7
Kennedy, Matilda, 9
Kennedy, Nelson, 9, 214n23
Kennedy, Nelson Edward, 10, 13, 194n52,
207n19, 212n9, 214n23, 214n27, 215n4,
215nn11–12, 215nn14–15, 216n31, 217n34,
217n1; Grandfather Kennedy, 6, 9,
38, 50, 86–87, 90, 94, 96–98, 207n19,
214n23, 214n28, 215n4, 215n14, 216n31
Kennedy, Sampson Edward, 5, 190n18,
215n15, 216n31, 217n34
Kennedy, Sarah Angeline, 9, 205n29,
211n36, 218n10
Killebrew, Thomas, 8, 221n43
Killebrew, William (Bill) Thomas, 36,
202n3, 205nn28–29, 235n9; Uncle
Billy, 16, 35, 40, 174, 204n19, 219n22
Killebrew, William Marion, 8
Kirby, Mr., 146–48, 151
Kirksey, Kentucky, 22, 197n96
Knight, Elaine, ix, 3, 20, 198n114
Kodak, 69, 210n20

Lady Baltimore cake, 77
Lambert, Judith (Judy) Killebrew, 3
LaTrue, Larry, 145, 149, 151
Lattimore, 66
Laura Lewis, 70
Lige, 232
"Little Brown Jug," 27, 201n16
Little Zion Cemetery, 13
Little Zion Primitive Baptist Church, 10
Little Zion, Tennessee, 2–3, 5–9, 16, 19, 35–38, 40, 87, 112–13, 190n15, 202n1, 202n7, 203n10, 205n30, 211n28, 214n27, 215nn3–4, 217n1, 218n12, 220n40, 221n41, 235n9
Lockridge's Mill skirmish, 193n44
Lord High Executioner grammarian, 163
"Love is Fair," 27
"Love's old Sweet Song," 144

Mamie, Miss, 178–79, 198n97
"Marryin' squire," 39
Martin, William, 6
Mason, Tennessee, 13, 22
Mattie, Miss, 64–65, 175, 179–80
Maude, Miss, 173
May, Miss, 167–69
Mayfield, Kentucky, 48–49, 206n14
Mayo, George T., 19, 202n7, 219n22
McLemore, John Christmas, 5, 190n15
McWherters, 4
McWherter, Almus, 8, 221nn42–43
McWherter, James, 6
McWherter, James Monroe, 8, 221n42
McWherter, William, 8
Memphis, 4, 8, 13, 22, 29, 32, 60, 64, 66, 70, 90, 138–39, 147–50, 162–65, 168, 176–77, 179, 191n27
Memphis Conference, 11, 79, 197n94, 200n2, 210n26, 211n33, 212n3, 213n21, 214n29, 223n17, 223n2, 229n1, 230n8

Methodist Discipline, 30, 54, 207n1
Methodist Episcopal Church, South, 11, 29, 189n9
Mississippi, 5, 12, 22, 80, 212n5, 214n19
Mississippi River, 5, 8, 12–13, 16, 20, 23, 96, 119–23, 133, 145, 153, 155, 159, 189n12, 191n30, 201n17, 201nn19–20, 204n22, 205n31, 210n21, 212n5, 220n33, 220n40, 222n9, 223n15, 225nn9, 229nn76–77, 230nn4–5, 230n10, 231n1
Moore, Calvin Simpson "Simp," 8, 13, 194n53, 202n2, 202n6, 203n10, 205n20, 205n29, 211n36, 214n26, 216n22, 218n10, 218n12, 223nn14–15, 235n9; Grandpa, 36–37, 41, 111–18, 130, 202n6, 204n21, 211n36, 215n14, 216n22, 218n10, 223n34
Moore, Emma Smith, 194n53, 218n10
Moore, James Silas (Uncle Jim/Jimmy) 39, 49, 204n16, 206n18
Moore, John Trotwood, 137, 227n44
Moore, Lemuel Potter (Uncle Potter), 39, 89, 95–96, 214n26, 216n23
Moore, Martha Emily, 194n53, 218n10
Moore, Mary Viola, 194n53, 218n10
Moore, Ruth Paralee McWherter Hart, 6, 202n2, 203n9, 211n29, 214n26, 216n22, 217n7, 219n26, 223n14, 223n15, 235n9; Mrs. Ruth Paralee Hart (Mrs. Thomas Green Hart), 6, 8, 119–24, 203n9, 204n20, 217n7, 227n8, 218n9, 219n25, 220n28, 220n31, 220n39; Mrs. Ruth Paralee Moore (Mrs. Calvin Simpson Moore)—Grandma, 33, 37–41, 71–72, 95–96, 110–14, 116–24, 193n47, 197n100, 204n20, 211n29, 216n22, 218n7, 223n14; Paralee, 7–9, 13, 37, 118, 124, 194n55, 202n2, 202n6, 203n8, 204n16, 207n17, 217n6, 218n9, 220n37, 221n41

256 Index

Moore, Sarah Angeline Kennedy, 9, Mrs. Calvin Simpson Moore, 205n29, 211n36, 218n10
Moore, Sarah Annie, 205n25, 206n15
Moore, Silas Reuben, 8, 138n38, 194n51
Moore, Simon Peter, 203n8
Moore, William Issac, 194n53, 218n10
Moores, 4
Morgan's Raiders, 42, 205n26
Murray, Kentucky, 4, 13, 22, 197n96, 206n9, 207n6

National Cloak & Suit Company, The, 167, 234n41
Nelly, 54–55
Night riders, 17, 129–30, 222nn7–8
Nordberg, Erik, ix
North Fork (Obion River), Tennessee, 6, 16, 42, 191n30, 201n19, 202n1, 204n22, 217n3

Obion, Tennessee, 14, 197n96, 200n2, 208n10, 208n12, 211n38, 221n6, 231n1
Obion and Forked Deer country, 96, 216n26
Obion County, Tennessee, 14, 200n2, 208n10, 208n11, 211n38
Ogilvie, Charles Dr., ix
"Oh, Dem Golden Slippers," 23, 212n12
Ohio, River, 22, 210n26, 223n17, 229n76
Old Bess, 23
Old Calico, 30
"Old Country," 41
"Old Dan Tucker," 42, 205n24
Old Dick, 23, 51, 53–56, 72, 80, 83, 86–87, 110, 155, 186
Old Kate, 174
Old Molly, 37, 95
Old Scratch, 97, 146, 216n28, 228n73
Old Watch, 96, 100

"Onward Christian Soldiers," 85, 213n16
"O Promise Me," 39, 204n14
Ore's Spring (Ore Springs, Weakley County, Tennessee), 113, 218n15
Ozark Mountain people, 148, 229n78

Palmersville, Tennessee, 5–6, 8–9, 22, 39, 190n18, 191n24, 199n138, 202n1, 203n9, 204n26, 212n9, 217n7, 220n28, 220nn39–40, 221n41, 221n43, 235n9
Panama Limited, The, 132
Panic of 1819, 5
Panic of 1893, 12
Panic of 1907, 210n23
Paris, Tennessee, 8, 37, 136, 202n1, 218n15
Parsons, Jim Henry, 73–75
"Pass Me Not O Gentle Savior," 157
Patterson, Malcom Governor, 222n7, 227n8
Pea Eye, Roscoe and High Pockets, 176
Phillips, E. Harrell, 11
Phillips, Old Mrs. Charity, 182
Pigg, Old Doc, 185
Pittsburg Landing, Tennessee, 79, 212n6
Prenshaw, Peggy Whitman, 2
Price, Sterling, 119, 193n46, 219n27
Primitive Baptists, 10, 16, 35, 202n4
Prince Albert, 176, 236n16
Pryorsburg, Kentucky, 12, 22, 197n96, 206n9, 207n6, 230n4
Punch and Judy show, 38, 203n11

Queen Isabella, 166, 234n36
Queen Victoria, 166, 234n35

Rankin, Quinton, 222n8
Reelfoot Lake, 17, 33, 89, 129, 176, 183, 201n20, 215n2, 222nn7–8
Ridgely, Tennessee, 197n96

Roach, Greg, ix, 3, 219n21
Roosevelt, Franklin, 1
Roosevelt, Theodore, 163, 210n21, 232n18, 233n23, 233n30

Sarton, Jessie Blanche, 172,
Savannah, Tennessee, 14, 76, 211nn38–39, 220n36
Sawyer Landing, 120
Sears and Roebuck, 12, 14, 24, 197n89, 200n8, 234n40, 234n41
Sedalia, Kentucky, 12, 14, 22, 197n96, 206n9, 230n4
Selmer, Tennessee, 13, 86–88, 214n22
Seth Thomas clock, 84, 213n15
Shelby, Isaac, 5
Shiloh, Battle of, 8, 12, 22, 43, 79, 85, 130, 205n31, 212n6, 213n17, 213nn19–20, 223n13, 223n15
Shiloh, Tennessee, 2, 8, 12–13, 22, 43, 79–80, 84–88, 130, 138, 197n96, 205n31, 211n39, 212nn4–7, 213n17, 213nn19–20, 223n13, 223n15, 229n4
Shiloh National Cemetery, 213n17
Shiloh National Military Park, 85, 213n17
Shivaree, 16, 42–43
Sinclair Oil Company, 21
Smith, Robert "Bob," x
South Carolina, 5, 97
Sparks, Mayor, 168
Squire Griggs, 19, 114–18, 124
Squire Killebrew, 43–44, 205nn28–29
State Militia, 17, 125, 129–31, 133, 221n6
Strong, Bob, 28–29, 30
Sullivan, Old Bill, 57–58
Sunset Cemetery (Dresden, Tennessee), 14, 21

Taylor, R. Z., 228n8
Teddy Bear, 69, 210n21

Tennessee River, 76, 79–80, 85, 160, 211n34, 211n39, 212n5, 229n4, 230n4
"Throw Out the Lifeline," 56, 207n3
"Tiger," (Mr. Tigrett), 17, 160–61, 166, 168; Mr. Tigrett, 160–63, 165–69
Tinsley, Doctor, 179, 181–82
Tipton County, Tennessee, 13
Travelyn, Mrs., 115

Uncle Charlie (Leroy Simpson Moore), 13, 19, 111–13, 116–18, 217n6, 218n11, 218n14, 219n21
Uncle Church, (Churchill Edwin Bondurant), 75, 211n37
Uncle Clabe, 42, 205n24
Uncle Harris, (Green Harris Kennedy), 93, 215n
Uncle Israel, 41, 204n21, 204n21
Uncle John, (John Calvin Moore), 93, 215n11
Union City, Tennessee, 1, 8, 190n17, 191n30, 204n17, 208n10, 208n13, 209n1, 221n, 122n14, 221n6, 222n6
University of Tennessee Press, ix, 3
U.S. News and World Report, 10, 21
"Unkissle" (Uncle Israel), 41

Washington Post, 2
Weakley County, Tennessee, 1–6, 8–10, 13, 19, 21, 35, 39, 71, 75, 90, 96, 190n14, 191n30, 193n32, 193n44, 195n65, 195n68, 19n99, 199n131, 199n138, 200n2, 202n1, 202n3, 204n17, 204n18, 204n22, 205n30, 221n28, 212n9, 214n25, 214n27, 215n3, 215n4, 215nn8–9, 217n1, 217n7, 218n10, 218n12, 218n15, 218n17, 220n28, 220n40, 221n41, 231n1, 233n27, 235n9
Weakley County Historical and Genealogical Society, ix, 3, 189n8, 198n114, 228n69

Wells, Thomas G., ix, 3
West Tennessee Land Company, 222n16
West Tennessee Normal School, 13
"When the Roll is Called up Yonder," 83, 213n13
White River (Arkansas), 120, 220n35
Wilderness Road, 96–97, 216n24, 217n34
Williams, Harrison, 2

Wilson, "Weepy," 184–85
Wingo, Kentucky, 13–14, 22, 197n96, 207nn6–7, 208n9, 208n11, 230n4

Yell County, Arkansas, 8, 217n47, 220nn29–30
"You've Got to Be Carefully Taught," 19

Zack, 180